Smothered *and* Covered

Smothered *and* Covered

Waffle House and the Southern Imaginary

Ty Matejowsky

The University of Alabama Press | *Tuscaloosa*

The University of Alabama Press
Tuscaloosa, Alabama 35487-0380
uapress.ua.edu

Inquiries about reproducing material from this work should be addressed to the
University of Alabama Press.

Typeface: Minion Pro

Cover image: Waffle House sign; detail of photo by Jon Tyson on Unsplash
Cover design: Lori Lynch

Cataloging-in-Publication data is available from the Library of Congress.
ISBN: 978-0-8173-2144-4
E-ISBN: 978-0-8173-9430-1

To my neighbor, friend, and longtime editor,
Martha Heine, the RBG of Dean's Reserve

Contents

Figures

Preface

My first visit to Waffle House did not disappoint. It was one in Covington, Louisiana, next to the Country Inn and Suites, a stone's throw from the onramp to the east–west Interstate 12. I was traveling with my wife and kids a few days before Christmas 2008 from our home in Orlando to visit relatives in Texas. Having covered a little more than half the distance the previous day, we were up early, way before the sun and complimentary hotel breakfast, in fact, facing down a full day's journey in the confined quarters of our cramped minivan.

Hundreds of miles of highway lay ahead, snaking us through the Pelican State's infamous chemical corridor, a.k.a. "Cancer Alley," past the imposing density of East Texas's Pine Curtain, and finally into the expansive Prairies and Lakes region just outside of the Dallas–Fort Worth metroplex. Forgoing coffee and breakfast before hitting the road was a complete nonstarter, so an alternative dining venue had to be found lest we succumb to some iffy convenience store fare somewhere along the way or, worse, endure the sort of predawn crankiness that can easily cast a pall over a family road trip.

With limited funds and few available choices, the nearby Waffle House seemed like our best and only option. Bundled against the morning chill, we trudged through the darkened motel parking lot, across an access road, past two 18-wheelers idling under some sodium-vapor streetlights and toward the eerily illuminated greasy spoon. Getting closer, the frigid air was tinged with smells of petrochemicals and cooking oil. Few cars were on the road at this hour. Almost none were parked outside the eatery as we approached its glassed entrance.

Once inside and out of the cold, we encountered a restaurant deep in the throes of graveyard-shift tedium. A skeleton crew of waitstaff milled about while two or three customers sipped coffee at the breakfast counter under the harsh globe lights installed overhead. Tinsel and other touches of holiday cheer adorned restaurant windows and walls in a mock semblance of yuletide merriment. Behind the counter, a line cook used a steel spatula to maneuver some bacon, eggs, and hash browns around the flat metal griddle. The food he prepared sizzled with the familiar sounds of spitting grease. Seemingly the worse for wear, a lone figure lay slumped across the tabletop of a padded laminate booth strewn with the detritus of a partially consumed meal. Maybe his impaired state explained the standoffish vibes coming from the waitstaff as we waited to be seated.

After what felt like several minutes, we finally just piled into one of the many unoccupied tables already provisioned with menus, utensils, and ceramic mugs. One of the Waffle House servers eventually acknowledged our presence as I searched for a highchair for my one-year-old son. She brought over some Coca-Cola tumblers filled with ice water alongside a pot of coffee, all the while apologizing for not assisting us sooner. Once we ordered, I braced for the inevitable challenge of keeping a toddler and two young children occupied while waiting for breakfast. Unlike other family eateries, this Waffle House did not provide crayons and coloring sheets as a simple way to entertain kids before the food arrives. Fortunately, the restaurant jukebox proved too enticing for them to ignore. As they flipped through the machine's various CD selections, my wife and I enjoyed some hot black coffee. There was no way of knowing that the next hour or so would help spark the germinal idea for writing this book.

When I state that my inaugural Waffle House visit failed to disappoint, I am not really referring to exemplary or even adequate food or customer service. Neither am I suggesting that the restaurant's unpretentious ambience and bare-bones trappings were the sort that buoyed my spirit while heading out the door. I suspect few people visit Waffle House with those kinds of expectations anyway. Rather, for me, the overall experience of breakfasting at Waffle House for the first time more than lived up to its uncharitable billing as "the poor suffering redheaded bastard stepchild of American restaurant chains" (Goad 2014). By this point, most Americans have heard of or encountered some kind of memorable events at Waffle House. The twenty-four-hour diner has become synonymous with all kinds of extreme or offbeat occurrences. The sometimes uncouth behavior exhibited by Waffle House patrons reflects the chain's unofficial standing as a nocturnal refuge for the drunk and disorderly.

This brings me back to the inebriated customer sprawled across the nearby booth. Soon after our food arrived, I saw him lift his head from the table, sit up, blink a few times, inspect his surroundings in a bleary-eyed sort of way, and then slowly rub his eyes. Almost immediately, he nodded off again, this time with his head tilted back and mouth agape. Within seconds, he started snoring, at first quietly, then with more guttural intensity. My wife and I exchanged glances, suppressing the urge to laugh. His labored breathing quickly punctuated the otherwise subdued atmosphere of the all-night eatery. Unfazed, the Waffle House employees paid him little attention. They lingered about the open-kitchen area seemingly waiting for their shift to end. My five-year-old daughter, entirely unbound by adult social conventions, pointed out the obvious, stating, "Mommy, that man is snoring really loud."

Fifteen years ago, this tragicomic figure could have easily been me or one of my college friends collapsed, well past the point of tipsy, in a restaurant booth in the dead of night. Back then, many a weekend outing unceremoniously ended at some budget all-night eatery just like this one, hovering over a greasy breakfast that I probably did not want and surely did not need. In retrospect, all I can say is God bless each and every one of the indefatigable servers who tolerated our lack of propriety if occasional jackassery. If, as the poet William Blake once wrote, "the road of excess leads to the palace of wisdom," then mine certainly passed through more than a few twenty-four-hour greasy spoons like this Waffle House.

It was around this point the guy bolted awake. Standing up rather shakily, he shouted, "Check!," before his knees buckled and he fell back unsteadily into his seat. This outburst might have been funny if it did not completely unnerve everyone in the eatery. One of the waiters hurried over to attend to him. When he stood up again, I got a better view of his gray business suit and flashy jewelry. His silver rings laden with turquoise stones reminded me of Stuntman Mike from Quentin Tarantino's *Death Proof*. His world-weary countenance called to mind Billy Bob Thornton in *Bad Santa*.

"You already paid your bill."

"I did."

"You most certainly did," the waiter said, not hiding his annoyance.

"Oh, I just wanted to make sure. You see, I'm in the business," he said inexplicably before sitting back down.

Wide awake now, the guy, with a notable sense of urgency, began fidgeting with the contents of the condiment caddy atop the cluttered table. Carefully inspecting and rearranging the sample-size packets of butter and jelly, he duly ignored the squeezable bottles of mustard and ketchup also close at hand, much to my relief. Once these items were sorted, his attention turned to the half-empty water tumbler, and he used a spoon to mix its icy contents. Doing our best to ignore the racket this created, we continued eating, just trying to finish up our meals and hit the road. Abruptly, he knocked the tumbler over, spilling water and ice cubes across the tabletop. A sheepish smile spread across his face as if he finally realized that his Waffle House welcome was now completely worn out. Getting up to leave, he headed toward our table rather than the exit. He told my wife, "You've got smiley eyes." Under other circumstances, this might have caused offense, but considering where we were, she and I just took it in stride. The guy then ambled out of the restaurant and into the early morning cold. Soon I settled our check and we were back on the highway traveling to Texas. I jotted the entire episode down in a pocket notebook that I keep with me for just such occasions.

It was some years later in my Anthropology of Fast Food class at the University of Central Florida (UCF) that the incipient impetus for a book-length examination of Waffle House further coalesced. One of my undergraduates chose the twenty-four-hour eatery for his end-of-term project, which entailed critically analyzing a corporate restaurant chain from an ethnographic perspective. His late-night research took place at an East Orlando Waffle House near the UCF campus. After reading his work, I could not help but wonder whether the number of alcohol-fueled encounters he documented was accurate or how much his observations of dodgy diner operations were reliable or just hyperbole. Of all the student projects I graded that semester, his probably resonated with me most as it not only echoed my own 2008 experience but also raised questions that seemed likely to benefit from scholarly consideration.

As I warmed up to the idea of pursuing Waffle House as a new research direction, these are the sort of questions I mulled over: How can Waffle House remain popular with diners much less stay in business with so many customers raising a ruckus under its roof? Similarly, how does the chain reconcile the family-friendly image that the restaurant industry seemingly favors with its checkered reputation as a late-night hangout for the chronically unsober? Finally, how do matters of region and class identity figure into the dining public's apparent love-hate relationship with the iconic eatery? When considered altogether, this research terrain seemed ripe for critical exploration, as most profiles of Waffle House cater to popular audiences and appear in mainstream publications or online venues.

As I delved into this topic, it became apparent that multiple versions of Waffle House appear to coexist simultaneously. For every gauzy account showcasing the Atlanta-based eatery as a special embodiment of working-class character, another emerges whereby the all-night diner is depicted as a pure distillation of corporate restaurant mediocrity that lends itself to various kinds of antisocial incidents. In all of these characterizations, however, what remains undisputed is the chain's regional affiliations to the American South. Few media accounts fail to mention such popular associations. In fact, they are often approached as among the most definitive aspects of Waffle House operations.

So, if Waffle House is a crowd-pleasing mass-market Fannie Flagg novel for some, for others it comes much closer to a gritty Harry Crews book where the threat of oddball mayhem, especially in the small hours stretching between dusk and dawn, might be anticipated. What seems missing from most if not all of the reportage on Waffle House are perspectives that look beyond simplistic dialectics of high/low cuisine or good/bad taste. The discursive space between such artificial endpoints remains a place rife with research possibilities. Over subsequent pages, a more nuanced view of Waffle House emerges that challenges prevailing notions about the brand and its conflicted relationship to today's South.

As no extended scholarly work has been published on this restaurant brand, there is a real opportunity to showcase what Waffle House symbolizes and/or means to southerners and nonsoutherners alike. Presently, no narrative nonfiction books critically examine Waffle House as a cultural phenomenon, regional icon, or embodiment of the South's often contradictory character. The books that have been published on the restaurant chain tend to be self-published personal diaries (Horne 2018), company-authorized histories (Heath et al. 2005), religious inspirational meditations (McBrayer 2013), or glossy photo books (Cash 2019).[1] Much written about the chain by journalists and others is presented in either a sensationalized or sentimental way (see introduction). Critically unpacking the iconic eatery from a more disinterested, social scientific, and (hopefully) humorously engaging perspective will not only elucidate the tensions between these opposing viewpoints but also highlight the discursive spaces wherein a more realistic and nuanced portrait of Waffle House emerges.

I intend to produce a more thoughtful account of Waffle House that neither privileges nor dismisses the brand based on recent media coverage and popular opinion. Even though the restaurant is widely viewed as a retail punchline due to all the late-night antisocial behavior that reportedly takes place there, it is also used by Federal Emergency Management Agency (FEMA) to accurately assess storm severity and disaster recovery (Ergun et al. 2010). Food scholars have not presented these sorts of dualities in a comprehensive and considered way. Indeed, it is in the exploration of this terrain where I aim to make my strongest contribution to the academic and social scientific literature on southern foodways and corporate restaurant chains.

My anthropological training and continued focus on manifestations of fast-food and fast-casual restaurants both in global and local contexts ideally situates me for writing a book such as *Smothered and Covered: Waffle House and the Southern Imaginary.* In fact, I am quite excited about critically examining this topic as I see it as revelatory for understanding much about the South and Red State America in the third decade of the twenty-first century amid the aftermath of the contentious 2020 US presidential election and the January 6 Capitol Insurrection. No less integral in pursuing this project is my background, living nearly my entire life within the real and imagined landscapes of today's Bible Belt. The various ambivalences I retain from this experience afford me enough critical perspective to craft a candid, albeit evenhanded, take on Waffle House's unique dualities within southern life and America's chain restaurant foodscape.

So, although I was born in the South—Bossier City, Louisiana, to be exact—and grew up on its western fringes in a small east-central Texas town somewhat equidistant between Houston and Austin, I really only consider myself a southerner by default. Even today, raising a family in greater Orlando, this label still seems an odd fit. While the region's southernmost expanse in the Sunshine State most certainly bleeds into central Florida—Floridians often say about their state "the further north you go, the more southern it gets"—any inclination toward fully embracing a southern identity continues to elude me. Perhaps I just internalized a broader, less parochial perspective coming of age as a child of television in the 1970s and 1980s. That, or maybe I am more deeply southern than I can either recognize or readily admit, particularly in my mannerisms and outlook on life.

Whatever the case may be, during my formative years and later as a teen, I found it curious that so many in my hometown and extended family for that matter could feel such strong affiliations or abiding allegiance to the South whether as a region or state of mind. These place-based feelings of pride, sometimes verging on overestimations of self-regard, for nothing more than being born in this part of the country, felt akin to taking credit for someone else's bygone accomplishments. Add to this all those upbeat expressions of regional (White) identity so factually untethered to the historical outcomes of the American experience, wherein those supporting secession and slaveholding were soundly defeated in 1865, and I could only wonder what continues to animate this particular marshaling of facts toward a counternarrative of defiant southern exceptionalism.

Seeing bumper stickers or T-shirts proclaiming "The South Will Rise Again," "American by Birth, Southern by the Grace of God," or "You Wear Your X, I'll Wear Mine" was fairly common growing up, just as hearing popular country songs by the likes of Hank "Bocephus" Williams Jr. with titles such as "If the South Woulda Won" and "If Heaven Ain't a Lot Like Dixie." Reconciling the open expression or tacit approval of such sentiments—never mind the continuing practice of naming public schools with integrated student bodies after Confederate luminaries (see chapter 4)—with southerners' reflexive hospitality and vibrant food traditions has always struck me as a particularly tough nut to crack. Hopefully, over the chapters that follow, not only will I provide a bit more clarity on this conundrum, but readers will also begin to see the US South and Waffle House with a new set of eyes.

When considered altogether, this book presents a timely and nuanced portrait of Waffle House, one that transcends the sort of one-dimensional characterizations promulgated by popular Internet tropes and essentializing media narratives. Longtime restaurant aficionados and even those unfamiliar with the chain stand to gain deeper insights about Waffle House's unique position within local foodscapes and its wider cultural impact across the South with the contextualization of these superficial descriptions. As Waffle House's more subtle, shaded, and underappreciated qualities assume sharper clarity over subsequent chapters, a less simplistic and/or dismissive rendering of the restaurant emerges. Readers can get a better sense about what aspects of the chain's contested status are deserved or unwarranted or some combination thereof.

In challenging long-held perceptions about Waffle House and its significant but by no means exclusive working-class clientele, opportunities also arise to delve deeper into articulations of regional identity, particularly those related to the southern imaginary, a concept grounded in contemporary film studies but applicable across multiple disciplines including anthropology and food studies. Described as "an amorphous and sometimes conflicting collection of images, ideas, attitudes, practices, linguistic accents, histories, and fantasies about a shifting geographic region and time" (Baker 2011), this idealized amalgamation of meaningful (un)realities continues to loom large at multiple levels of US modernity, allowing us to anchor information into some semblance of an orderly system of signification.

If anything, it plays a vital role not only in delineating an intersubjective southern mythos that many Americans find appealing and others continue to question but also in perpetuating contested spaces where material realities and aspirational yearnings reverberate and clash. Whether disseminated by Hollywood, Madison Avenue, Nashville's Music Row, or other purveyors of resonant media content, popular understandings of today's South do not always align with the lived experiences of everyday Americans in the past or present.

Just as *American Cinema and the Southern Imaginary* (2011:2) authors Deborah E. Baker and Kathryn McKee forgo any claim of "access to a real, historically knowable South or an authentic southerness that has somehow been corrupted" or romanticized over time, I too dismiss possessing any such privileged knowledge while researching and writing this book despite my moderately southern upbringing. That stated, invoking the southern imaginary, with its "evocative, overdetermined, and contradictory impulses and its many critical and theoretical resonances," proves useful vis-à-vis Waffle House (Baker and McKee 2011:2). In myriad ways, Waffle House's disputed status within America's (fast-)casual foodscape echoes these tendencies, subsumed as it is within the broader political, economic, and sociocultural sweep of a region seemingly fated to forever amend, justify, double-down, and/or compensate for so many aspects of its collective heritage.

Against this sometimes emotionally charged backdrop, it is probably no overstatement to suggest that the Waffle House we now recognize as an iconic albeit oft-beleaguered all-night eatery would probably not engender its current range of reactions had it emerged in any other regional context. Indeed, the affinities/aversions people living on both sides of the Mason-Dixon Line express toward Waffle House variously intersect with the southern imaginary. No matter how effective this resonant touchstone has become in conveying "the largely pre-reflexive parameters within which people imagine their social existence" (Steger and James 2013:23), the southern imaginary remains a complicated and unfinished tapestry of frayed fabric and colorful stitchwork that Waffle House continues to embody in profound and subtle ways.

Acknowledgments

While I spent many months at home hunched over my laptop on the dining room table or secluded away in my office at the University of Central Florida (UCF) grinding this book out, it bears both mentioning and emphasizing that this work did not emerge strictly from my own personal initiative or efforts. Without the help, support, and inspiration of others, the book would remain nothing if not a figment of my intellectual imagination, a project that failed to coalesce into a coherent work of publishable material.

From UCF, particularly within the Department of Anthropology (my home for some two decades), I would like to acknowledge the help and support from Sarah Barber, Tosha Dupras, Beatriz Reyes-Foster, and John Schultz as well as Lisa Hass, Tiffany Chestnut, and Puck Winchester. You guys helped me make this book a reality in ways you may not realize. Also, I would like to thank Rebecca M. Murphey from the UCF Library who assisted me in tracking down some hard-to find-source material. Likewise, I would like to say thanks to the UCF College of Sciences, particularly, its Sabbatical Committee, for granting me a semester off in fall 2019 to work on this project. Finally, a big shout out to my undergraduate research assistant from spring of 2019, Brittany Hagedoorn, who pretty much left no stone unturned searching out so many Waffle House news stories. Thank you, Brittany!

From the University of Alabama Press, I acknowledge the continual help and support of my editor, Wendi Schnaufer. It was a pleasure working with her and receiving her encouragement and valuable feedback throughout this process. Also, thanks to all of the anonymous reviewers who provided such insightful comments that helped elevate this work in so many ways. If this book comes anywhere close to meeting its stated objectives, it is because you helped me dig deeper and look in new directions.

On the home front, I want to thank my lovely wife and wonderful kids for putting up with me as I commandeered part of the house to work on this book amid the close quarters of the global pandemic. To Bonny, Fletcher, and Griffin, you guys continue to inspire me in myriad ways. ("Hey, your dad wrote another book.") To my wife and best friend, Lorena Parker Matejowsky, you have always been my best sounding board and source of encouragement. Thanks to all of you. Let's celebrate by going to Waffle House!

Last, this work owes much to my abiding admiration for the underdog. To paraphrase some Guns N' Roses liner notes from 1987, thanks to all the teachers, preachers, and cops who never believed.

Smothered *and* **Covered**

Introduction

House of Waffles

Perhaps no other US restaurant chain enjoys the same level of good-natured notoriety and blue-collar cachet as Waffle House. This iconic all-night greasy spoon remains a perennial fixture along the highways and byways that crisscross the Bible Belt's suburbanizing rural landscape, sort of like the fast-casual equivalent of variety store giant Dollar General.[1] Waffle House's yellow/black signage and minimalist box design are familiar features of the motel and strip mall parking lots that dot the street-level fabric of towns and cities across this part of Red State America.

Here, the near ubiquity of the corporate logo—eleven square letter tiles spelling out the company name like something on *Wheel of Fortune*—attests to the brand's cultural relevance region-wide (Junod 2009; Blinder 2018). Today, even Truist Park, home of Major League Baseball's Atlanta Braves, boasts its very own scaled-down Waffle House eatery, the company's only ballpark venture, sole non-twenty-four-hour location, and first to sell beer (Brasch 2018). If McDonald's is the US restaurant brand that best represents America to the rest of the world, then Waffle House arguably stands as its regional counterpart, functioning as symbolic shorthand for a resonant South that persists in the public consciousness like so much legible narrative. A South that no matter how real or imagined remains altogether distinctive in ways both subtle and significant and yet, paradoxically, highly emblematic of the variegated tapestry of today's United States.

Launched some seventy-five years ago by metro Atlanta neighbors Joe Rogers Sr. (1919–2017) and Tom Forkner (1918–2017), Waffle House's corporate footprint is considerable, extending north into Pennsylvania and as far west as Arizona. By last count, more than two dozen states now have one or more Waffle House restaurants.[2] Despite such national reach, most of the chain's 1,990 stores remain clustered in the American Southeast and Gulf Coast (Freeman 2017), primarily operating as company-owned branches

Figure I.1. Waffle House, Wilmington, North Carolina. RedCom Productions/Shutterstock

with only around 20 percent managed and run as franchises (Scheiber 2017). Georgia alone has over 440 locations, roughly one-quarter of all Waffle House outlets, found mostly within or near Atlanta, with a per capita ratio of one Waffle House restaurant for every twenty-four thousand Georgians (ScrapeHero 2020). This number more than doubles the combined totals of what is found in North Carolina and Florida, the states with the two next highest concentrations of Waffle House eateries (ScrapeHero 2020).[3]

While the scale of Waffle House operations is surely impressive numerically speaking, its geographical scope still remains subordinate to that of other industry leaders. In fact, it is fair to assume that Waffle House privileges its regional ubiquity in and around what was once popularly called "Dixie" (Cooper and Knotts 2017) well above any concerted push into new

if possibly more far-flung territories. Rival breakfast servers Denny's and IHOP are, by way of comparison, found in all fifty states with each making significant inroads in overseas markets. Although Waffle House lacks such international presence, it still surpasses these competitors in terms of sheer numbers, as IHOP operates about 1,840, mostly US, outlets,[4] with Denny's close behind at 1,700 restaurants.[5]

Tellingly, but not coincidentally, Waffle House's long-standing operational stronghold in the South roughly approximates a map of the NCAA Southeastern Conference (SEC). This collegiate athletic conference is well-known to college football fans as it encompasses fourteen member institutions within eleven contiguous states stretching from Texas in the west to South Carolina in the east and Florida in the south to Missouri in the north

(Wilson 2017). This geographical slant, coupled with a signature menu anchored by waffles, grits, hash browns, steak, eggs, pork chops, sweet tea, coffee, biscuits, gravy, pecan pie, and other inexpensive regional favorites, places Waffle House in clear contention for the South's quintessential roadside diner/breakfast counter. Despite their popularity and pervasiveness, neither Denny's nor IHOP can readily lay claim to such a distinction.

A veritable microcosm of messy American modernity (Swenson 2018), Waffle House's dependable, if sometimes lackluster, products and service are only unavailable under the most extreme of circumstances. The 24-7 eatery stays open every single day of the year, including Thanksgiving and Christmas, shutting its doors only when natural disasters such as tornadoes or hurricanes strike. For this reason, FEMA adopts the so-called Waffle House Index, an unofficial metric that helps gauge storm severity and appropriate disaster response based on the number and timing of Waffle House closings and reopenings in affected areas.[6] While extremely disruptive in terms of normal sit-down dining and the company bottom line, even 2020's coronavirus pandemic could not keep the chain from providing locked-down customers hearty meals whether through home delivery or curbside pickup. In fact, when Georgia controversially emerged as one of the first states to lift or relax weeks of COVID-19 restrictions in late April 2020, Waffle House promptly reopened its dining areas statewide, allowing customers to return for in-house service, albeit in a somewhat limited capacity (Crane 2020).

This ostensible inability to cease operations not only underscores Waffle House's enduring convenience and accessibility, it also reinforces the restaurant's nocturnal allure. Like the graveyard shift depicted in Edward Hopper's *Nighthawks*—only one much less metropolitan and *noir*—third-shift Waffle House remains a favorite haunt of hungry travelers, insomniacs, law enforcement officers, and others keeping vampire hours. It is not for nothing that the weekend party crowd regularly seeks refuge here amid the pallid fluorescent lighting and vinyl-laminate tabletops after local nightspots close.

Although not as kitschy, pricey, or deliberately nostalgic as the more family-friendly Cracker Barrel—another sit-down eatery whose menu and brand identity are inextricably rooted in regional foodways and culture (Cooley 2015:148–54; Stanonis 2008 ["Just Like Mammy"]:226)—Waffle House nevertheless occupies a special niche within the increasingly diverse (fast-)casual dining scene of today's South. In a sense, Cracker Barrel is where folks go for lunch with family after Sunday morning worship and

Waffle House is where they end up with friends after a night of barhopping winds down. Ostensibly, the more sophisticated Cracker Barrel wields an air of comparative respectability among today's dining public. It does after all operate its very own on-site gift shop plying countless patriotic and mid-twentieth-century American knickknacks, ready-to-wear, and consumables to patrons coming and going from its simulacrum general store dining area. From a marketing perspective, Waffle House is relegated to an almost "country cousin" status.

For many, Waffle House's position defies easy categorization or consensus by dint of the Janus-faced role it plays in southern lifeways and the sometimes intense reactions it engenders in those living on both sides of the Mason-Dixon Line. Known to many nonsoutherners through myriad pop culture references (see chapter 5), news accounts, and occasional encounters on road trips or family vacations, Waffle House continues to resonate among Americans of all stripes in ways that few other corporate chains quite approach. By now, even those hailing from more northerly climes are well aware of the brand and its distinct sociocultural associations despite living hundreds of miles away from the nearest location.

To be sure, Waffle House's standing in the popular consciousness is informed by various complexities and contradictions. Core features such as a no-frills layout and down-home breakfast fare do much to endear the all-night eatery to everyday diners. The product and operational simplicity, however, belie a deeper, more nuanced reality. Indeed, if Waffle House represents something more than the sum of its constituent parts, it is likely because the restaurant differs from competitors in ways not always appreciated by the dining public. In truth, there is often more than meets the eye with regard to Waffle House operations. Even for something as ostensibly straightforward as ordering food, the company uses some special approaches rarely encountered elsewhere.

When it comes to placing orders between guests and waitstaff and between waitstaff and cooks, the restaurant employs some highly idiosyncratic practices that really only make sense within the context of Waffle House. While these distinctive features originated in the 1980s, partially to reduce order turnaround time, their initial conception was not part of some grand marketing scheme or company effort to engage diners in new or novel ways. Rather, they emerged in a much more organic and bottom-up approach through both customer initiative and employee innovation. Today, these practices play an inextricable role in shaping restaurant operations, adding new levels of charm and distinction to the Waffle House brand (Lotz 2015).

Customers use a special proprietary lingo that is printed on the restaurant's laminated table menus when ordering hash browns. Often called cottage or home fries in other parts of the United States, these sides of fried potatoes are included with most breakfast orders, just as McDonald's offers french fries with nearly every lunch or dinner meal. The first customized options for hash browns—"chunked" (with diced ham) and "covered" (slathered with melted cheese)—officially debuted nationwide on February 9, 1984. Some years earlier, restaurant managers in Greater Atlanta noted this concept after observing their kitchen staff adding unusual toppings to the hash browns they made for themselves or friends (Lotz 2015). Recognizing its promising sales and dining potential, Waffle House soon incorporated this new offering into its normal breakfast repertoire.

Since the 1980s, diners have also proven quite imaginative in conceiving unique toppings of their own. The "country" (with sausage gravy) hash browns Waffle House now serves are based on popular customer requests from Texas (Lotz 2015). Nowadays, patrons enjoy a wide range of alternatives in how their hash browns can be prepared. Offerings are listed in

Figure I.2. Waffle House menu. Eric Glenn/Shutterstock

descending order from top to bottom on the restaurant menu, denoting when they first became commercially available. If diners want hash browns topped with sautéed onions, they say "smothered." If they want them with cut-up tomatoes, they say "diced." Other possibilities include hash browns that are "scattered" (spread on the grill), "peppered" (with jalapeño peppers), "capped" (with mushrooms), "topped" (with chili), or served "all the way" (with all available toppings). These pan-fried favorites can even come without any special topping or preparation or with various combinations of the above options (e.g., "smothered, covered, and chunked")[7] for the more culinary adventurous.

Arguably more complicated and less well-known than such specialized hash browns is the elaborate communication scheme developed between Waffle House waitstaff and grill operators for all meal orders. This novel messaging system uses a specific symbolic code involving the precise placement of various accoutrements such as condiment packets, utensils, pickles, and cheese slices on individual plates to denote order information. Based on this intricate system of visual shorthand and nonverbal cues, cooks not only know what orders belong to which plates but also how to prepare dishes. ESPN sportswriter Dave Wilson (2017) was the first to really publicize this previously unnoted "mark" system, writing, "A jelly packet at the bottom of the plate signifies scrambled eggs. Raisin toast is signified by a packet of apple butter. A mustard packet facing up means a pork chop. Face-down means country ham. A pat of butter is a T-bone, and its place on the plate determines how the steak is cooked, from well-done at the top to rare at the bottom." Such regimentation helps streamline restaurant operations, mitigating some of the confusion and noise that can muddle kitchen–sales floor communication during peak business hours.

The lines of messaging between waitstaff and behind the counter personnel are further refined through the "pull, drop, and mark" system, which is used company-wide. Andrew Knowlton (2015)—a journalist who penned the well-received *Bon Appétit* article "What It's Like to Work at the Waffle House for 24 Hours Straight"—notes that after servers jot down customer orders, the servers occupy a designated spot on the floor and yell them out to the kitchen grill: "Pull" means to pull whatever meat they indicate from the fridge (e.g., "Pull two sirloins, one bacon"). They then yell, "Drop," which indicates how many hash browns to drop on the grill (e.g., "Drop three hash browns, two in the ring!"). And finally, there is the "Mark," which tells the grill-operator what the actual combination is. The server might holler, "Mark steak and eggs medium over medium on two, country ham and eggs scrambled!" (a steak cooked medium with eggs over medium, and scrambled eggs with country ham).

This sort of under-the-radar sophistication cuts against the grain of what most mainstream Americans think about Waffle House. Thanks to a near continuous stream of news and Web stories that skews mostly toward the reductive, the brand assumes particular dimension in the public mind even as it still means different things to different people. Indeed, if the portraits of Waffle House that emerge from such coverage fall along a continuum, then one dominant media narrative distinguishes one endpoint, while an increasingly salient counternarrative characterizes the other. So far, the sorts of broad-brush characterizations touted at either end of this spectrum have not been fully reconciled with one another much less adequately explored by food scholars and others interested in intersections of corporate brand identity and southern foodways and culture (Edge, Engelhardt, and Ownby 2013).

The persistence of such dichotomous thinking about Waffle House is understandable considering how the twenty-four-hour breakfast diner seems to engage the public imagination in mostly one of two ways. At one extreme, restaurant operations and clientele are approached as something akin to late-night punchlines synonymous with mediocre food, petty crimes, drunken brawls (see chapter 3), after-hours tedium, and all variety of southern "backwardness" (Stanonis 2008 ["Introduction"]:2). The strange or sometimes cartoonish behavior showcased in these accounts (e.g., "Former Psych-Ops Soldier Wearing Clown Suit Arrested for Smoking Meth at Waffle House"—*Raw Story* headline from Athens, Georgia, March 4, 2016; or "Man Found Living on Roof of a Waffle House"—*Gawker* headline from Augusta, Georgia, May 10, 2011), coupled with the frequent involvement of local law enforcement, does much to elicit all kinds of snarky labels or unwanted characterizations that actively subvert the kind of carefully crafted corporate images typically favored by the restaurant industry (Brown 2011; Gettys 2016). In fact, when the chain does make the headlines these days, people do not expect to read about the food.

Waffle House's growing stature as an inadvertent lightning rod for so many oddball occurrences works to shift focus away from the simple service model and southern-inspired menu selections on which the company originally built its name. If anything, it adds a measure of sideshow distraction to restaurant operations that few other fast-casual eateries regularly face. Unsurprisingly, many Waffle House detractors, and doubtless even some regular patrons, enjoy applying catty nicknames to the eatery such as "WaHo" or the "Florida Man" of restaurants (Gettys 2016). More cutting perhaps, some simply drop the "W" from the chain's name when discussing the breakfast diner, rebranding it as "affle House" (i.e., "Awful House"). While such dubious distinctions hold an undeniable entertainment value and staying power of sorts, they are now increasingly countered by a growing reappraisal and warts-and-all appreciation of Waffle House in mainstream American life.

Almost diametrically opposed to the kind of pithy tabloid treatment mentioned above is an emerging chorus of voices that opts to look past the obvious police blotter and *News of the Weird* story angles to celebrate much of what Waffle House actually offers consumers. In this more boosterish strain of media coverage—where food is foregrounded and bad behavior considered local color—the brand's popular status in the South and elsewhere is approached in ways that do nothing so much as effectively humanize the eatery and its widely attributed blue-collar customer base.

Like segments of the popular Food Network show *Diners, Drive-Ins and Dives* (2007–present), where celebrity chef host Guy Fieri travels around the country in a flashy convertible championing ordinary Americans' penchant for down-home restaurant cuisine, the profiles of Waffle House coming from this side of the media spectrum are much more generous, if occasionally heavy-handed, in their praise or lack of judgment. As a counterweight to those who seemingly go out of their way to denigrate Waffle House, however, they serve as something of a corrective measure or counteractive ballast, helping restore a semblance of balance to the brand's frequently beleaguered image.

Within this context, both Waffle House and its clientele are cast as irrepressible underdogs that, despite an overt lack of sophistication and the derision of self-appointed tastemakers and gourmands, embody an Everyman ethos whose charm and appeal remain all but impervious to changing tastes and trends. A whole subgenre of contemporary fiction known as grit lit elevates such narrative tropes by equating the no-nonsense lifestyles of the so-called Rough South as necessarily more viable and authentic culturally speaking than what is encountered elsewhere (Vernon 2016).[8] When viewed through optics such as these, the open-kitchen eatery comes to symbolize all that is honest and credible about today's Bible Belt and the dining preferences of everyday southerners (Locker 2017 [14 Things You Didn't Know]). The late intrepid celebrity chef Anthony Bourdain says as much in a 2015 segment of his popular CNN program *Parts Unknown* wherein he made a late-night visit to a Charleston, South Carolina, Waffle House with fellow chef Sean Brock. For Bourdain, Waffle House is "an irony-free zone where everything is beautiful and nothing hurts; where everybody regardless of race, creed, color or degree of inebriation is welcome. Its warm yellow glow a beacon of hope and salvation, inviting the hungry, the lost, the seriously hammered, all across the South, to come inside. A place of safety and nourishment. It never closes. It's always, always faithful, always there for you."

It is not hard to miss the quasi-religious overtones of this quote, seeing as Waffle House is made to sound something like that most central and oftentimes contradictory of southern institutions, the Evangelical church (Wilson 2004; Jones 2020). Such characterizations are surely intentional as they appear in an idiom that deeply resonates with contemporary southerners.

Seemingly on the same pluralistic Waffle House wavelength as Bourdain is National Magazine Awards' two-time recipient Tom Junod who penned a brief if also kinetic appraisal of the brand in *Esquire*'s March 2009 issue. Toward the end of the piece, the Atlanta-based Junod notes: "There are a lot of Black people who won't go to a Denny's because of that chain's history of discrimination; there are a lot of gay people who won't go to a Cracker Barrel for the same reason. There isn't anybody who won't go to a Waffle House, though, because you can always find a Waffle House that suits you, and every Waffle House waitress greets you the same way."

Writing for the *Harvard Crimson*, Roey L. Leonardi, a native South Carolinian reaffirms such sentiments, stating:

> I wish I could pinpoint what keeps me coming back. Perhaps it's the knowledge that Waffle House will welcome six bleary-eyed high school seniors who can't help but order the entire menu on Saturday night, just as it will welcome families in their Sunday best and truckers who've driven across countless state lines the night after that. Waffle House does not ask you to be more than you are, and you treat it much the same. It is a mutual openness, a shared warmth. You laugh until you ache beneath the fluorescence which illuminates everything: grease and mop water on the kitchen floor, just enough quarters counted and stacked on top of a laminated menu, the tattoo on the wrist of a waitress who will call you "baby" when she asks if you need a drink to-go. (2020)

Even as Bourdain, Junod, and Leonardi celebrate the kind of "letting your hair down" behavior that often maligns the chain, they also approach Waffle House and by extension the South itself as sites of human imperfections that are paradoxically sites that are perfectly human. Overall, the tension existing between these opposing viewpoints about Waffle House creates a compelling discursive space for understanding how popular articulations of brand identity and regional foodways take root and gain resonance across diverse domains of contemporary American life.

In the introduction to the 2007 edited volume *The Restaurant Book: Ethnographies of Where We Eat*, anthropologists and food scholars David Beriss and David E. Sutton approach chain and independent restaurants as more than just out-of-the-home dining venues. They consider restaurants as "total social phenomena" (2007:3) since they not only "provide a context in which questions about, ethnicity, gender and sexuality all play out" (2007:1) but also a space where "many . . . core concepts used to define cultural worlds—such as the distinction between domestic and private life, or the rules surrounding relations with kin or with strangers—are challenged" (2007:1).

For Beriss and Sutton, an eatery like Waffle House embodies the corporatized and sometimes dizzying nature of "postmodern life" partially by assuming "the symbolic work previously reserved for monuments and parades, representing the ethos of cities, *regions[,]* ethnic groups, and nations" (emphasis added) (2007:1). In the South and elsewhere, "restaurants . . . define urban landscapes, reflecting and shaping the character of neighborhoods or even the reputation of whole cities and *regions*" (emphasis added) (2007:3). Such actions help reaffirm aspects of geographical identity, foregrounding regional cuisine and showcasing the (nostalgic) imagery and semiotics that convey meaning to so many. Within restaurant kitchens, regional tastes, flavor principles, and cooking styles often gain maximal expression. Similarly, dining areas provide settings where the interior design (visual decoration and layout style), graphic design (corporate logo, menu items, and appearance), and sound design (musical atmosphere) of restaurants work to engage consumer sensibilities, oftentimes cultivating a distinct identity tied to geographical place (Pardue 2007:71).[9]

Although Waffle House can be characterized in various ways, few would deny its core southern credentials, particularly given the restaurant's signature bill of fare and historical roots (Dyer 2008). Whether it is Bob Moser writing for *Rolling Stone* aptly describing Waffle House eateries as "square-shaped terrariums of Southern culture" (2018) or the satirical newspaper *The Onion* running the fake headline "Mason-Dixon Line Renamed IHOP–Waffle House Line" over an obviously doctored but nevertheless hilarious 2001 photo of an "official" North–South border sign replete with both chains' corporate logos, associations between Waffle House and the South enjoy considerable currency in the public mind. Even as sociologists, historians, and others continue to question just how different the South is from the rest of the United States (Lassiter and Crespino 2009; Isenberg 2016; Vance 2016), many southerners persist in maintaining or even nurturing their own distinctive identity vis-à-vis others just as they have for generations (Cobb 2005). Such geographical and cultural connections between Waffle House and the South remain firmly embedded in popular thinking even though the chain never directly references them in-store or online.

Indeed, one would be hard pressed to find any overt mention of the region on restaurant menus, promotional displays, or social media postings on Facebook, Twitter, and Instagram. Truth be told, the chain seems more inclined to go in the other direction when it comes to promoting its eateries. Rather than openly tout its southern heritage, the company opts for a more generalized approach, one partially informed by its ongoing aversion to radio or television advertising. A Waffle House magazine entitled *Inc* for "inclusion" was launched in 2007, but the in-house publication is not meant for a mainstream audience and, thus, has a limited circulation (Rawson 2013:221). Such narrow marketing bandwidth within today's ever-shifting mediascape complicates Waffle House's ability to cultivate a coherent brand identity amid so much outside caricature and competition.

For example, its current marketing slogan of "America's Best Place to Eat" does little to evoke Waffle House's long-standing southern bona fides.

Figure I.3. Waffle House waffle. Eric Glenn/Shutterstock

If anything, it comes across as somewhat uninspired if not completely in-nocuous. Newbies to the restaurant can be forgiven for not immediately drawing a connection between the chain and this tagline seeing as it is so conceptually and geographically diffuse. The fact that its namesake prod-uct—the waffle—is decidedly European in origin with most common asso-ciations linking this small, crisp, battered delicacy to Belgium and France and not the American South only heightens this kind of disjuncture.[10]

Perhaps the closet Waffle House actually does come to acknowledging its regional affiliations is the company's recent cosponsorship of a National As-sociation for Stock Car Auto Racing (NASCAR) racing team. Like the afore-mentioned Dollar General—another southern-affiliated chain associated with inexpensive merchandise, blue-collar clientele, and yellow/black color scheme (Turner 2018)—Waffle House has embraced this popular genre of motorsports as a way to connect with its customer base. As a distinctly southern pastime—one that traces its roots first to the souped-up speedsters of Prohibition-era bootleggers running contraband in and around Atlanta and later to the supercharged automobiles of Daytona Beach hot-rodders racing up and down the hard pack sands of area shorelines—professional stock car racing has morphed into a hypercorporatized multimillion-dollar enterprise.

This sport attracts a rabid following of mostly white working-class south-erners who experience the thrill of this highly commercialized undertaking either on television or in person at NASCAR's nearly two dozen concrete speedways found nationwide (Daniel 2000). Given the significant overlap between the racing and restaurant brand's core audiences, Waffle House's decision to ink a 2016 endorsement deal with Sprint (now Monster En-ergy NASCAR) Cup Series #43 driver Aric Almirola appears to be a highly shrewd and lucrative business arrangement.

Suffice it to state, much like its place of origin, Waffle House deals with more than its fair share of cultural baggage. Even though the stereotypes that serve to define everyday perceptions of the brand and region are not al-ways accurate or necessarily deserved, they still maintain enough currency within public thinking to make them difficult to fully transcend. Probably more so than any other part of the United States, the American South con-tinues to grapple with a historical legacy steeped in a sometimes celebrated, sometimes disdained, interplay of race, class, religion, and politics. For na-tives and non-natives alike, any honest assessment of this complex heritage necessitates a need to acknowledge that there is much to both commemo-rate and criticize. Notably, foodways provide a viable context for teasing out many of these regional intricacies in ways that resonate across both scholarly and general audiences (Edge 2017).

The centrality of food in the contemporary and historical South remains something both uniquely expressed and highly variegated (Egerton 2002; Ferris 2014; Reed 2018:173–226). From the Louisiana Creole cuisine of the Gulf Coast to the Lowcountry fare of the Carolinas and Georgia, from the game and farm foods of southern Appalachia, to the pit barbecue of east Texas, an eclectic array of cooking approaches and dishes works to define the character of southern foodways in both obvious and understated ways (Knipple and Knipple 2014). Indeed, this regional foodscape encompasses a wide range of knowledge, beliefs, and practices that reveals almost as much about its distinctive cultural and socioeconomic milieu as it does the virtues and shortcomings that characterize southern cooking's ongoing legacy (Edge 2017). Certainly, few other regions can boast a more diverse and sumptuous culinary character than the American South (Cooper and Knotts 2017:18–20).

Southern foodways are rooted in various West African, European, and Native American traditions that blended together over time to create what for many is the ultimate comfort cuisine (Ferris 2014). Grits, greens, skillet cornbread, sweet tea, pit barbecue, buttermilk biscuits, hushpuppies, fried chicken, chitterlings, and battered catfish are but some of the perennial favorites that continue to whet the appetites of locals and nonlocals alike. Whether home-cooked or restaurant prepared, a love for such down-home fare does much to bridge the historical divisions that still cleave along well-established lines of class, race, politics, and education. Of particular relevance to Waffle House is the special reverence that southerners attach to the full morning breakfast (Stanonis 2008 ["Just Like Mammy"]:217–18). With vastly more protein, fat, and caloric content than what is typically served in something like a continental breakfast, the eggs, bacon, sausage, and other heavier offerings of this full morning meal enjoy a distinguished status within the contexture of southern foodways.

The starchy ingredients and lard-rich recipes long favored at full breakfast and Waffle House possess a distinct gustatory appeal that often overrides more distant worries about their long-term impact on individual health and overall well-being. To wit, few diners likely dwell on the dangers of high blood pressure or clogged arteries while sitting down at 3:00 a.m. to signature Waffle House dishes such as the Pork Chop Breakfast. In the main, Waffle House is not the sort of restaurant one frequents for healthy dining, despite the chain adding the chicken-centric Light Corner to its menu in 2010. Most customers simply want something familiar and inexpensive to eat with little or no concerns beyond satisfying their immediate hunger. So, even as the kind of southern cooking featured at Waffle House deeply resonates with local palates, it also proves anything but cost-free when consumed regularly or even intermittently.

The South's aggregate health profile consistently ranks among the nation's worst, in part because so much of its everyday restaurant cuisine relies on the easy availability of unhealthy, animal-sourced, and processed foods containing high concentrations of sugar, sodium, and fat. This culinary bent, in turn, contributes to one of the highest incidences of serious noninfectious diseases including obesity, hypertension, and type-2 diabetes (Kogler 2017). The shift toward smaller portions and nutritious breakfast ingredients and menu options (whole grains, egg whites, fresh fruit, kale, steel-cut oats, lean sausage, and turkey bacon) embraced elsewhere has yet to significantly take root in today's South.

Without confusing correlation with causation, it bears noting that states now experiencing the nation's highest obesity rates—Mississippi, Louisiana, West Virginia, Alabama, Oklahoma, Arkansas, South Carolina, Arkansas, and Texas—are also the ones where Waffle House proliferates (Jitchotvisut 2014; Kaiser Family Foundation 2018). No less troubling, Waffle House country also leads the nation in rates of adult smoking, sleep disturbances, low fruit and vegetable consumption, low exercise, and low life expectancy (Maddock 2018; Kaiser Family Foundation 2018). Preliminary data from the 2020 coronavirus pandemic suggest the American South absorbed a disproportionate share of the fallout from COVID-19 due to a tragic interplay of historically undercapitalized medical infrastructure, high poverty rates, structural racism, and government officials at multiple levels of authority who failed to fully or expeditiously implement mitigation strategies to slow the virus's spread (Fausset and Rojas 2020; Newkirk 2020; Vestal 2020).

Amid this sort of disjuncture, Waffle House continues to plot its own course much as it has over the past seven decades. Unlike the competition, the open-kitchen eatery never really developed a marketing palette sophisticated enough to help fend off bad press or rehabilitate lingering characterizations. Other chains with southern affiliations negotiate these complexities in part by touting a well-crafted brand image (Edge 2017:109–26), usually one based around some old-fashioned aesthetics and evocative historical imaginaries that harken back to simpler, albeit storybook, interpretations of the past.[11] Such efforts can serve as a touchstone of sorts for shaping public perceptions about their restaurant operations and countering some of the more reductive narratives promulgated by media and other sources. Waffle House is left somewhat flat-footed in this regard given its long-standing unwillingness to embrace the sort of marketing platforms and approaches favored by other chains within today's (fast-)casual dining scene.

So, if Cracker Barrel's wholesome corporate identity conveys a kind of sanitized, Mayberry version of the prewar South where Jim Crow, lynching, Lost Cause nostalgia, and racial injustice never really happened (Tolentino 2016; Penman 2012), then Waffle House evokes something much less innovative and/or thematic. Similarly, if Popeyes Louisiana Kitchen (formerly Popeyes Chicken & Biscuits) can rebound from years of slumping sales in the 2000s in part by introducing a sassy fictional spokesperson named Annie (played by actress Deidrie Henry) as a way to authenticate the chicken chain's distinctive New Orleans roots and Cajun cooking style (Morrison 2014; Smith 2016), then Waffle House lacks a similar focal point to highlight the diner's southern-inspired menu and unpretentious ambience. Even the Bubba Gump Shrimp Company—a seafood restaurant based on the 1994 Oscar-winning Tom Hanks's blockbuster *Forrest Gump*, a film unafraid to explore some of the dark corners of everyday life in the segregated South—coalesces around one of the most beloved and noble characters in recent movie history to sell their brand of shrimp, fish, and assorted Cajun and Creole cuisine. Absent such a thematic hook, Waffle House stands notably apart from the competition.

Arguably, it is this absence or downplaying of resonant core concepts that leaves the twenty-four-hour diner less resistant to outside caricature or ridicule. Without an overarching premise that consistently articulates what Waffle House means across multiple contexts, the restaurant becomes something of a blank canvas wherein consumers, comedians, pundits, journalists, and others wield considerable sway in characterizing the brand in any way they see fit. However inadvertently, Waffle House ends up ceding much of its messaging authority to external events and personalities that almost always gravitate toward one of the aforementioned narrative frameworks. Even if this hands-off approach keeps the restaurant in the public eye in a "no such thing as bad publicity" kind of way, it becomes something entirely different when the Waffle House name intersects with hot-button issues such as gun violence and racial discrimination.

So, less by design than default, the no-frills eatery seems to lag behind the curve when it comes to delineating a sophisticated brand identity that sets the tone for how the chain is perceived whenever it is drawn into the spotlight for reasons either good or bad. Such passivity becomes increasingly problematic in today's highly mediated and overly politicized social media landscape. The multiplicity of opinions and online reviews proliferating across the Internet, coupled with the ability of consumers to rapidly mobilize or disseminate information, makes corporate messaging an increasingly tricky proposition in the Digital Age.

For chains like Waffle House, simply sitting back and letting events play out can invite all sorts of preventable complications. For a start, it makes heading off any potential public relations crisis, much less actively mitigating the fallout from one fast unfolding, particularly onerous. Moreover, it hinders efforts to enhance company prestige or capitalize on good news whenever something auspicious occurs.

Much like the South itself, Waffle House provides a context that seems to bring out the best and worst of people. Without overgeneralizing or failing to appreciate the sweeping scope of such a statement, both restaurant and region possesses what Drive-by Truckers front man Patterson Hood terms "the duality of the Southern thing." As a native Alabaman and emerging alt-country/southern rock icon, many of Hood's lyrics, music, and writings reflect his ambivalences of growing up artistic and self-aware in the contemporary South. In specific terms, this "duality" speaks to the sense of pride and shame that many southerners vacillate between or experience simultaneously when confronting their regional heritage.[12]

Hood gained widespread notice for articulating such sentiments in his 2015 *New York Times Magazine* op-ed "The South's Heritage Is So Much More Than a Flag." In the piece, he thoughtfully unpacks many of the complexities of southern identity vis-à-vis heated debates over publicly flying the Confederate battle flag in the second decade of the twenty-first century. While openly celebrating southern contributions to music, art, and civil rights, Hood ultimately calls for the flag's removal in the wake of the Charleston church shooting by a twenty-one-year-old white supremacist Dylann Roof, who killed nine African Americans who were attending an evening prayer service (Hood 2015).

No matter how overt or veiled, the darker impulses to which Hood alludes do much to subvert the stereotypical hospitality long associated with the American South (Szczesiul 2017). A predisposition toward displays of kindness, warmth, and graciousness, especially to those acquaintances or strangers deemed (near-)equals, is something that dates back to antebellum times. Whether genuine or superficial, these expressions of mannered generosity still inform many of the social interactions experienced throughout the region. Certainly, no other part of the United States has cultivated a reputation so closely aligned with reflexive politeness and folksy friendliness. The prevailing deference toward others amid ongoing exclusions based around race, gender, class, sexuality, faith, and politics within this socially conservative and religiously fundamental milieu remains one of the enduring paradoxes of regional culture.

At Waffle House, these regional idiosyncrasies often get magnified or exaggerated to the point where long-standing characterizations about the South are readily reified. Much as the warped contours of a funhouse mirror draw attention to certain traits over others, restaurant operations seem to accentuate the light and dark extremes of the American South and not much else. At least that is how it appears to anyone following recent coverage of the iconic eatery either in traditional media or online. For every clip of choppy cellphone footage of a drunken free-for-all (see chapter 3) or ugly racist incident at a Waffle House (see chapter 4), there are acts of kindness and selflessness by restaurant staff/clientele that go viral, helping reaffirm one's faith in humanity. For every minor or serious criminal infraction that calls into question basic human decency or even common sense, there are other Waffle House encounters so ridiculously bonkers that only the truly humorless among us would fail to appreciate their comedic value.

A number of recent episodes illustrate these highs and lows in sometimes lurid, sometimes poignant ways. Indeed, within a roughly six-month span beginning in December 2017, Waffle House made headlines for reasons both farcical and tragic. It even grabbed attention for a simple act of kindness that challenges prevailing notions about millennial entitlement and self-centeredness. While any random timeframe would likely include some kind of newsworthy Waffle House story given the public's long-standing fascination with the restaurant, the events that occurred during this particular months-long stretch evoke the darkness and light associated with the chain in highly resonant ways. The good, bad, and abhorrent details presented in the following accounts speak to how Waffle House is now something more than just a greasy spoon where hash is slung and orders drunkenly slurred. For better or worse, it has become yet another place in American life where our better angels and baser instincts manifest themselves, sometimes with truly devastating results.

To start, the twenty-four-hour eatery garnered national notice a few weeks before Christmas in 2017 when customer Alex Bowen stumbled, hungry and slightly inebriated, into a seemingly deserted South Carolina Waffle House at around 3:30 a.m. After waiting nearly ten minutes without any service, the vodka-emboldened thirty-six-year-old floor installer and Army vet took matters into his own hands, slipping behind the counter for some impromptu griddle action. Bowen soon uploaded a series of Facebook selfies of himself mugging for the camera and cooking a double Texas bacon cheesesteak with extra pickles as the restaurant's sole employee snoozed nearby. After cleaning the grill, Bowen quickly stole away into the night with no one from Waffle House ostensibly the wiser (Held 2017).

Returning some hours later to pay for his ill-gotten grub, Bowen promptly received a Waffle House apology, a mild reprimand about the hazards of customers in the kitchen, and, in a brilliant display of public relations spin, an actual job offer. Emerging less unscathed, the offending worker earned a full week's suspension for sleeping on the job. Perhaps because Bowen's restaurant joyride embodied many of the evocative tropes now associated with drunken Waffle House revelry, the incident promptly went viral, eventually getting coverage from major news outlets including *USA Today* and *NPR* (Held 2017). Depending on one's perspective, Bowen's antics raise some intriguing questions about how much such behavior is emblematic of today's social media sensibilities where documenting outlandish deeds is *de rigueur* or a clear case of white privilege that would likely produce an entirely different outcome if committed by a person of color.

Waffle House was in the national spotlight again in March 2018 for reasons much less comical but arguably more inspirational. During rush time at a Waffle House in La Marque, Texas, a town just north of Galveston, customer Laura Wolf snapped a photo of eighteen-year-old waitress Evoni Williams pausing to assist an elderly regular, Adrien Charpentier, sitting at the counter with a portable oxygen tank unable to cut up his ham dinner. Wolf's late father also experienced hand trouble, so Williams's unselfishness struck a responsive chord with her. After some internal debate, Wolf posted the image to social media praising the teenage waitress's compassion with a caption that partly read, "I'm thankful to have seen this act of kindness and caring at the start of my day while everything in this world seems so negative. If we could all be like this waitress and take time to offer a helping hand" (Soong 2018).

Williams's altruism soon earned considerable online accolades after Wolf's post went viral. In fact, within a matter of days, it had been shared tens of thousands of times. Once the story came to La Marque mayor Bobby Hocking's attention, things took an even more improbable and heartwarming turn. For her kindness, the city not only issued a proclamation naming March 8 Evoni Williams Day but it also provided the soft-spoken Waffle

House waitress a $16,000 scholarship to Texas Southern University, a public historically Black university located just up Interstate 45 near downtown Houston. In a workplace ceremony, a grateful and teary-eyed Williams accepted an oversize check, answering questions from a throng of journalists as the mayor, Waffle House staff, family, and friends looked on, saying, "I would want someone to help my grandmother or grandfather" (Soong 2018).

The positive vibes and residual goodwill generated by William's story for Waffle House were abruptly overshadowed a few weeks later by a mass shooting at a restaurant located in the Antioch neighborhood of Nashville, Tennessee. At around 3:25 a.m. on April 22, 2018, a partially clothed gunman exited his pickup armed with an AR-15 semiautomatic rifle and fatally shot two people in the parking lot. The assailant, later identified as twenty-nine-year-old Travis Reinking, then entered the building, spraying bullets at those inside, killing one and fatally wounding another. Eventually wrestled to the ground and disarmed by wounded restaurant patron James Shaw Jr.[13] Reinking fled the scene only to be captured over a day later after an intensive manhunt. Besides the four fatalities, two other victims were hospitalized with serious injuries (Moser 2018).

This Waffle House tragedy unwittingly thrust the company into the national conversation on gun violence. Public opinion on the issue remained raw after a series of mass shootings including the Marjorie Stoneman Douglas High School shooting in Parkland, Florida (February 2018—seventeen killed), the church shooting in Sutherland Springs, Texas (November 2017—twenty-five and an unborn child killed), and the Las Vegas mass shooting (October 2017—fifty-eight killed), leaving many Americans feeling anxious, angry, and devastated. Reinking, who had a long history of mental illness and erratic behavior such as trying to breach the White House perimeter in 2017 and believing singer Taylor Swift was stalking him, used previously confiscated firearms that were subsequently returned to him by his father to perpetrate the massacre. Reinking was eventually deemed too incompetent to stand trial and committed to a mental facility for treatment.

In response to the tragedy, Waffle House offered to pay for the medical expenses of those injured and the funeral costs of those killed. Yet, while companies like Dick's Sporting Goods stopped selling assault-style weapons and Delta Air Lines, United Airlines, MetLife, Hertz, and others formally severed ties with the National Rifle Association (NRA) in the Parkland shooting's aftermath, Waffle House did not follow a similar tack after the Antioch incident. Considering that their presumptive clientele of working-class southerners largely overlaps with staunch supporters of the Second

Amendment and NRA, the Reinking shooting placed the breakfast chain in a rather tricky spot politically. Beyond calling for unity in the days after the shooting, praising the actions of Shaw and law enforcement in Reinking's eventual apprehension, and somberly paying tribute to those killed and wounded, the chain never directly addressed, much less took sides in, America's ongoing gun debate. Clearly, pursuing a more activist stance on the issue poses numerous pitfalls for a company so closely associated with the South and traditional southern lifeways.

Compounding the ill effects of the Antioch shooting were calls for a national Waffle House boycott by Bernice King, youngest daughter of civil rights icons Martin Luther King Jr. and Coretta Scott King. King took to Twitter in early May 2018 to call for such action after cellphone footage surfaced of a police officer in Warsaw, North Carolina, choking and then slamming twenty-two-year-old Anthony Wall to the ground outside a Waffle House location. Wall, dressed in formal attire, had stopped at the all-night eatery with his sister after accompanying the sixteen-year-old to her high school prom. Local law enforcement was called to the restaurant after a Waffle House employee confronted the couple for sitting at a table that had not yet been cleaned. Video of the subsequent altercation with the police was posted on Facebook and quickly went viral, prompting King (McKibben 2018) to tweet: "Family, lets stay out of @WaffleHouse until the corporate office legitimately and seriously commits to 1) discussion on racism, 2) employee training, and 3) other plans to change; and until they start to implement changes. newsobserver.com/news/local/art . . . 9:06 AM—May 10, 2018."

What happened to Wall was just the latest episode in a spate of incidents involving racial profiling allegations and the violent arrests of young African Americans at Waffle House. In a 2013 essay "'America's Place for Inclusion': Stories of Food, Labor, and Equality at the Waffle House," Katie Rawson notes: "Since the 1990s Waffle House has had more than twenty cases of racial discrimination filed against the company. The majority of these cases involve white employees refusing to serve or harassing minority customers. In several of the trials, the defendants were found not guilty; in others, Waffle House Inc. settled with the plaintiffs" (2013:230).

In fact, less than a month before the Wall altercation, two Alabama Waffle House incidents drew scrutiny to the treatment of African Americans. The first involved twenty-five-year-old Chikesia Clemons, who was forcefully arrested in the early morning hours of April 22, 2018, at a Waffle House in Saraland, Alabama, for allegedly stealing fifty-cent plastic cutlery

(Richards 2018). Cellphone footage of the altercation shows police officers pinning Clemons to the restaurant floor in such a way that left her breasts exposed. In the clip, one officer can even be heard threatening to break her arm. The arrest drew swift condemnation by various civil rights and social justice groups. After a sit-in at the restaurant the following day, representatives of chapters of the National Association for the Advancement of Colored People (NAACP), Black Lives Matter (BLM), and Street Peace America met with corporate officials at the Waffle House headquarters in metro Atlanta to discuss their concerns (Haag 2018).

Directly on the heels of protests against Clemons's violent arrest, Waffle House made the news again for the ill-treatment of another Black woman at one of its Alabama locations. Even without police involvement, what happened to Jacinda Mitchell at a Pinson Waffle House eatery was not the kind of press coverage that any fast-casual chain striving to attract a diverse customer base would ever find welcoming. The thirty-something Mitchell posted a forty-five second video to YouTube documenting the local Waffle House's locked doors that prevented her from accessing the eatery even as white customers continued eating inside and restaurant personnel performed various graveyard-shift duties all but ignoring her efforts to gain entry. Before fleeing the scene after a white customer pressed hard against the glass,[14] apparently threatening to shoot her, Mitchell states that "they have the doors locked and they have customers in here, and they're saying that they're closed. The customers are eating and they happen to be white customers, and I am African-American" (Thorton 2018).

Upset by her denial of service, which incidentally occurred within hours not only of Clemons's April 22 arrest just a few hundred miles away in Saraland, Alabama, but also the tragic mass shooting at the more geographically proximate Waffle House in Antioch, Tennessee, Mitchell nevertheless dismissed calls to sue Waffle House, stating that she uploaded the clip to make both the general public and corporate office aware of her mistreatment at this particular store. For its part, Waffle House sent Mitchell a formal letter of apology after her viral cellphone attracted significant media buzz throughout Alabama and beyond. The company's ham-fisted inclusion of a gift certificate "redeemable toward a free meal valued up to $15" prompted Mitchell to immediately mail it back (Thorton 2018).

With the Antioch tragedy and all three alleged racist incidents falling within such a brief twelve-day span in the spring of 2018 (Murphy 2018), Waffle House appeared to occupy a rather curious if also decidedly precarious position within popular thought at this particular moment in time.

On the one hand, the eatery still enjoyed a surfeit of public support and sympathy in the immediate aftermath of the Tennessee restaurant shooting (Moser 2018). On the other hand, three controversial and highly visible Waffle House encounters that viscerally called into question the company's treatment of Black customers seemed indicative of a deeper and more troubling pattern of restaurant discrimination (see chapter 4).

For other companies, this string of events could easily coalesce into a major public relations disaster, one with serious financial implications expedited by a major exodus of once-loyal brand customers. The potential for such outcomes is doubtless compounded as a social media boycott spearheaded by the daughter of a slain civil rights icon proceeds to attract considerable press attention, spotlighting some unflattering aspects of company operations. Despite facing such strong headwinds going into the summer of 2018, Waffle House ultimately weathered this turbulent period not so much through crisis management but more by indirectly capitalizing on the residual goodwill it enjoyed in the wake of the Antioch restaurant shooting. Bernice King's call to action never really achieved the kind of sustained momentum needed to effectively shift public opinion away from a well-established and culturally resonant brand. In fact, even today, Waffle House continues to stand by its policy of employees calling the police whenever they feel threatened on the job (Horton and Siegel 2018).

When considered altogether, the incidents discussed here suggest an escalation, if not possible culmination, in the dichotomous tension that characterizes Waffle House's often contradictory public profile. Is Waffle House an unfortunate example of a restaurant chain where racist and discriminatory behavior all too easily finds expression, or is it an oasis of friendly service and simple grub amid unassuming surroundings as founders Joe Rogers Sr. and Tom Forkner originally envisioned (see chapter 2)? Efforts to reconcile such light/dark extremes are tempered somewhat by the chain's putative standing as the South's quintessential breakfast counter/roadside diner. With so many paradoxes interwoven into the sociocultural fabric of today's South, it is unsurprising that similar discontinuities also emerge within the social and symbolic schema of Waffle House. The fact that the eatery serves as an unofficial "petri dish" (Filloon 2017) of everyday life in this part of the United States helps to contextualize such disjunctures, rendering them much less inexplicable to outside observers.

Still, most aspects of day-to-day restaurant operations fall short of anything approaching the sensational or newsworthy. It would be near impossible for the company to stay in business much less consistently earn profits if its workaday operations were continually plagued by such extreme and dubious encounters. Despite popular depictions of Waffle House online or in other media as a hotbed of boorish or antisocial conduct, most of what goes on at the eatery is so ordinary and routine that it hardly warrants consideration. Customers arrive at the diner, find seats, peruse the menu, make small talk with waitstaff, order food and drinks, eat what is on their plates, listen to the jukebox, pay for their meals, and leave without incident. Such goings-on occur thousands of times a day; most come nowhere near warranting a cellphone video or emergency call to 911.

Even as the chain's public image is closely aligned with all kinds of outlandish and atypical behavior, the particulars of the situation prove something much less revelatory. At Waffle House, friendly and/or competent service, courteous or disinterested (sober) clientele, and uneventful meals remain the norm rather than the exception. Niceties like these often get lost in the barrage of sensationalized depictions that hones down the subtlety of what the restaurant actually provides. The overamplification of its more problematic aspects works to obscure and diminish how the chain truly engages customers in everyday settings. Since routine Waffle House operations seldom measure up to the headline-grabbing hype that captivates large segments of the dining public, a sizable disjunction between brand identity and everyday reality persists. The company's disinclination or inability to wrest full control over the restaurant narrative has emerged as one of the defining, if not overlooked, aspects of the Waffle House brand.

What follows is a critical meditation on Waffle House that works to (1) demystify the lingering stereotypes that characterize the open-kitchen eatery in popular thought and (2) disentangle some of the intricacies and incongruities that define restaurant operations in the South and nationwide.[15] As an enduring, albeit easily caricatured, corporate brand, Waffle House blends the sensational with the mundane in ways not always appreciated by everyday diners or contemporary food scholars. Although Waffle House is now widely viewed as a southern dining institution of sorts, this iconic status confers as much, if not more, notoriety as it does public recognition. Given its rather unique standing within the (fast-)casual foodscape of today's South, the breakfast chain offers a viable context for considering both the interplay between restaurant foodways and regional culture and the long-standing paradoxes inextricably embedded in southern life (Edge 2017).

Beriss and Sutton (2007:3) note that restaurants "form a bustling microcosm of social and symbolic processes focused on the formation and maintenance of identities in the context of highly sensory environments." Such abstract processes gain significant expression in the case of Waffle House as the chain both reflects and reifies much of what it means to be southern and less-affluent in the first quarter of the twenty-first century. The sights, smells, tastes, sounds, and tactile sensations of eating at this restaurant do much to express the budgetary considerations and parameters of palate exhibited by its target clientele. Menu offerings and restaurant ambience further evoke the regional and class-based sensibilities of the night owls, road-weary travelers, families, college students, and blue-collar types who commonly frequent Waffle House.

Over the pages that follow a more thoughtful and nuanced portrait of Waffle House emerges that neither privileges nor dismisses the brand based on recent media coverage and popular Internet tropes. The sometimes celebrated, sometimes derided restaurant chain assumes new levels of distinction when considered through the critical lens of food studies analysis. Heeding Beriss and Sutton's call "to further scholarly exploration of the multiplex ways that restaurants can be situated in our contemporary world" (2007:8), this book examines how Waffle House fits within the cultural, political, and socioeconomic milieu of today's Bible Belt and the role it plays in shaping the contours of regional identity vis-à-vis other parts of the country (Cobb 2005).

Organization

The book comprises five chapters that approach Waffle House from various points of view and perspectives. Drawing on information culled from the available scholarly literature and mainstream media accounts, findings presented over subsequent sections work collectively to delineate a less reductive take on the all-night eatery. Unlike much of what now informs public discussions about Waffle House, this work explores the discursive terrain where restaurants serve, in the words of Beriss and Sutton, as "social and symbolic spaces" discernibly linked to "larger historical and politico-economic processes" (2007:4).

Chapter 1 situates Waffle House within a broader examination of historical working-class southern eateries, in general, and roadside diners and breakfast/lunch counters, more specifically. The cultural and sociohistorical relevance of these mom-and-pop restaurants is considerable seeing as they not only served as flashpoints of "political participation" (Cooley 2015:148–54) in urban communities during the civil rights era but also anticipated the rise of Waffle House and other all-night restaurant chain eateries in towns and cities throughout the Southeast and Gulf Coast. Chapter 2 traces Waffle House's history from its humble origins in metro Atlanta to its current status as a fast-casual success story and veritable icon of southern identity. The details of how this open-kitchen eatery carved out a viable presence within the (fast-)casual foodscape of today's South by serving popular comfort food in many ways parallels historical developments that have transformed communities region-wide over the past seven decades.

Chapter 3 examines the dark side of Waffle House by considering the range of petty infractions, drunken escapades, and serious criminal offenses that the chain seemingly elicits. Although it may be tempting to view the inclusion of these accounts here as a lurid or gratuitous gesture, the fact remains that for many Americans Waffle House is synonymous with these sorts of goings-on. Various theoretical and material explanations can elucidate why the restaurant is so often viewed as a hub of odd criminal activity (Melbin 1987). Chapter 4 builds off such analysis by examining intersections of Waffle House and race. Like many restaurant chains in the South and elsewhere, Waffle House has frequently fallen short when it comes to ensuring that all of its clientele and staff are treated fairly and equitably. Even though the brand now touts itself as "America's Place for Inclusion" (London 2006; Rawson 2013) after making strides to better engage employees, diners, and surrounding communities since the early 2000s, a number of recent incidents and legal actions complicate such company efforts.

Chapter 5 shifts focus to reflections of Waffle House as a popular cultural phenomenon. By cataloging and critiquing the chain's myriad intersections with film, television, stand-up comedy, literature, professional/collegiate sports, and popular music, among other media/entertainment genres, this discussion helps synthesize the chain's complicated legacy in ways meaningful to southerners and nonsoutherners alike.

1

Waffle House Precursors

Diners and Lunch/Breakfast Counters

Waffle House is situated within a broad social and historical framework. Acknowledging this, as this chapter does, is both necessary and illuminating, as so many of the menu items and dining amenities now available to Waffle House customers were developed and pioneered decades ago by the owners/operators of diners, lunch/breakfast counters, and other simple eating venues. In more ways than one, Waffle House emerges as the modern equivalent of these so-called greasy spoons by virtue of its no-frills dining format, inexpensive food offerings, and unpretentious ambience. Whereas in decades past everyday folk could get quick and simple meals at various independent mom-and-pop eateries (e.g., breakfast/lunch counters) located in urban neighborhoods or along a gradually integrated interstate highway system (e.g., roadside diners, twenty-four-hour truck stops), these kinds of nonchain outfits now seem like quaint throwbacks, given their ostensibly subordinate position to the hegemony of (inter)national chain eateries.

Dining Out

Dining outside the home at restaurants—once the special domain of travelers and the affluent or moderately well-off—has become an inextricable aspect of everyday life thanks to the proliferation of various (non)chain eateries that help define the foodscapes and built environments of towns and cities across the unfolding work-in-progress that is today's United States. Whether it is pricey haute cuisine or inexpensive fast food, most Americans take for granted the availability of restaurant-cooked meals (Crowther 2013:178–79). Few of us can remember much less conceptualize a time when places of public eating were not widely encountered or readily frequented.

The convenience, variety, and novelty that these establishments offer meet a real need for individuals and families, especially those grappling with the incessant demands imposed by the oft-callous realities of a shareholder-first market economy. As millions of Americans continually strive to make ends meet or strike that ever-so elusive work-life balance, expectations about household meal preparation/consumption no longer invite the same level of care or consideration that they once did. Indeed, finding alternatives to this core domestic task has become less and less problematic with the wide variety of prepackaged or ready-made meal options available to consumers. Ongoing advances in digital/delivery technology further expedite everyday meal consumption at home.[1] Like so many aspects of household modernity, food production/consumption has been gradually externalized and/or parceled out to sources operating beyond the domestic sphere.

When time is money and productivity paramount, going out and paying for meals prepared by others becomes a viable and sometimes unavoidable necessity, one that challenges long-standing aversions to consuming food in the presence of strangers (Spang 2000). Even as the hectic pace and tight schedules dictated by work and family obligations continue to define the modern condition for so many, such pressures do not and cannot negate our inherent need to eat. No matter what else is happening day to day or hour to hour, time must always be set aside for eating.[2] With so many aspects of people's lives now externally oriented beyond the home (e.g., work, school, and travel), it is fair to suggest that the preparation and consumption of breakfast, lunch, and dinner belong as much to the public domain as they do the domestic.

The shift in this form of meal eating from a largely private household endeavor to something widely accomplished in the public realm stems from continuing changes in our prevailing political economy. Today, with so much of what it means to be human subsumed into the seemingly all-pervasive schema of hyperdrive global capitalism—where maximizing behaviors associated with wage-labor, commodity sales and capital accumulation are accorded near-universal validity—it is unsurprising that patterns of how and when we take our meals are so heavily market determined. As various processes of industrialism, Fordism, post-Fordism, and McDonaldization transformed conditions of labor and family life across Europe, North America, and most of the world beginning in the eighteenth century and dramatically accelerating in decades thereafter, notions of time and work schedules assumed a calendrical precision that now rigidly defines the existence for millions around the globe. In fact, such alterations in how we conceptualize and organize everyday life are so far-reaching and profound that few give them a second thought.

As places of employment and business, restaurants like Waffle House are both a part of and an outcome of such processes. Their daily rhythms and operations reflect the timetables and social arrangements fostered by a prevailing market economy that ostensibly attains greater hegemony with every passing year. Conditions of global capitalism and neoliberalism subject populations worldwide to aspirational promises of better living through consumption and material acquisition just as they shape the contours of ordinary existence, in part, by reconfiguring local foodscapes to the point where the presence of both chain and nonchain eateries is seemingly ubiquitous. Anthropologist Gillian Crowther (2013:179) notes that, nowadays when it comes to dining outside the home, "we are used to a wide range of choices, and to the idea of eating in public; this has not always been the case, and it has an acquired set of social behaviors that we now take for granted. If we look back at this history of public eating establishments we can see that it has taken awhile for this activity to become unproblematic, either for the individual or for state authorities."

Although the core concept of restaurants remains virtually unchanged since they first emerged in eighteenth-century France as venues for feeding paying kitchenless customers (Spang 2000), these enterprises have changed dramatically in both form and practice over subsequent centuries. Indeed, today's global restaurant scene is nothing if not highly variegated and capitalized, catering to the diverse needs, preferences, and sensibilities of a wide range of clientele and socioeconomic demographics.[3]

At a deeper level, the restaurants we frequent and styles of cuisine we ultimately embrace convey more than just culinary preference and pocketbook realities. In a distinctly multiscalar way, they also communicate something about us as people. As Crowther notes, "public eating was born of necessity, but has flourished as a means to communicate individual and group identity" (2013:183). Within the context of the southern imaginary, where wide-angle expressions of regional character assume powerful reification through, among other things, prevailing styles of cooking, cuisine, and hospitality, a restaurant like Waffle House becomes something more than a popular eatery given its strong geographical affiliations to the American Southeast and Gulf Coast.

Unsurprisingly, this hypercompetitive market sector represents a significant share of the gross domestic product (GDP) for the United States and other countries, generating billions of dollars annually. According to the latest National Restaurant Association's figures, US eateries were on track to produce some $799 billion in 2017 sales. Employing nearly 14.7 million workers—approximately 10 percent of the US workforce—the million-plus restaurants operating nationwide collect nearly half of every American-spent food dollar (*National Restaurant News* 2017).

With so much variability in this retail form operating worldwide, few would deny the restaurant's cross-cultural adaptability and meme-like replicability across both time and space. As a quality of life measure, in fact, the vibrancy of a city's or region's corresponding restaurant scene figures prominently in how locals and visitors viewed it. The cosmopolitanism and semiotics of "progress" that so many cities and regions strive to cultivate is intimately bound up with the number, quality, and types of public dining venues available to consumers. Even in developing contexts throughout the global South, corporate restaurant chains and their mom-and-pop counterparts now flourish alongside the more traditional venues operated by (semi)stationary market stall vendors and mobile street hawkers, significantly altering the urban fabric, eating habits, nutritional regimes, and consumer sensibilities at the community level (Matejowsky 2018; Searcey and Richtel 2017).

The sorts of restaurants that ultimately emerge and thrive within any given locale, however, do not arise in a vacuum (Haley 2011). That quaint little neighborhood bistro on the corner or the cookie-cutter fast-casual breakfast chain adjacent to the motel parking lot are both products of larger political and economic forces whose influences can seem vague and largely disconnected to the realities of everyday life, particularly for consumers just grabbing a quick bite. As material fixtures and social hubs embedded within the schema of municipal commerce, however, restaurants add body and sinew to the retail morphology of local foodscapes. Myriad factors affect their scope and character as they develop and operate over time, coalescing into what are often highly dense and competitive public dining scenes.

Restaurants: Structure versus Agency

Like other abiding features of human social life, restaurant scenes like those found in the American South (Edge 2017:109–216) are situated within a prevailing social structure. These overarching frameworks establish the parameters that constrain or influence peoples' actions or decision-making (Elder-Vass 2010) including those related to food production and consumption. As socially constructed features of human existence, structures are born out of a complex interplay of historical trends, policy decisions, macroprocesses, disruptive geopolitical events, and shifts in political economy, all of which filter down to the local level. There, they shape the lived experiences and foodways of ordinary people, privileging some and disadvantaging others (Elder-Vass 2007; Haley 2011).

Few people question the legitimacy or normative value of social structures given their all-encompassing reach. Most simply internalize their validity and unconsciously accept them as the way things are (Sewell 1992). Our internalized norms, institutions, and social arrangements reflect these enduring macrolevel structures in ways that create a set of patterned conditions that effectively dictate what is and is not possible in human social life. Within social structures, overt and implicit considerations of race, gender, class, religion, and other factors further inform and reinforce the decisions and actions we eventually take. So much so, in fact, that it is sometimes tempting to view humans as little more than pawn-like analogues operating within the scripted rules and fixed outcomes of an elaborate board game. Even as scholars debate the finer theoretical points of social structures as workable schemes for understanding and organizing the social playing field in which humans exist and operate, these conceptual models exhibit a remarkable staying power within the social sciences and elsewhere (Hays 1994).

Yet, while individual behavior is constrained by long-standing institutional priorities and the situated constraints imposed by others, humans display varying levels of agency vis-à-vis the restrictions to which social structures subject them. However unconscious, human agency plays a vital role in how we ultimately conceptualize our efficacy on events and then enact it upon the world. Whether it is purposeful goal-oriented activity, unconscious involuntary action, or some combination thereof, agency both transcends and challenges the primacy of structure in dictating how human affairs unfold.

This is certainly true when it comes to how we negotiate the intricacies and mundanities of established foodscapes and restaurant scenes. These critical spaces provide settings for expressions of local foodways and wide-ranging behaviors associated with production and consumption (Beriss and Sutton 2007). Animating all this is the autonomous behavior of individuals and households whose entrepreneurial initiative, consumer choices, and other forms of human agency contribute to the overall viability of regional dining scenes among other things. Indeed, within public dining contexts across the South and elsewhere, the actions of restaurant owner/operators and consumers do much to determine the specifics of eating meals at the local level. So, although the "structure versus agency" debate remains unresolved, primarily in terms of ascertaining which side is wholly or mostly responsible for producing or curtailing generative human outcomes (Elder-Vass 2010), this dichotomous framework does prove useful in elucidating the dynamics and institutional arrangements that give body and form to the everyday realities of human existence, including those related to regional foodscapes.

Restaurant Scenes and the American South

Much can be gleaned about a society or region by considering the array of restaurants and cuisine styles favored by food consumers. The prevailing tastes, migration/settlement patterns, ethnic compositions, diasporic experiences, and employment conditions of populations all gain expression through the range and variety of eating venues available. The eateries prevalent in any given urban locale, for example, serve as much as a window into current consumer sensibilities as they do the connective tissue that links movements of people and capital over time. As microcosms of society writ large, local/regional restaurant scenes reflect shifting socioeconomic and political arrangements, conveying plenty about the material and cultural changes unfolding within overarching social orders (Beriss and Sutton 2007).

The American South fits into such processes. The regional foodways of southern states can be viewed as the ongoing culmination of myriad culinary traditions, population migrations, historical developments such as those related to the transition from a largely agrarian and slave-based plantation way of life to a more urbanized wage-labor mode of existence, and the increasingly coordinated marketing efforts of (inter)national restaurant and food industry conglomerates (see introduction). The distinctive restaurant scenes encountered in this part of the country also illuminate the people, events, and processes that define southern life both in the past and continuing today.

No matter how easy it is to retrospectively view these critical food spaces as perennial aspects of regional life—ones that seems to emerge somehow fully formed or without much prior effort or enterprise—such notions capture neither the transformative scope nor considerable breadth of the macrolevel processes shaping their incremental development and operational viability. As a collective mirror that reflects our diverse heritage, culture, and history, the kaleidoscopic constellation of restaurants and foodways operating regionally or nationwide is nothing if not deeply reflective of how we arrived at a particular place and time. Whatever relevance and/or success a chain like Waffle House currently enjoys, its popular status among everyday Americans remains something arguably best understood within the South's unfolding historical and sociopolitical narrative.

Setting the Stage

As processes of industrialization, wage labor, and urbanization accelerated in mid- to late nineteenth- and early twentieth-century America, transformations in the basic fabric of US society commenced with real, albeit often asymmetrical, impacts. While unevenly distributed geographically or historically, the overarching legacy of these changes remains pervasive. Thanks to the development of a heavy industrial base (e.g., steel production, shipbuilding, auto manufacturing, mining, and other capital-intensive enterprises)—one that attracted considerable inflows of (inter)national capital and labor—northeastern and midwestern communities around the Great Lakes underwent major political and socioeconomic shifts during this time. Recent European arrivals and those seeking employment from other parts of the United States (e.g., the Great Migration[4]) added new dimensions of demographic character to these regions subsequently labeled the Rust Belt and Northeast Corridor (Hurley 2001:26–38).

Similar changes took place much less rapidly and/or visibly elsewhere in America. In towns and cities throughout the South, various structural and historical factors precluded more robust and widespread industrial/economic development until after World War II. Among other things, a fragmented regional infrastructure, Jim Crow segregation, the lingering effects of the Civil War/Reconstruction, and centuries of enslavement of Africans contributed to socioeconomic and political conditions largely incompatible with the sort of sweeping changes already transforming many northern states. In the American South, agrarian economies and rural lifeways continued to hold sway over much of everyday existence just as they had over previous decades. Although slower to transition away from this more insular mode of living—at least compared with other US regions—what eventually became known as the Bible Belt could remain impervious to encroaching modernity for only so long, eventually succumbing to its more transformative influences in ways both profound and subtle (Cobb 2005).

Indeed as the Sunbelt emerged as a viable geopolitical and socioeconomic region contained within the contiguous United States beneath the thirty-sixth parallel (everything under this latitude stretching from Florida to California) beginning in the 1950s and continuing today, the demography of southern and Gulf Coast states assumed new dimension and character. Thanks to relatively warmer climates, surging numbers of Baby

Boomers looking for economic opportunities and retirement options as northern deindustrialization intensified in the 1970s, and the growth of the aerospace, defense, and petroleum industries, the prominence of southern and southwestern states expanded dramatically, introducing all sorts of human, economic, and cultural capital into that swath of the country now covered by Waffle House's considerable corporate footprint. The higher wages and associated benefits associated with this kind of economic development must be taken into account in allowing many southerners to transcend their agricultural and blue-collar roots to experience some measure of middle-class status during these years (Schulman 1994; Haley 2011). Such developments played a significant role in the emergence of a viable regional consumer culture and restaurant scene.

The demographic character of the Sunbelt, in general, and South, more specifically, underwent additional change and nuance beginning in the mid-1990s and accelerating over subsequent decades thanks to the profound economic and political changes wrought by 1994's North American Free Trade Agreement (NAFTA). As many of those displaced on both sides of the US-Mexico border scrambled to mitigate the fallout of having their previous livelihoods upended—especially poor Mexican subsistence farmers who no longer could compete in the new economic playing field—the demographic profile of the US South became much more international if also Hispanicized in character. As John T. Edge points out in *The Potlikker Papers* (2017), the contributions of these new transplants have done much to alter and enrich established southern foodways.

Southern Meal Procurement

Notwithstanding the kind of aforementioned North/South asymmetries, few aspects of national life could remain unaffected by these major shifts in political economy, including local foodways. As the twentieth century progressed, many tasks previously centered around daily meal preparation/consumption became increasingly divorced from their domestic roots. When it came to production, the autonomy that for so long characterized household procurement of food, ingredients, and cooking materials gradually ceded ground to developments in America's burgeoning consumer economy. Expanded availability of canned goods, processed fare, and other nonperishable items mass produced and transported from afar significantly elevated the US food industry's influence over local kitchens and pantries (Cobb 2005). The concurrent rise of small independent groceries, many of which subsequently grew from local general stores into regional and national supermarket chains, further diminished the sort of self-sufficiency that had heretofore characterized household preparation of snacks, breakfast, lunch, and dinner.

Even as such retail advances slowly took root across the American South, domestic cooking responsibilities still adhered to normative gender patterns. Female household heads, usually wives or mothers or among more well-off southern families hired African American domestic help, disproportionately oversaw meal preparation and cleanup duties. Their male counterparts, usually husbands and fathers, primarily pursued traditional breadwinner roles outside of the home (Sharpless 2010). Even though the conveniences afforded by new grocery innovations, as well as those stemming from technological improvements in electrification, refrigeration, and transportation, helped ease many everyday burdens for affected homemakers, such advances did little to alter the gendered divisions of labor still so prominent across US households.

Around this time, restaurant dining for blue-collar workers started coming into its own thanks to a growing labor force and concomitant demand for accessible and affordable meal options before, between, and after work shifts (Sheumaker 2017:61). Paying for non-home-cooked meals became both necessary and feasible for scores of southerners and nonsoutherners alike as numerous daily activities extended beyond their traditional domestic base including wage-labor industrial/manufacturing jobs. In part, these post–Civil War developments, coupled with expectations about consumer possibilities, prefigured the rise of an expansive service sector that would operate alongside US manufacturing for decades before finally supplanting it in terms of aggregate economic/employment clout in the 1970s.[5]

During this period of intense socioeconomic and demographic change, shift workers at various factories, plants, shops, mills, mines, and other places of blue-collar employment became financially able and circumstantially compelled to seek out snacks and inexpensive non-home-cooked meals (Sheumaker 2017:61). Demand for low-cost dining did not go unheeded locally for long. Various entrepreneurs and aspiring restauranteurs across the country began finding ways to accommodate the mealtime needs of the nation's labor force. Although some workplaces maintained on-site commissaries where workers could purchase food for personal consumption, the kind of sit-down eateries that emerged and thrived as mainstays of mid-twentieth-century foodscapes initially began as small-scale family-run enterprises.

In fact, early mobile ventures peddling food to places of employment likely stand as the first manifestation of such simple restaurant operations.

Historian Helen Sheumaker (2017:61–62) notes that, during the second half of the nineteenth century, "wagons with prepared foods would travel to worksites, and in 1872 the first lunch wagon, the Pioneer Lunch Wagon, rolled up into Providence, Rhode Island, offering boiled eggs, coffee, and pie. By 1889, lunch wagons were found in towns of any size that had a factory. The New England Lunch Wagon Company had a chain of almost 300 wagons up and down the New England coast."

Quickly morphing into actual physical stationary businesses whose architecture and aesthetics emerged as integral and eventually iconic aspects of mainstream America's restaurant foodscape, these cottage industry endeavors aimed at providing hearty meals to a hungry, price-conscious clientele. Morning, noon, or night, customers could choose from an array of fried or grilled foods simply prepared on flattop griddles or other cooking appliances in open-air or closed-kitchen settings. Core breakfast fare at these utilitarian eateries included coffee, scrambled/fried eggs, bacon, grits, omelets, hash browns, waffles, and pancakes. Some perennial lunch and dinnertime favorites were Salisbury steak, deep fried chicken, meat loaf, hamburgers, steak and deli meat sandwiches, baked beans, french fries, coleslaw, soup, chili, baked pies/cobblers, iced tea, and sodas.

Whether in small company towns or densely populated urban areas, these independent and later chain operations performed valuable services to local workforces, in part, by feeding growing numbers of wage earners, particularly during weekday lunch and breakfast. Signature features of these historical working-class restaurants included but were not limited to no-frills table/counter service, short-order cooking, daily lunch/breakfast specials, and simple décor. Increased automobile use and the ongoing integration of America's transportation system intensified demand for new establishments of this type. Soon, various hamburger stands, roadhouses, around-the-clock truck stops, and other roadside eateries became common fixtures along America's heavily traveled roadways and city streets. In no small measure, these chain and independent ventures helped expedite the pace and extend the breadth of US manufacturing and commercial enterprise by keeping workers continually fed and on the go, reconfiguring the street-level fabric of an increasingly car-centric America in the process. According to Philip Langdon in *Orange Roofs, Golden Arches: The Architecture of American Chain Restaurants* (1986:36),

> the urban chains that had grown up between the 1880s and 1920 . . . pushed
> right up against the sidewalks and attracted customers who arrived on

foot or from trolleys, subways, and other mass transportation systems. But instead of sharing sidewalks with neighboring buildings, these new restaurants often pulled away from other structures—not far at first, but far enough to permit a fundamentally different approach to exterior design. Here, in its incipient stage, was one the critical changes in twentieth-century chain restaurant design: the beginning of the abandonment of tight, densely urban patterns of development. Standing as separate objects, the new restaurants had the potential to achieve strikingly individualized personalities. It is no accident that this transformation began in the 1920s. By 1920 the number of motor vehicles in the United States had nearly quadrupled in just five years, to a total of 9.2 million cars, trucks and buses.

Restaurant Antecedents

To understand Waffle House's overarching significance within the regional foodways of today's South, especially vis-à-vis the southern imaginary, it is useful to consider some of the antecedent restaurant types referenced here in greater detail. The cultural and sociohistorical relevance of these mom-and-pop restaurants extends beyond serving food, as they not only served as flashpoints of "political participation" (Cooley 2015:148–54) in urban communities during the civil rights era but also anticipated the rise of Waffle House, Denny's, IHOP, and other all-night corporate eateries in towns and cities throughout the Southeast and Gulf Coast.

Whether urban breakfast/lunch counters, small-town greasy spoons, or twenty-four-hour truck stops located along lonely stretches of interstate highway, these predecessors of "America's Best Place to Eat" developed numerous operational and aesthetic qualities over the years that continue to find expression in Waffle House and its various chain restaurant rivals. For many southerners, the near ubiquity of these mom-and-pop outfits prior to the rise of McDonald's, Burger King, Hardee's, Bojangles, and other corporate fast-food outfits during the postwar era evokes a genuine sense of dewy-eyed nostalgia for times gone by. In fact, these early independent establishments are now so fondly remembered that they pretty much qualify as veritable distillations of that kind of Route 66 roadside Americana whose timeless appeal cuts across both regional and generational divides (Sides 2004).

Even though nonexclusive to the US Southeast and Gulf Coast, this variety of eatery did much to shape popular twentieth-century restaurant dining when it came to general amenities and available menu items. From offering everyday working folk and others various comfort food to crafting an unpretentious casual atmosphere that had no aspirations toward posh sophistication, these Waffle House precursors established a basic template of service/cuisine that has been replicated for decades by so many fast-casual breakfast chains. Less concretely but no less significantly, they also set a standard for public expectations about dining within what is arguably perceived as the most quintessentially blue-collar of America's various restaurant genres.

Notably, Waffle House was neither the first nor only southern-affiliated all-night breakfast chain to replicate the operational format pioneered by the independent blue-collar restaurants discussed herein. Toddle House—started in 1929 by Houston lumberman Jacob Cox Stedman before relocating a year later to Memphis, Tennessee, where it thrived with new investors including the local Britling Cafeteria and highway-coach carrier Dixie Greyhound Lines—successfully ran hundreds of franchises nationwide in part by adhering to the winning formula developed by roadside diners and other mom-and-pop eateries in the 1920s and earlier. Famous for its cottage-style brick buildings, distinctive blue roofs, twin chimneys, conduction cookers, compact dining areas, and "No Tipping Allowed" policies (Dowdy 2019:39–41; Sherman 1987), Toddle House operated more than two hundred built-to-plan locations in some ninety US cities during its 1950's heyday. In 1962, the parent company of Toddle House business rival Steak 'n Egg Kitchen purchased the Memphis-based brand, ditching the Toddle House name and placing the new acquisitions under its own restaurant banner or one of its other restaurant holdings (Lauderdale 2011).

Interestingly, Toddle House also operated two nearly identical lines of eateries mostly located in and around Memphis but also found elsewhere across the United States. The first was Harlem House, which catered exclusively to African Americans in the decades prior to desegregation (Lauderdale 2011); the other was the broader-focused chain known as Hull House (Langdon 1986:35–36). A short-lived revival of the Toddle House brand occurred in the 1980s with the eventual operation of some forty-five such namesake eateries mostly located in Florida. These much larger ventures enjoyed a few years of success before shuttering in the early 1990s (Lauderdale 2011; Sherman 1987).

As detailed in chapter 2, Toddle House's sway over Waffle House's early years is both considerable and unsurprising seeing as how Joe Rogers Sr. worked as a restaurant regional manager prior to cofounding Waffle House with Tom Forkner in the mid-1950s (Rogers 2000:59–99). In fact, even today the influence of Toddle House is readily apparent in Waffle House operations. Customers need look no than the double-sided table menus awaiting them while being seated. Here, patrons will notice among other available breakfast favorites a subsection near the top of the laminated placard devoted to four different egg-based dishes officially known as Toddle House Omelets. As an apparent nod to its corporate progenitor, the naming of these select offerings provides a small tip of the hat to the Toddle House brand. As a gesture, it no doubt highlights the connection between the two chains even as it probably goes unrecognized by all but the most old-school of Waffle House clientele.

Despite the distinct advantages that come with national brand recognition and significant branch/franchise capitalization, today's Waffle House remains firmly embedded within a tradition of inexpensive sit-down eateries and simple casual dining. In conspicuous and also nuanced ways, the twenty-four-hour chain embodies the archetype and ethos of these earlier operations, providing its mostly southern clientele no-nonsense restaurant experiences replete with familiar cuisine and standardized service. With few exceptions, Waffle House continues to draw the bulk of its customer base from one end of the socioeconomic spectrum. To be sure, few Americans nowadays associate the popular open-kitchen eatery with the kind of high-end establishments typically frequented by the South's more genteel and moneyed coat and tie crowd.

To posit that most affluent or moderately affluent southern diners do their best to steer clear of Waffle House is surely not hyperbole. These better-off individuals/households occupy a privileged position within the social hierarchy where menu prices hold little or no sway over decisions about where to eat. For some within or approaching this upper echelon, even those highly exclusive and pricey upscale eateries typically regarded as "fine dining" remain real and reasonable options. Most hardcore and casual Waffle House customers would likely never consider patronizing such high-priced restaurants, much less feel welcome visiting them. In fact, the socioeconomic divide between these opposing ends of the public dining spectrum is so extensive that they remain all but irreconcilable. Overall, ongoing racial, gender, and class divisions continue to inform public eating practices in towns and cities across the South much as they did in the past.

Waffle House remains one of the few low-cost eateries that still attracts its share of non-working-class clientele. Under certain circumstances, particularly on the weekend once local night spots close and dining possibilities significantly narrow, the restaurant's consumer profile assumes a decidedly less uniform socioeconomic character. At such times, with few out-to-eat options readily available, the chain's customer composition skews more and more heterogenous as hunger, convenience, and perhaps some level of intoxication compels those averse to Waffle House to seek out exactly what "America's Best Place to Eat" has to offer.

As will be discussed in greater detail throughout chapter 3, part of Waffle House's resonant appeal lies in the nocturnal allure it wields over not only its core customers but also those normally disinclined from eating there. After sunset, especially during that stretch between midnight and daybreak, a more diverse cross-section of today's dining public finds its way to the restaurant, some looking for a quick bite, others forestalling the night's inevitable end. Unsurprisingly, many of the hijinks and felonious behaviors that subsequently splash across broadcast/digital/print media occur within this particular timeframe.

When Waffle House slips into this new and arguably liminal mode of operation, early risers just starting their day invariably cross paths with those who have yet to call it a night. Compounding such graveyard-shift incongruities is the arrival of the "ironic consumption" crowd (Warren and Mohr 2019), who derive some level of (inebriated?) satisfaction by patronizing establishments far afield from their usual restaurant haunts. Partly to confound established social expectations about when and where to eat and partly to differentiate themselves within and among peer group(s),[6] these privileged and mostly college-aged individuals undertake this sort of self-aware restaurant slumming almost as an end unto itself. Social media's performative dimension and increased currency within today's interactional arrangements figures prominently in such self-conscious dining practices.

Yet, no matter whether or how much Waffle House becomes another putative working-class good/brand (e.g., Pabst Blue Ribbon [beer], Dickies [work apparel], or trucker hats [mesh/foam ballcaps favored by 18-wheeler drivers in the 1970s]) appropriated by urban millennials, Gen-Z'ers, or Internet tastemakers in a seemingly endless quest for authentic hipster credibility vis-à-vis obscure or down-market products, Waffle House's restaurant pedigree remains inextricably rooted in those noncorporate ventures from decades past dedicated to meeting blue-collar dining needs in the South and elsewhere. Unlike their trend-conscious counterparts who dabble in bottom-range retailing as feigned gestures of consumer sincerity, chain regulars rarely if ever embrace such higher-level ulterior motives when patronizing Waffle House. For them, the breakfast counter remains an unassuming dining establishment that offers affordable comfort food in simple surroundings, almost like a quaint throwback to the so-called Joe Six-Pack eateries of yesteryear.

Classic Roadside Diners

Of all the working-class dining formats to which Waffle House traces its roots, the classic American diner is probably the closest approximation. This decades-old variation of the nineteenth-century horse-drawn lunch wagon approaches near legendary status within today's highly corporatized food-scape given its putative position as a twentieth-century icon of mass consumerism (Hurley 2001:21–105; Gutman 2000).[7] Whether open all night or primarily meeting the everyday breakfast/lunchtime needs of US wage earners, the roadside diner of yore enjoys an undeniable staying power that few other sit-down restaurant types can credibly rival. Far from relics of some bygone era—at least in terms of their abiding influence—old-school diners have an impact that extends well into the twenty-first century, serving as touchstones from which today's fast restaurants draw inspiration and as all-American archetypes readily employed by the US cultural industry.

Pop-culture depictions of this quintessentially American eatery persist across multiple entertainment and artistic genres. Portrayals of diners in film (*Diner*, *Cars*, *Pulp Fiction*), music (Suzanne Vega's *Tom's Diner*; Tom Wait's *Nighthawks at the Diner*), television (*Alice*, *Seinfeld*), literature (*Fried Green Tomatoes at the Whistle Stop Café*), and fine art (Norman Rockwell's *The Runaway*) remain both resonant and pervasive, attesting to their enduring legacy. So, too, does the National Register of Historic Places, which includes two seminal northeastern railcar diners—Poirier's Diner in Providence, Rhode Island, and Munson Diner in Liberty, New York—on its list of historically significant buildings/sites designated for preservation and protection. Moreover, the generic catchphrase "Eat at Joe's"—a placeholder slogan highly evocative of mid-twentieth-century eateries operated by eponymous regular-guy proprietors—has crept into the American vernacular, conveying an Everyman ethos now almost universally accorded to US roadside diners.

During its popular heyday in the decades immediately preceding/subsequent to World War II, this groundbreaking concept in eating meals outside of the home distinguished itself largely by dint of its ubiquity and conspicuity. Of the roughly six thousand diners operational midcentury, most were located east of the Mississippi River, serving some 2.4 million customers each day (Nagle 1951).[8] Analogous to manufactured homes with regards to production/mobility and to railroad cars with respect to size/dimension, these moderately capitalized prefabs filled an important need not only for hungry blue-collar workers seeking inexpensive meals but also for aspiring and mostly immigrant entrepreneurs looking to mount the bottom rungs of restaurant retailing. However modest, roadside diners became both literal and figurative vehicles for upwardly mobile early and mid-twentieth-century Americans hoping to transcend their socioeconomic status and achieve a measure of socioeconomic success, making headway toward some individualized variation of the much-vaunted American Dream.

That the geographical clustering and production/assembly of roadside diners occurred mainly in northeastern states before expanding elsewhere are doubtless unsurprising given the trajectory of those wholesale sociopolitical and economic changes transforming early to mid-twentieth-century America previously discussed in this chapter. Early on, before diners were produced as prefabricated structures at one of several different northeastern factories,[9] enterprising restaurateurs found the narrow width and extended length of old railcars ideal for tapping the dormant potential of urban/roadside lots heretofore unutilized for retail development. These small albeit high-traffic locations—never really commercially exploited before—suddenly became viable real estate by squeezing converted rail wagons into their confined dimensions for the expressed purpose of serving simple and inexpensive meals to ordinary working folk.

Such distinctive spatial/operational aspects gave these start-ups a comparative advantage vis-à-vis more established brick-and-mortar eateries, mainly when it came to seizing new opportunities in local retail commerce. Many diners, in fact, established operations directly adjacent to factories and other place of blue-collar employment to directly serve workers, cultivating something of a captive audience (Hurley 2001). By expanding the scope of where and how meal eating outside of the home occurred, first-generation diners provided wage earners affordable meal options that exploited emerging changes in American labor and manufacturing, helping democratize local dining scenes in the process by broadening the parameters of who exactly gets to patronize sit-down restaurants.

Before this, paying for meals in the public sphere reflected distinct class boundaries, as few beyond travelers and/or the (moderately) affluent could afford the associated costs of going out to eat. Without the pricey meals or fancy accoutrements of eateries frequented by better-off Americans, a kind of cultural baggage soon developed around diners that persisted far into the twentieth century. These not always positive connotations largely stemmed from their humble origins and price-conscious clientele. For many, diners' perceived shortfalls and subordinate standing vis-à-vis other eateries proved difficult to fully transcend even as these blue-collar establishments proliferated nationwide. Unlike the sit-down family restaurants that would soon flourish across urban and roadside America, a reputation for wholesomeness remained elusive for roadside diners, even as they continued to engage significant segments of the dining public.

So, although widely touted nowadays as a US institution of sorts, popular attitudes about roadside diners were not always uniform or laudatory, especially during their years of commercial prominence just before and after World War II. Back then, colloquial and dismissive labels such as "greasy spoons" effectively took root, informing public perceptions about how these eateries fit within emerging restaurant hierarchies. Dissociating standard diner fare/operations from prevailing stereotypes about poorly prepared and/or mediocre cuisine proved challenging, given the inability of most diner owner/operators to blunt such negative characterizations through trade groups, responsive marketing efforts, and/or advertising promotions. Speaking to the *New York Times* in 2011, *Roadfood* (1978) coauthor Michael Stern stated, "In the '20s, '30s, and '40s, for any restaurant that strove to serve better food the term 'diner' was anathema. It meant greasy food and the dark and dirty side of eating" (Newman 2011).

Despite such common and widespread sentiments, diners still connected with consumers during these years for reasons beyond their convenience and inexpensive fare. In fact, some patrons actually preferred that proprietors incorporate changes only sparingly if at all. Writers such as Blake Ehrlich— whom Andrew Hurley spotlights in *Diners, Bowling Alleys and Trailer Parks: Chasing the American Dream in the Postwar Consumer Culture* (2001:80)— disfavored diners moving away from their simple blue-collar roots, viewing it as imperative that every effort to retain their basic character be made. For Ehrlich and other midcentury Americans, roadside diners' down-to-earth charm, particularly when manifested through unpretentious and/or earthy customer and employee behavior, deserved preservation if for no other reason than its overt lack of sophistication. Never knowing what to expect from other customers when visiting one of these down-market eateries remained a significant aspect of their appeal.

Also, part of what helped elevate roadside diners for regulars and non-regulars alike was the restaurant's highly idiosyncratic curbside appeal. For motorists traveling along the nation's turnpikes and city streets, the distinctive aerodynamic look so emblematic of the era's classic prefabricated stainless steel model vividly stood apart from the rather humdrum designs and layouts sported by other contemporaneous dining establishments. Customers approaching from the outside were greeted by a conspicuous blend of gleaming reflective surfaces and smooth subtle curves, creating a distinct tableau that appeared almost as timeless as it did ahead of its time. In ways both understated and substantial, these roadside eateries visually punctuated the often drab street-level fabric of towns and cities, adding a real cosmetic flair to local surroundings.

Assorted exterior features including low-slung metallic facades, flashy neon signage, car-friendly curbside spaces, and sleek Art Deco accents worked collectively to grab the attention of highway travelers, blue-collar workers, and others in the dining public. Echoing the clean lines and streamlined styles of motor vehicles rolling out of Detroit's various auto-assembly plants during these years, the aesthetics of mid-twentieth-century roadside diners conveyed a real sense of forward momentum, modernity, and optimism prior to the restaurant genre's eventual 1960's decline and gradual mid-1980's reemergence (Gutman 2000). So evocative was the attention-grabbing architecture of these iconic roadside eateries, in fact, that long-time Waffle House rival Denny's adopted this decidedly retro look for dozens of its franchise operations beginning in the early 2000s and continuing today (Newman 2011).

No less integral to classic American diners' overall aesthetic is the distinctive array of décor accents and hallmark features found inside these roadside eateries. The dining/kitchen areas of most first-generation diners sported cohesive interior looks largely the result of their signature boxcar designs. The extended lengths and narrow widths of these prefabricated eateries limited their inner/outer dimensions, placing clear constraints on restaurant functionality, affecting how employees/customers could utilize interior spaces. Unlike other sit-down establishments of the time, stainless steel railcar models lacked the sort of floor-to-ceiling partitions that helped segregate kitchen personnel from paying customers. Raised counters and open-air kitchens fostered a distinct set of spatial/interpersonal arrangements that narrowed the social distance between restaurant guests and employees, reifying the democratic tendencies nowadays so frequently attributed to these Waffle House precursors.

With physical barriers separating the dining public and nonwaitstaff workers all but absent, customers were close to the visceral stimuli inherent to the meal preparation process. For starters, restaurant patrons' proximity to diner food production—with its inescapable sights, sounds, and smells emanating from upright coffee percolators, metal kitchen implements, and grease-spitting flattop griddles among others—added layers of sensory sensation to mealtimes beyond those directly rooted in the gustatory experience. Spoken and unspoken interactions with diner personnel amid backdrops of overlapping customer conversations further solidified the intrinsic chumminess. In these and other ways, roadside diners assumed a place in American foodscapes deeply informed by their on-site amenities and particular spatial arrangements.

Ongoing advances in kitchen/restaurant technology also proved to be important to diners' proliferation across US foodscapes during the first third of the twentieth century. As Sheumaker (2017:62) notes, "Several changes to food preparation technology contributed to the rise of the American diner: the electric toaster in 1924, percolators, sliced bread in 1928, and even new materials such as Formica plastics that were slick and easy to care for. Diners became the lower-tier restaurants of choice."

Such innovations/developments expanded diner menus and improved service, helping consolidate classic roadside diners' look in the minds of most Americans. Once inside, patrons encountered various features that nowadays seem entirely inextricable to the archetypal US diner. Interior touches such as Formica/vinyl laminate tabletops, swivel counter stools, glass-enclosed dessert displays, black/white checkerboard floors, padded booths, and windows/walls made of translucent glass bricks left an indelible mark on US restaurant retailing, establishing core design aesthetics that effectively foreshadowed local (fast-)casual and fast-food scenes for decades to come. Similarly, table/counter service where cash-paying customers settled their dinner bills at registers located directly adjacent or near restaurant exits became something of an industry standard.

So, depending on the perspective, classic American diners' popularity/notoriety largely rested on their cuisine, clientele, consumer amenities, or some combination thereof. Whatever the extent to which these restaurants publicly resonated, few were exempt from the sociopolitical issues confronting everyday Americans in the decades both before and after World War II. Even though matters of racial segregation/disparities were familiar to US public dining scenes—in fact, they were very much the norm—reactions to such inequalities eventually came to a head during the civil rights era. Although not embedded in collective memory in quite the same way as the early 1960s' nonviolent sit-in protests at southern retail store lunch counters (Cooley 2015), roadside diners, too, became subject to bottom-up efforts to effect social change via public dining (Hurley 2001:84–92).

During these years, as African Americans and other minority groups

pressed for equal standing with their more socially and economically privileged white counterparts, accessing restaurant offerings became a point of
contention. As work life made dining outside of the home a reality for so
many Americans of color, any push toward racial inclusion appeared pretty
much a foregone conclusion. This, coupled with the fact that restaurants
were some of the few social spaces easily disrupted operationally through
targeted civil disobedience, made such efforts a logical form of protest. For
proprietors, many of whom harbored racial prejudices themselves, sorting
out ways to accommodate the dining needs of nonwhites—who increasingly
represented a significant paying clientele—without alienating their white
patrons proved both unwieldy and ultimately ineffective in quelling mounting opposition to race-based exclusions nationwide (Hurley 2001:87–88).

Before the federally mandated desegregation of the mid-1960s, diner
owner/operators maintained the status quo through some variation of segregated dining sections or by allowing takeaway purchases through rear
doors/side windows but no table service for nonwhites. Such efforts were
more readily feasible in the Jim Crow South, where a decades-long two-
tiered caste system, undergirded by various cultural and legal practices,
permeated nearly all aspects of everyday life. Indeed, the southern imaginary's dark and ugly side must engage this all-prevailing system of American apartheid. Until the race-based exclusions so deeply interwoven into
the fabric of US restaurant retailing were finally reversed, the democratic
characterizations so often retroactively applied to roadside diners remained
far from complete. Yet, although long overdue, the end of segregated dining
practices in the American South and elsewhere did little to change the diner
industry's overall economic fortunes.

As a restaurant concept, roadside diners effectively peaked sometime
early in the civil rights era. After years of growth beyond their geographical
northeastern stronghold, diners experienced a gradual decline in consumer
interest and material quality, ceding ground to emerging chain drive-ins,
fast-food joints, sit-down family eateries, and other establishments offering
new types of customer experiences and restaurant offerings. In some ways a
victim of their own success, these independent eating venues reached a numerical saturation point during these years. Increased competition caused
proprietors to look beyond their primary blue-collar base and try new approaches to capture the dining public's patronage. As owner-operators began catering to the tastes and sensibilities of new clientele—middle-class
households and those with more discretionary income—a notable shift in
the overall character of roadside diners emerged. It seemed that the changes

that writer Blake Ehrlich warned against midcentury had finally begun in earnest.

According to Hurley (2001:92), by the early 1960s, "the diner had been transformed into a safe and inviting middle-class institution, but in straying from its traditional social niche it also became more vulnerable to competition. As restaurants with diverse regional and class lineages converged on the middle-income family market, a variety of commercial dining formulas and styles were synthesized into a uniform standard. This was not good news for the diner industry; as the diner lost its distinctiveness it also lost its competitive edge."

Over subsequent years, the once-ubiquitous roadside diner became a rather scarce commodity along US highways and city streets. As the 1970s transitioned into the 1980s, in fact, few classic dining car models remained operational much less profitable. Many simply closed or were demolished, making way for chain restaurants like Waffle House and Denny's that leveraged their capitalization and franchising clout to offer consumers similar fare/amenities in settings less wedded to bygone eras.[10] After years of declining sales and dwindling customer counts, some diner owner/operators ultimately adopted an "if you can't beat 'em, join 'em" attitude and purchased fast-food franchises of their own (Hurley 2001:101).

Most of the classic diners that survived these lean years, however, soon encountered a growing resurgence of interest in retro-restaurants similar to these blue-collar eateries of yore. Around the time Barry Levison's 1982 film *Diner* (coincidentally?) hit theaters (Hurley 2001:83–84), the stainless steel variety of roadside diner experienced a kind of cultural rebirth that in hindsight appears less about simple food and friendly service and more about the wistful nostalgia and Reagan-era Americana embraced by so many middle-aged Baby Boomers of the time (Gutman 2000:208–21). Although other popular twentieth-century roadside operations (e.g., drive-in movie theaters) that piqued the US imagination in terms of attracting customers or sustaining public interest fell by the wayside, the classic American diner somehow clicked with prevailing retro-sensibilities, recapturing a bit of the popular cachet that had notably slipped away over previous decades. Quite simply, and against most reasonable expectations, this dining format went from something fast approaching obscurity to a restaurant genre gaining ground toward indisputable icon status.

From the mid-1980s onward, independently owned/operated roadside diners, particularly the prefabricated railcar types, have enjoyed an outsized influence over US restaurant retailing that far exceeds their scant numbers. The old-school metallic versions that never ceased operations, in fact, are now viewed almost as much as tourist attractions as they are iconic roadside eateries (Gutman 2000), what with their eye-catching looks and rare presence in local foodscapes. The mid-1980's classic diner revival gripped the imagination of both the dining public and restaurant industry in ways that went beyond simple patronage. To wit, various regional/national restaurant chains ended up co-opting roadside diners' classic retro-design when establishing local retail operations across various US markets (Hurley 2001:92–95).

Besides Denny's adoption of signature diner aesthetics for several of its franchise locations early in the twenty-first century, other lesser-known brands have similarly embraced the iconic stainless steel look for their (sub) urban dining venues. A case in point is the fast-casual brand 5 & Diner, an Arizona-based restaurant chain with franchises and company-owned branches in Phoenix and Surprise, Arizona; Orlando, Florida; and Worcester, Massachusetts; as well as a commercial presence in Iowa and Oklahoma. Launched in 1989, 5 & Diner restaurants evoke a distinct sense of neon-tinged roadside Americana, especially in their capacity as nighttime gathering spots for local hotrod enthusiasts and weekend automobile clubs (Wang 2012).

Just as Cracker Barrel promotes its locations as concept/themed restaurants—basically Disneyesque replicas of old-fashioned country stores replete with front-porch rockers and checkerboards atop rustic pickle barrels—so too does 5 & Diner tout its eateries as modern-day equivalents of archetypal mid-twentieth-century diners. With few service or aesthetic features too small to disregard, 5 & Diner chain eateries strive to provide customers with an idealized dining experience through its detailed architecture and operations highly reminiscent of times gone by. The metallic facade, neon lighting, and aerodynamic accents so closely associated with the historic working-class diners of years past are conspicuously foregrounded in their various eateries. If anything, 5 & Diner's unapologetic embrace of the American roadside diner's classic look illustrates just how facsimiles of this restaurant type still hold the US consumer imagination in thrall (Wang 2012).

Lunch/Breakfast Counters

If roadside diners represent the quintessential greasy spoons that once dotted America's expansive highway system with such eye-catching flair, then lunch/breakfast counters stand somewhat removed from the more conspicuous out-to-eat options with regards to their overall numbers and aesthetic curbside appeal.[11] As the archetypal low-priced eateries of yesteryear primarily encountered in downtown settings, lunch counters' rise followed on the heels of the early twentieth-century diner boom, exploiting untapped possibilities in America's increasingly diverse consumer economy. Ordinary working folk's newfound ability/need to eat outside the home created opportunities for those entrepreneurially savvy enough to reconfigure the diner concept into something not only better reflective of blue-collar realities but also potentially profitable for aspiring owner/operators.

Right around World War I, new expectations about where and how public dining could occur gained traction as lunch counters took root locally. Whether in small agriculturally oriented towns or mid- to large-sized cities with varying demographic and geographic characters, low-cost eateries of this type added both depth and variety to local restaurant scenes. Patrons often referred to them as "luncheonettes" given their limited spatial dimensions, business hours, and standard bill of fare. The fact that these venues tended to experience their primary business rush right about midday also informed this designation. In many cases, the terms *lunch counter* or *luncheonette* were used interchangeably to describe any small-scale neighborhood restaurant/café serving simple inexpensive fare to wage earners in primarily urban contexts.

Sometimes these labels even applied to those aforementioned first-generation dining cars. Many lunch counters approximated roadside diners with respect to basic amenities/equipment, menu items, and their core blue-collar clientele, yet these scaled-down establishments lacked diners' prefabricated architecture and visible presence within the street-level fabric of US towns and cities. Most distinguished themselves from competitors not only through the novel niche they soon occupied in local foodscapes but also the one they eventually inhabited in the public imagination. Being both innovative and affordable dining options for Americans on both sides of the Mason-Dixon Line, the lunch counters that subsequently etched themselves into the popular consciousness were the ones prevalent during the civil rights era.

As sites of everyday food consumption, this variety of lunch counter operated within larger brick-and-mortar commercial ventures not traditionally associated with food preparation/service. Whether affiliated with regional/national discount chains (e.g., Kmart), five-and-dime variety stores (e.g., Woolworth's, Kress's, or J. J. Newbury's), or other twentieth-century commercial establishments offering cost-conscious working people multiple lines of merchandise for reasonable prices, these designated dining areas resonated across multiple segments of the dining public, including city dwellers with newfound discretionary income and those looking to grab a quick bite while out shopping for other items (Cooley 2015).

Decisions by these discount retailers to convert part of their sales areas to on-site restaurant facilities including soda fountains and open-air kitchens prior to World War II anticipated future chain store expansion into areas beyond their original purview of dry goods, ready-to-wear, sundries, toiletries, and other assorted inexpensive to midpriced merchandise. Over subsequent years, this diversified approach became something of an industry standard. The banks, eateries, optometrists, and tax services found nowadays in big box retailers like Target and Wal-Mart and walk-in clinics currently operating inside chain variety drugstores such as Walgreen's and CVS owe part of their emergence to these sales floor dining facilities.

These brand retailers' gradual transformation of their namesake stores from simple variety outlets to something approaching highly capitalized one-stop shopping venues proved beneficial for sellers and customers alike. Exploiting conditions of economies of scale, select discount chains leveraged their increasing purchasing power in the decades after World War II to redefine where and how consumers obtained store merchandise. Taking this approach nationwide before finally putting it into global hyperdrive, such tactics enhanced customer convenience and patronage, helping lower prices for countless staple items across multiple lines of merchandise for millions worldwide. Walton's 5 & 10—subsequently global retail behemoth Wal-Mart—started in Bentonville, Arkansas, surely stands as this retail method's most enduring bellwether, transforming built environments and redefining consumer expectations both nationally and internationally.[12]

To suggest that meeting myriad consumer needs all under one roof lacked adverse outcomes is clearly erroneous,[13] particularly as it relates to the ill effects such intensive business practices caused neighboring independent outfits over time. Such sentiments seem patently obvious for Americans who lived through the accelerated post–World War II corporatization of local retail scenes. As Wal-Mart and other chain outlets proliferated in urban peripheries, and customer flows shifted away from their traditional downtown bases, a gradual hollowing out of US city centers became visibly manifest by the mid-1980s. These developments and the events leading up to them significantly eroded lunch counters' viability as potential dining sites with so many prospective patrons gravitating outward to new and arguably more prosperous outlying areas.

Unable to wield the same sort of hardball tactics that discount chains successfully deployed against their suppliers/wholesalers to eke out additional savings for their clientele, mom-and-pop ventures found themselves severely undercut both logistically and financially in trying to attract consumer dollars. The associated costs of remaining competitive vis-à-vis highly capitalized big box brands steadily eroded local retailers' profitability, edging them farther and farther along the slippery slope toward a "race to the bottom" situation in which shuttering or declaring bankruptcy loomed ever-present. For many small businesses, such outcomes became unavoidable.

Such dismal prospects were entirely unforeseeable to those would-be restaurateurs looking to seize unrealized opportunities within early twentieth-century America's expanding retail landscape. As possibilities of dining out increasingly filtered downward into US working-class households both before and after World War I, potential variations on established restaurant formats came to the fore as viable commercial endeavors. Integrating sit-down eating options within the sales floors of conventional retail operations transitioning into one-stop shopping ventures held genuine promise as a winning formula for reasons both apparent and not so patently obvious. Perhaps more than anything else, the high probability for success of this new approach hinged on the fact that the consumers already converging within downtown business districts and inside store sales areas represented a considerable captive audience ideally situated for commercial exploitation.

With chain store owner/operators now making inexpensive cooked meals and soda fountain fare available to their clientele, adding another stop to everyday shopping excursions became less and less a necessity for hungry customers/urbanites going about their day. These new consumer conveniences enhanced both dining and shopping experiences in towns and cities across the United States. Yet, as noted, not all lunch counters operated as designated dining areas within mainstream American discount retailers. The lunch counter label assumes almost as much relevance for those twentieth-century sit-down restaurants/cafés offering inexpensive no-frills cuisine to blue-collar clientele primarily in downtown locations as it does the more well-known eateries affiliated with the bargain and mid-priced variety stores and chain retailers considered herein.

However, it is these latter retail/restaurant hybrids more than other lunch counter varieties that retain such a staying power within popular thought, as their legacy remains inadvertently subsumed within some of recent American history's more turbulent episodes. For reasons that extend beyond conventional restaurant retailing, the emergence, success, and gradual disappearance of this unique dining innovation is perhaps forever overshadowed by its initially dubious but ultimately transcendent association with some pivotal moments in America's post–World War II Civil Rights Movement, which I discuss in this chapter.

Without accounting for individual quirks characterizing certain local operations, several key features emerged to collectively define the prototypical store lunch counter both within the restaurant industry and across the dining public. These innovative dining venues—similar to most classic roadside diners, urban cafés, and other contemporaneous freestanding eateries—sported uniformed waitstaff, open-air kitchens/prep areas, simple dining counters with stainless steel/chrome accents, raised revolving chairs for single diners, and booths with Formica/vinyl laminate tabletops for couples/groups. Such abiding features would later find expression in Waffle House and other simple chain eateries.

Notwithstanding such core traits, store lunch counters primarily distinguished themselves from other blue-collar dining establishments in terms

Figure 1.1. Waffle House counter and open-air kitchen, Mount Pleasant, South Carolina. Chris Perello/Shutterstock

of physical and operational scale, requiring much less financial overhead, operational capital, and car-centric amenities. Moreover, they needed fewer employees to take customer orders or perform various behind-the-counter cooking and prep work. In fact, it was often the case that rather than hiring new personnel to assume such duties, store managers simply required existing sales floor staff to carry out various kitchen and counter tasks as part of their shift work (Plunkett-Powell 1999:142).

Including simple dining components within preexisting commercial facilities held undeniable crossover potential that many store owner/operators quickly seized upon (Cooley 2015). For a variety of reasons, not the least of which was how it expanded consumer offerings and kept paying customers on-site longer than was previously typical, this enhanced reconfiguration of store sales floors not only added new wrinkles to downtown retailing but also foreshadowed the communal food courts that subsequently thrived in US shopping malls, airports, college campuses, and various other public settings. Numerous chain/independent retailers embraced this hybridized approach. With the possible exception of Kress's five-and-dime variety stores, perhaps none remains so pioneering and historically connected to these sit-down operations than onetime retail giant F. W. Woolworth Company, more commonly known as Woolworth's (Plunkett-Powell 1999:140–65).

Beyond its more narrowly focused candy/confection counters—introduced in 1886—Woolworth's first real foray into in-store dining occurred in the spring of 1910 when select northeastern stores began test-marketing the sale of fresh root beer, ice cream, and hot dogs (Plunkett-Powell 1999:150). Any lingering doubts about the profitability of offering customers easily prepared inexpensive fare were effectively dispelled within a few months. At this stage, the company was well into its fifth decade of retail operations, maintaining over 250 stores on both sides of the Atlantic, drawing thousands of daily customers attracted by the brand's accessibility and reasonably priced merchandise. In fact, by this point, Woolworth's had become all but synonymous with qualities such as value, reliability, and convenience. In light of such popular sentiments, the firm's launch of on-site restaurant venues seemed nothing if not a shrewd and logical next step (Plunkett-Powell 1999).

According to Karen Plunkett-Powell (1999:151) in *Remembering Woolworth's: A Nostalgic History of the World's Most Famous Five-and-Dime*, "On August 31, 1910, the first official F. W. Woolworth & Co. eatery opened on 14th Street, New York City. Managed by J. U. Troy, it was known as the Refreshment Room, a phrase Woolworth had picked up in England. This original restaurant was a far cry from the Formica-counter décor of later Woolworth's luncheonettes. The room was located in the rear of the store, in a space measuring twenty-seven by sixty feet. The dining area featured sixteen Carrera-marble glass-topped tables and a forty-foot glass-topped counter. Behind the scenes, modern kitchen equipment hummed."

Following this in-store eatery's initial success, this groundbreaking concept in non-home-cooked dining was quickly duplicated in other Woolworth's outlets first across the US Northeast and then elsewhere. Boasting an original menu where nothing cost more than a dime, the Refreshment Room's affordability readily aligned with the brand's reputation for low prices. However popular, not all store locations boasted sales floors sizable enough to accommodate the original Fourteenth Street Woolworth's Refreshment Room's established dimensions. Those lacking the requisite space to encompass such novel retail facilities were promptly retrofitted to house smaller versions of this dining innovation.

In part, such remodeling efforts expedited Woolworth's switch to the iconic lunch counter format, effectively setting the standard for how it and other department/variety brands went about serving the dining public over subsequent years. In terms of consumer impact, such moves cannot be underestimated. Like roadside diners, Woolworth's store lunch counters and those of its mom-and-pop and chain competitors emerged as convenient mealtime options for ordinary Americans looking for affordable meals/snacks. Their proliferation across US downtown settings proved something of a retail boon in the years immediately preceding the Great Depression. In fact, "by 1928, the company was proud to announce 90 million meals per day were being served in Woolworth's coast to coast" (Plunkett-Powell 1999:152).

Enticed by friendly service and affordable prices, ordinary working folk continued to be attracted to Woolworth's lunch counters both before and after World War II. Indeed, up until the 1940s, the chain served complete meals that never cost more than twenty-five cents (Plunkett-Powell 1999:140). Simple cuisine/desserts anchored Woolworth's stationary menu during these years. Americans had their choice of various selections including "steaming coffee, malted milk shakes, apple pie á la mode, baked muffins, pizza, tuna salad with a pickle wedge, banana split house boats, fresh-squeezed orange juice, even chicken chow mein on a bun" (Plunkett-Powell 1999:140). Regional favorites reflecting the nuanced particulars of local palates often supplemented these core items. Whether servings of peach pie at Georgia Woolworth's or biscuits and gravy at Tennessee locations, enterprising owner/operators increased profitability and consumer good-will by catering to such established tastes (Plunkett-Powell 1999:140).

Beyond regional cooking, Woolworth's lunch counters also cultivated loyal followings through special in-house promotions. Some of these in-store efforts included enticing customers to restaurant/retail facilities through upbeat gimmicks whereby customers received free/discounted food based around games of chance. Others involved working with US farmers—whether at the local or regional level—to create supplemental menu offerings based around available agricultural surpluses (Plunkett-Powell 1999:153). To wit, the lunch counter's signature "year-round" turkey dinner emerged out of Woolworth's utilizing whatever holiday poultry went unconsumed at Thanksgiving or Christmas (Plunkett-Powell 1999:153).

Such novel approaches even informed everyday interactions designed to streamline order turnaround. Like present-day Waffle House employees, Woolworth's lunch counter workers—mostly uniformed and aproned women—developed their own proprietary "food lingo" to expedite counter to kitchen communications, hastening the completion of all purchases. For instance, employees taking orders would holler to short-order cooks "Adam and Eve on a Raft" if customers wanted two poached eggs on toast or "Gentleman Will Take a Chance" if they purchased side orders of hash (Plunkett-Powell 1999:154–55). As Woolworth's lunch counter jargon gained in popularity, some of its more resonant terms like *mayo* and *BLT* became part of the American vernacular.

With variety/discount store lunch counters, in general, and Woolworth's luncheonettes, specifically, occupying such significant space within mid-twentieth-century American foodscapes, it is not altogether surprising that the era's prevailing sociopolitical issues, especially racial injustice, encroached upon local operations in various ways. Particularly in southern states where Jim Crow continued to privilege the white majority while marginalizing people of color, transgressing this two-tiered system's pervasive legal and sociocultural apparatus carried genuine risks even for something as simple as dining out. Multiple times, in fact, mob violence and bloodshed ensued when nonwhites attempted to access the same restaurant services as their white counterparts in the Deep South (Plunkett-Powell 1999:162).

For reasons that become subsequently clear not only in this chapter but also in chapter 4 as specifically related to Waffle House, those seeking redress for long-standing institutionalized practices of racial oppression utilized these widely accessible lunch counter facilities as sites of "political participation" (Cooley 2015). Specifically, the concerted efforts of select

African Americans targeting a national brand like Woolworth's brought maximum leverage and visibility to their social justice cause. Building on the momentum achieved through *Brown v. Board of Education* (1954), the Montgomery bus boycott (1955–56), the Little Rock Nine (1957), and the Civil Rights Act of 1957, what eventually became known as the Greensboro sit-ins began modestly enough as a local protest against restaurant segregation, only to dramatically mushroom into a full-fledged national consumer boycott. Retrospectively, the Greensboro, North Carolina, sit-ins were recognized as a watershed moment in America's long and often bumpy road toward racial justice and equal opportunity.

In February 1960, four African American college students, subsequently known as the Four Freshmen, were denied counter service in the Whites Only section of downtown Greensboro Woolworth's and returned over successive days/weeks to continue their nonviolent quest for treatment equal to that which local white diners received. Ignored or dismissed by restaurant personnel on each return visit, the young men stoically occupied counter seating day in, day out, awaiting their chance to place orders. As Woolworth's refusal of service gained local media attention, the situation escalated, lurching toward some indefinite, possibly violent, confrontation. In fact, once press coverage spread beyond Greensboro, the prospects for spilled blood appeared all the more certain, heightening already-fraught racial tensions.

As winter turned to spring and spring became summer, scores of Black and white supporters and white counterprotestors descended on the demonstration site to witness firsthand the ensuing stalemate between lunch counter employees/management and the four seventeen- and eighteen-year-old demonstrators. Taunts and jeers from white locals opposing their civil disobedience—apparently spurred on by the Ku Klux Klan (Plunkett-Powell 1999:160)—raised the likelihood of a violent altercation against the Four Freshmen even more. As neither side appeared willing to back down, regular store operations all but ceased, essentially turning downtown Greensboro into ground zero for the fight for civil rights.

With intensified press coverage and growing protest numbers, the sit-in's impact began to cut into store profits. Income losses affected its Greensboro operations and those in more distant parts of the country as the protest continued to dominate US media cycles. By choosing a nationally recognized brand like Woolworth's—a company with hundreds of retail locations worldwide—student demonstrators effectively harnessed the boycott potential of a national audience increasingly sympathetic to their plight. Activists and consumers living hundreds of miles away, particularly in the US Northeast, launched Woolworth's protests of their own as a show of solidarity. Whether taking the form of storefront picket lines or shopping elsewhere, these efforts placed the discount chain in an increasingly untenable position. Had the Four Freshmen targeted a regional retailer or national chain with much less name recognition for their in-store protest it seems unlikely they could have rallied so much consumer support toward their cause (Hurley 2001:304–10).

For Woolworth's, the ongoing standoff in Greensboro and subsequent protests nationwide proved a public relations nightmare. The company's inability to compel one of its southern affiliates to peacefully resolve a particular matter, allowing it to spiral out of control, soon began to adversely affect all Woolworth's operations. Indeed, the months-long sit-in exposed the brand's flawed albeit unofficial approach toward addressing matters of race and equality.

According to Plunkett-Powell (1999:159), "the umbrella policy of the F. W. Woolworth Co. since the 1930s had been to cater to all Americans, regardless of race, color, and religious affiliation. Yet, the unspoken policy was to abide by the wishes of local store managers (based on the particular traditions of their geographical region) when it came to serving food to minorities." Given how the Greensboro sit-in significantly reversed Woolworth's popular brand image in just a few short months, ceding so much authority to local managers no longer appeared an approach worth pursuing. As public sentiment shifted more and more in the protestors' favor, company higher-ups sought some sort of face-saving offramp to help restore normality to Woolworth's operations and win back customer support. Behind-the-scenes negotiations between both parties in the summer of 1960 eventually lead to a breakthrough, allowing each side to walk away without needless bloodshed. With little fanfare and almost no advance warning, three African American Woolworth's employees—not the original Four Freshmen—received "official" service on the afternoon of July 25. Within less than a week, hundreds of other local Black residents patronized the lunch counter, signaling a return to something approaching regular operations.

While tensions seemingly lessened in Greensboro, elsewhere in the South segregated service and sporadic acts of violence against African Americans persisted at store lunch counters (Plunkett-Powell 1999:162). Only after the Civil Rights Acts of 1964 and 1965 did full restaurant desegregation officially commence (Plunkett-Powell 1999:163). With fewer and fewer restaurant owner/operators now willing to assume the legal penalties associated with refusing service to people of color, overt policies of racial segregation in public dining space all but ended. In a very real sense, the actions of the Four Freshmen and their supporters not only showcased the efficacy of nonviolent protest as a means of affecting social change but also how chain restaurants are variously linked to "larger historical and politico-economic processes" (Beriss and Sutton 2007:4), indelibly altering the fabric of US society.

With the benefit of hindsight, lunch counter operations—whether at Woolworth's or one of its various competitors—never really seemed to recover from the fallout of this pivotal episode in US race relations. To be sure, the years after the Greensboro sit-ins marked a new phase for this in-store dining format, what with new and more sophisticated dining options and shifting consumer tastes. According to Plunkett-Powell (1999:156), "the Woolworth food centers and luncheonettes that opened between 1963 and 1997 were more streamlined and less quaint than their predecessors. These were modern food facilities, geared toward a population always on the go, who demanded top quality 'fast food' at traditional Woolworth's prices."

Unquestionably, the popular rise of corporate fast food and concomitant hollowing out of US city centers throughout the 1970s and 1980s transformed local dining scenes nationwide. For lunch counter proprietors, these conditions carried both opportunities and risks. Yet, as economic and human capital fled downtown areas for more profitable suburban locales, most owners/operators found the prospect of reinventing their operations a decidedly uphill battle. Unlike classic roadside diners—another blue-collar dining format stuck on a downward trajectory during these years—store lunch counters never experienced any sort of a nostalgia-tinged reassessment by Reagan-era Baby Boomers or others.

If anything, they appeared as quaint vestiges of a bygone time before consumers flocked to shopping malls and fast-food outlets in outlying suburban areas. As the twentieth century drew to a close, the writing was essentially on the wall as far as the viability of the store lunch counter format was concerned. Plunkett-Powell (1999:156) notes that "in the summer 1997, the last of the Woolworth's luncheonettes and cafeterias started closing down in North America." By this point, what was once a hallmark feature of downtown shopping districts and department/variety stores all but faded into obscurity. In their wake, new types of chain eateries and restaurant hybrids emerged to capture the imagination of the US dining public. Among this new breed of popular sit-down venues was the putative southern icon Waffle House.

Fast-Casual Restaurants

Of all the labels currently embraced by industry insiders and chain restaurant aficionados to describe (dis)similarities within America's public dining scene, perhaps nothing better applies to Waffle House than the broadly used if sometimes hard to pin down *fast-casual* designation (e.g., Chipotle Mexican Grill, Dickey's Barbecue Pit, and Panera Bread). Situated a notch or two above the near ubiquitous fast-food classification (e.g., McDonald's, Burger King, Subway, and KFC) and somewhere below the slightly more upscale casual-dining category (e.g., Applebee's, Red Lobster, TGI Friday's, and Olive Garden), the fast-casual genre encompasses both the midpriced cuisine enjoyed by so many Americans, as well as the specific retail arrangements in which such meal production and consumption occurs (Toast 2021).

If fast-casual eateries incorporate some of the best of what corporate fast food has to offer customers in terms of convenience and standardization, they also apply lessons learned from casual dining's more concerted emphasis on restaurant ambience and cooking approaches. Viewed as an ostensible amalgamation of conventional corporate fast-food and casual sit-down dining, it is easy to consign Waffle House and its various fast-casual counterparts to an apparent middle ground, one that holds distinct market resonance across the United States and increasingly worldwide, nestled as it between these more readily discernable restaurant categories.

Yet, whether dubbed *casual*, *fast casual*, or *fast food*, the application of such terminology to today's various out-to-eat options comes with certain limitations. Classifying restaurants along these lines does demonstrate just how diversified meal eating outside of the home has become over the past several decades, and it also highlights the pervasive interpenetrative linkages now found among so many corporate restaurant formats. Because disaggregating these complexities is difficult, identifying distinctions among today's various US chain eateries should be approached with informed intuition rather than any sort of categorical exactitude. As with other typological schemes, pinpointing precise lines of separation among various classification categories presents challenges, as boundaries frequently bleed together, resisting overt demarcation.

Instead of adhering to any rigid type of hierarchical system with mutually exclusive characteristics and clear-cut borders, it is arguably more accurate to regard America's corporate restaurants as falling along a continuum with subtle or shaded differences among genres/operations. Accordingly, the terms *fast casual* and *casual* are sometimes consolidated into a more inclusive category conceptualized as *(fast-)casual*. This less narrowly defined classification functions as a de facto counterweight to corporate fast food's considerable footprint within the overarching context of today's chain eatery foodscape. Thus, although an inexpensive all-night greasy spoon like Waffle House remains part of this (fast-)casual schema, the space it occupies surely lies toward the spectrum's lower end, near the more-expansive fast-food category (Toast 2021).

From the 1970s onward, (fast-)casual has grown in popularity as a style of dining and overall restaurant numbers, thanks in part to a standardized production and service format that translates as easily across multiple genres of cuisine (e.g., seafood, Mexican) as it does across multiple regional markets. As an everyday staple of middle-class foodways in the United States and elsewhere, (fast-)casual dining represents an out-to-eat option that successfully melds the accessibility and familiarity of established fast-food brands like McDonald's and Burger King with some of the slightly more upscale touches encountered in traditional sit-down restaurants. The fact that some stay open all night only adds to their cachet among American diners.

Although never likely to be confused with fine-dining establishments, these eateries and the products they offer feel qualitatively different from those encountered at conventional corporate burger joints and fried chicken outfits. In truth, they often resemble augmented versions of traditional fast-food operations due to slight upgrades in (healthy) meal options and enhancements in décor and consumer amenities. Such modest refinements include trained waitstaff, fresh ingredients, and nondisposable tableware. Sometimes they even entail table service and beer/wine options. Some (fast-)casual restaurants sport drive-through windows like their fast-food counterparts and most now also offer curbside pickup for online takeout orders.

No longer relegated to major cities or suburban peripheries, (fast-)casual operations have extended their reach into small towns across the South and beyond. These restaurants occupy a discernible position within America's chain eatery landscape some level above standard fast food, particularly in terms of menu style, preparation methods, and relative pricing. This mainstream dining sector provides consumers looking to reap a little more for their dollars an array of choices that effectively satisfies any type of meal craving or appetite. Excluding alcohol sales, Waffle House easily fits within this category's extensive parameters.

As competition within America's (fast-)casual restaurant intensifies— what with the proliferation of these widely encountered establishments within or near so many highway exits, airport terminals, suburban shopping centers, and other sites within the built environment—individual chains look for innovative and enduring ways to distinguish themselves from market rivals. Partly through crafting distinct brand identities based around recognizable logos, resonant color schemes, clever marketing slogans, and evocative origin stories and mission statements and partly through developing successful dining concepts rooted in inviting décors, friendly table service, laidback atmospheres, and moderately priced menu items, such efforts establish a loyal base of repeat customers who frequent these full-service eateries ostensibly as much for their easygoing ambience as for their signature bills of fare (Toast 2021).

With so much (fast-)casual restaurant variety, and so many midpriced eating options available to today's consumers, it is probably unsurprising that chains routinely engage in targeted marketing to gain and/or retain competitive advantage within America's expanding out-to-eat foodscape. By focusing on one particular market segment as opposed to many, chains are nominally guaranteed some level of profitability that would otherwise prove elusive by trying to appeal to all diners. Just as Hollywood, publishing houses, music companies, and other players in the US cultural industry cater to the tastes and sensibilities of select demographic groups to effectively carve out a viable market niche, so too do (fast-)casual brands tailor their offerings in calculated attempts to win over key subsets of the dining public.[14]

In both concept and implementation, decisions by (fast-)casual chains to target specific market demographics in lieu of a more broad-based approach are quite intentional, informing myriad aspects of restaurant operations, including how popular brands engage the consumer imagination. For consumers, such efforts render distinctions among chains more readily discernible, helping them navigate the multiplicity of available dining options and make informed decisions about where and how public dining occurs. More to the point, they also help shape contours of meal eating outside of the home, contributing to matters of personal/geographical identity, as is argued throughout this book.

Waffle House—no exception to such retail practices—also orients its operations toward key segments of the dining public. Widely recognized for capitalizing on what cost-conscious southerners want in an all-night lunch/breakfast chain, the company offers a varied menu of inexpensive fare and simple restaurant facilities that consistently attracts its fair share of potential/repeat customers. Actively courting and gearing its eateries toward this market niche, Waffle House continually works to shore up its position vis-à-vis the (fast-)casual competition partly by selectively integrating new amenities/innovations into its operations and partly by remaining true to the original vision implemented by cofounders Joe Rogers Sr. and Tom Forkner back in the 1950s (see chapter 2).

Even though consumer trends come and go, Waffle House patrons can pretty much expect that the chain will deliver its dependable if sometimes uninspiring service/products without much in the way of complication or fuss. This baseline consistency in restaurant offerings doubtless plays a role in why the brand remains such an abiding fixture in the South's thriving chain foodscape. Moreover, it does not hurt that normally staid Waffle House dining can sometimes assume a decidedly raucous edge, given its long-standing reputation as a lightning rod for all kinds of "freak flag" behavior. However remote, the off chance that some left-field occurrence will punctuate ordinary restaurant operations—especially after dark—adds a sense of random excitement to mealtime proceedings arguably missing from most other (fast-)casual eateries (see chapter 3).

Prevailing public sentiments that conflate Waffle House with some variation of messy southern modernity notwithstanding, the company resists explicitly touting its geographical/cultural roots, as previously mentioned. Although not actively downplaying its regional bona fides, Waffle House nevertheless avoids overtly showcasing its southern affiliations in any of its marketing or consumer outreach. Again, one would be hard pressed to find evocative terms like "southern cooking" or "the South" mentioned in any of its promotional efforts. Similarly, resonant images such as the one found on Cracker Barrel's current logo—in this case, an elderly looking (white?) man in bib-overalls astride a front-porch rocking chair with his elbow resting on a rustic pickle barrel—remain all but absent in Waffle House signage or marketing. For Waffle House, this kind of indirect approach when it comes to crafting a viable corporate image vis-à-vis its perceived standing as a southern institution creates a vacuum of sorts, one leaving ample room for the southern imaginary's expansive tendencies to fill.

2

The House That Waffles Built

With some of the key elements of the historical/structural back-drop now documented (Isenberg 2016; Catte 2018), consideration of Waffle House's rise from an independent Atlanta-area greasy spoon to its elevated position within the (fast-)casual sector of today's chain restaurant scene is warranted. Paying particular attention to the interplay of events, personalities, and successes/failures that ultimately characterize the chain's decades-long journey from an essentially two-man operation in the 1950s to a widely popular brand with approximately 45,000 employees spread across some 1,990 retail locations in over 2 dozen states, what follows is a concise overview of company history/operations, demonstrating how the chain both exemplifies and subverts many of the tropes variously rooted in accepted southern imaginaries.

The rise of Waffle House as both a multimillion-dollar company with considerable name recognition and an iconic restaurant brand cultivating a wholesome corporate image frequently at odds with its oft-beleaguered public persona can be approached in various ways. Nowadays, it arguably stands as much as a veritable American success story readily steeped in the familiar tropes of entrepreneurial initiative and spirited can-do-ism as it does an episodic journey wherein the triumphs and setbacks of an enduring commercial partnership can sometimes oversentimentalize, sometimes underplay, the variegated realities of a decades-long business relationship, especially when refracted through the prismatic lens of the southern imaginary.

A useful construct for understanding the aspirations and yearnings of a region long accorded underdog status within the American experiment (Cobb 2005), the southern imaginary (pre)reflexively shapes the historicized idiosyncrasies, moralities, and pathologies of the Bible Belt into meaningful if also overdetermined expressions of cultural identity (Baker 2011). This swirling bricolage of narrative, imagery, and sentiment assumes particular resonance in the case of Waffle House. Much of the chain's public profile evokes the dualities and disparities informing core aspects of southern modernity (Blinder 2018; Moser 2018). As is argued here and throughout this book, such contradictions lend metaphorical heft to notions of Waffle House as a viable microcosm of the American South.

Bearing this in mind, attempts to decouple popular accounts of Waffle House's early stages and later achievements from this compelling framework present various complications given the enduring sway this intersubjective southern mythos holds over the hearts and minds of so many folks living on either side of the Mason-Dixon Line. The available details of how the chain emerged and expanded into a such quintessential aspect of America's restaurant foodscape exhibit basic narrative coherence when considered altogether. Just how deeply such backstory accounts like those characterizing Waffle House's regional rise ultimately penetrate the national consciousness remains an open question.

For decades, little information about the lives of Waffle House executives and cofounders much less anything about company finances made its way into the public sphere (Mote and Stansell 2020). Like its aversion to traditional restaurant advertising and promotion on television, radio, and in print, Waffle House has kept fairly mum on its inner workings all these years, even to the point where the sales figures and other data that actually do make it into the public record are not company provided but are rather rough calculations estimated by outside analysts (Mote and Stansell 2020). Speaking with the *Atlanta Business Chronicle* in 1988, Bryan Elliot, an Atlanta-based financial analyst, stated, "There are three types of companies. There are public companies that trade stock and have to share information. Then there are private companies that don't trade stock but are somewhat open about their operations and numbers. And then there are the companies that won't even acknowledge that they exist. And that is Waffle House. They are a very, very private and tight-lipped company" (Welch 1988).

So, with the general thrust in the public domain, but not so much the specifics of how company cofounders Joe Rogers Sr. and Tom Forkner took their original concept—in this case, a simple greasy-spoon venture launched just outside of Atlanta in Avondale Estates, Georgia, on Labor Day weekend in 1955—to a fast-casual chain of national repute, the broad strokes of a conventional bootstrapping narrative coalesce into an evocative origin story albeit one not necessarily appreciated outside of Waffle House's southern stronghold in and around the Big Peach. Barring some dramatized warts-and-all telling of Waffle House's origins and ascendancy along the lines of the 2016 Hollywood biopic *The Founder* starring Michael Keaton (as fabled McDonald's CEO and cutthroat fast-food visionary Ray Kroc), considerable discursive space remains available for a more nuanced rendering of the eatery's modest beginnings and eventual rise in the South's chain restaurant scene.

Waffle House both illuminates and casts shadows across the region's cultural landscape and established dining scene, so any generative recounting of its formative years and the personalities driving its success warrants consideration beyond the mainstream's essentializing gaze. The broad-brush characterizations already showcased in the accepted lore of today's South go only so far in revealing the underlying complexities and contradictions of Waffle House's unfolding corporate narrative. In contrast to the company's largely hands-off approach to managing its current public image vis-à-vis television/radio advertising and other mass media marketing (see introduction), Waffle House has taken small but decisive steps in recent years to tout a particular version of its early stages and accomplishments.

In shoring up its legacy this way, however, the chain still avoids any overt or official affiliation to the South whether as a cultural touchstone or geographical backdrop. The regional connections so widely attributed to

Figure 2.1. Waffle House founders Joe Rogers Sr. (left) and Tom Forkner (right) chat with seated customer, Norcross, Georgia, 2005. AP Photo/Ric Feld

Waffle House in popular sentiment, with many ascribing it southern icon status (Junod 2009; Blinder 2018), find little expression in portrayals of its corporate beginnings. Before marketing itself as "America's Best Place to Eat," Waffle House publicized its operations with the slogan "Good Food *Fast*." Neither catchphrase comes across as all that descriptive or anywhere close to evoking a popular brand image ostensibly rooted in this distinctive regional milieu. If anything, such generic messaging leaves considerable space for the open-ended variabilities of the southern imaginary to subsequently fill.

The Waffle House Museum

Indeed, those wanting a breezy or curated depiction of Waffle House's unique genesis need look no farther than the company's namesake museum housed in the original Avondale Estates location near the Atlanta suburb of Decatur. The venue opened in 2008 as the Waffle House Museum, becoming another stop on the local sightseeing circuit. The chain's birthplace sits inconspicuously enough on a corner lot along a busy stretch of roadway near a tire store and auto repair shop. Across the street stands a modern mixed-use complex with upper-floor apartments and ground-floor retailing. Its contemporary aesthetics serve as an obvious counterpoint to the Waffle House Museum's unassuming shoebox architecture.

Not continuously occupied by the company since its launch some sixty-five years ago, the original Waffle House location went through various business incarnations over the years. In 1973, Waffle House first sold the property to one of its store managers, who ran it as an independent grill minus the Waffle House name or company backing. The property changed hands more times over subsequent decades; notably operating as a Chinese take-out eatery whose heyday spanned most of the 1990s. Punctuating these extended periods of occupancy between Waffle House's original ownership and its museum phase was the occasional vacancy, leaving the building unused anywhere from a few weeks to a few months at a time. It was during these intervals of inactivity that noticeable signs of disrepair to the property became most visible (Auchmutey 2008).

By the time Waffle House repurchased the space in 2004, its unkempt appearance approached eyesore status within the surrounding area's street-level fabric. Where it once boasted clean lines and an inviting facade, the restaurant facility and adjoining property had gradually succumbed to the ravages of time. Minimal upkeep and ill-advised remodeling changes hastened its decline, leaving a commercial structure marred by pockmarked features and a weed-strewn parking lot. The shoebox-shaped building's empty storefront had become so rundown, in fact, that by the early twenty-first century most passers-by knew little of its novel position within metro Atlanta's urban heritage, much less its wider significance in regional food-ways (RoadsideAmerica.com 2002).

Exterior and interior work began in earnest once Waffle House reacquired the property in 2004. Beyond efforts to restore the company birthplace to its original look and realize its potential as a local tourist stop, other factors motivated the chain in taking on this project. Even as this venture mirrored ongoing gentrification work transforming neighborhoods throughout metro Atlanta, it was also implemented in a putative attempt to boost Waffle House's corporate profile and historical standing across the state and nationwide.

Although unlikely to achieve the same type of recognition as other iconic Georgia brands in altering the fabric of American consumerism, namely, Coca-Cola,[1] Home Depot, and Chick-fil-A,[2] Waffle House made deliberate strides in that direction with the 2008 launch of the Waffle House Museum. Establishing this unassuming showcase of company achievement and history provided Waffle House a new platform to tout its accomplishments. It can be viewed not only as a bid to burnish brand legitimacy within US retailing and America's (fast-)casual restaurant industry but also as a genuine attempt at shaping a coherent and resonant legacy, laying claim to whatever historical recognition the brand warrants for its myriad contributions to southern life and foodways.

Validating such efforts was the Georgia Historical Society's decision to formally classify the Waffle House Museum site as a historical landmark in 2012. To celebrate this special designation, an official commemoration ceremony took place on a sunny September afternoon in front of the diner's refurbished glass and brick facade. With dozens of well-wishers and local media in attendance, the event included the nonagenarian cofounders Rogers and Forkner as guests of honor. They unveiled the newly erected historical marker that stands eye-level near the museum entrance. Affixed to the top of a metal pole, the cast-aluminum "Alamo"-shaped plaque summarizes Waffle House's origins and achievements in just over one hundred words. Adding a touch of prestige and perhaps the definitive word on public understanding of how the breakfast chain emerged and thrived, the marker reads

At this location, on Labor Day 1955, Avondale Estates neighbors Joe Rogers, Sr. and Tom Forkner founded the first Waffle House. The name was inspired by the most popular item on the original menu. The restaurant's focus on fast-food and round-the-clock service reflected mid-century societal shifts toward an automobile culture. As suburbs and the interstate highway system developed through the region and the nation, Waffle House grew to include over 1,600 locations nationwide, becoming an American cultural icon open 24 hours a day, seven days a week. In 2004 Waffle House reacquired the original restaurant building and opened it as a museum in 2008. (Georgia Historical Society 2012)

The low-key Waffle House Museum offers a decidedly retro vibe that evokes an idealized version of southern urbanism and effectively downplays the darker undercurrents of mid-twentieth-century American dining—in effect, those rooted in white privilege and the segregated public eating practices of the time. The entire venue is rather small, unable to accommodate large numbers at any one time. A 1950's replica diner that looks something like a movie set serves as the museum's primary focal point. Each year, groups of senior citizens, school children, families, and curious sightseers filter through this old-school Waffle House facsimile, gaining insights into how today's iconic restaurant brand initially ran its operations.

Tours are free but almost always by appointment, usually on Wednesdays or Thursdays, in the late morning or early afternoon. About four times per year, the museum holds an open house for those who want to check things out without the hassle of securing reservations. Most of the time, however, due diligence in planning ahead effectively pays off. If not for the fact that Waffle House prides itself for seemingly never closing its doors or rarely turning anyone away from service, the museum's limited or irregular business hours would hardly warrant comment. However, this narrow window of accessibility represents something of a cool irony that in certain ways reflects the South's idiosyncratic character: a place of folksy friendliness and deep-rooted divisions based on class, race, politics, religion, and gender.

Upon entering the museum, guests find themselves in a lunch counter setting similar to those experienced by first-generation Waffle House clientele. This highly curated space features an open-air kitchen and fullback barstools among other postwar restaurant amenities. Simple wood paneling, framed menu prices, stainless-steel appliances, and shelves lined with dinnerware and provisions define the room's interior wall space. The raised counter seating offers visitors a convenient perch from which to learn about Waffle House's various accomplishments from tour guides well versed in company history.

Museum-trained volunteers serving as faux waitstaff help guide visitors through the facility during scheduled business hours. Displaying their knowledge of Waffle House lore in both scripted spiels and during question-and-answer sessions, guides almost always win audiences over by first wearing and then distributing those disposable paper hats sported by on-duty kitchen workers. Many visitors end up wearing the flimsy Waffle House headgear for the duration of their museum outing. Some even get a shot at winning inexpensive company swag by spinning a prize wheel once their visit winds down. Arguably the luckiest guests of all were those who got to meet Rogers or Forkner when either or both would drop by the museum for a quick visit in the years before their passing within months of each other in 2017.

No meals are prepared on-site, but a fully functional eatery is located a few blocks away for anyone craving simple breakfast/dinner fare. Occasionally, Waffle House parks its yellow/black food truck outside the venue, doling out free waffles, coffee, and sodas for museum guests. Capitalizing on the recent food truck craze, the company-sponsored mobile kitchen is wrapped in a large vinyl graphic/decal, making it look like an actual brick-and-mortar Waffle House restaurant on wheels. It is frequently rented out for weddings and other catered events in the metro Atlanta area and across the Southeast. The food truck is sometimes even deployed to assist disaster-impacted communities as it was in 2016 when residents of Baton Rouge, Louisiana, who experienced catastrophic flooding were provided free food (Snider 2018).

Besides the replica diner, the Waffle House Museum also includes an auxiliary space where guests can view an assortment of company artifacts and memorabilia spanning some sixty-five years of restaurant history. Objects on display or behind glass include old menus, framed photos, vintage uniforms, and assorted promotional knickknacks touting the Waffle House name. Collectively, these exhibited items convey a basic timeline that allows even those unfamiliar with the brand to appreciate the many changes that have transformed Waffle House since its founding decades ago. In fact, when everything in the old-school diner and memorabilia area is considered, a rather buoyant company narrative emerges that (understandably) privileges a sort of nostalgia-tinged Americana over any kind of textured or shaded approach.

Before Waffle House, There Was Toddle House

Numerous historical factors informed the Waffle House style and format of its initial operations in and around Atlanta in the decades before it achieved household status across the American consciousness (see chapter 1). Perhaps nothing exerted greater sway over the Waffle House brand both in the years leading up to and subsequent to its mid-1950's launch than the aforementioned Toddle House breakfast chain (see chapter 1). In fact, the Waffle House that so many recognize and respond to nowadays would not exist without the considerable influence of this once-popular Memphis-based eatery.

Toddle House's humble beginnings and eventual success as a company extend back to the Great Depression (1929–33), really to the America of Roosevelt's New Deal (1932–39), when the country was struggling to chart its way out of the devastating political and socioeconomic tumult that had negated so much of the prosperity of previous years. Starting as a fledging Texas diner venture by Jacob Cox Stedman in 1929 known as "One's a Meal," the chain relocated operations to Tennessee and rebranded as Toddle House once James Frederick "Fred" Smith assumed controlling interest in 1931 (Rogers 2000).

The ever-enterprising Smith charted out an aggressive company expansion plan that extended into the 1940s, even past his 1948 death, eventually peaking in the 1950s with more than two hundred Toddle House restaurants nationwide. His initiative and drive are widely credited with elevating Toddle House into a profitable regional chain with considerable national reach (Rogers 2000:65), but the momentum behind Smith's achievements proved unsustainable in the years after his passing. In fact, by the early 1960s, the Toddle House name had all but faded from the public sphere after a series of ownership changes (Langdon 1986:35–37).

Toddle House's peak phase, just as its corporate footprint attained maximum geographical range, coincided with Waffle House's mid-1950s arrival. Toddle House innovations and in some instances its managerial shortsightedness, particularly as it related to advancement opportunities for enterprising employees, profoundly shaped Waffle House's future direction both immediately and over the long term. Rogers, a onetime Toddle House vice president, admitted as much stating, "If Toddle House would have offered ownership to the management team, there never would have been a Waffle House" (Scheiber 2017).

So, if Toddle House established a viable blueprint for meeting the everyday dining needs of a largely blue-collar clientele in simple surroundings, then Waffle House subsequently elevated and expanded this formula, going on to create not only an enduring 24-7 sit-down eatery with some 1,990 locations nationwide but also an iconic restaurant brand with considerable cultural cachet in the twenty-first-century South. The DNA of Toddle House remains overtly imprinted on current Waffle House operations—the afore-mentioned Toddle House Omelet—just as it finds discernible expression in other aspects of today's restaurant foodscape.

As a no-frills chain eatery with distinctly southern affiliations, Tod-dle House projected a coherent brand image primarily through its distinc-tive restaurant look (Langdon 1986:39). At the height of brand popularity, few could mistake Toddle House franchises for anything else, as how all looked so much alike both outside and inside. Adhering to a unique built-to-plan architectural design and kitchen preparation and service scheme, most Toddle House outlets varied little from one another in terms of aes-thetics and amenities. Earlier iterations of Toddle House were prefabricated twenty-four-by-twelve-foot buildings delivered via flatbed trucks to local sites and meant to be manned by one employee but later ones were con-structed on-site with more durable materials and were somewhat larger. The portability of first-generation Toddle Houses proved decidedly advan-tageous to the chain's burgeoning success. As Langdon writes (1986:36), "It eliminated the need to purchase permanent building sites. The restau-rants could adjust to changes in automobile traffic and public transporta-tion routes, and they could occupy lots that real-estate speculators were willing to lease only on a short-term basis—in some instances a mere thirty days at a time. Any chain that could pick up its building and move would obviously have a stronger hand in negotiating with land-owners."

With only minimal variation, the modest and yet distinct outward ap-pearances of Toddle House outlets encompassed whitewashed cottage-style buildings with brick or faux brick exteriors and blue roofing bracketed by dual ornamental chimneys. Copper canopies enclosed by glass vestibules de-fined customer entrances. Primly manicured lawns accented by simple shrub-bery and flowerbeds, sometimes surrounded by white picket fences, and elevated street signs featuring two short-order cooks holding aloft steam-ing restaurant grub enhanced such roadside aesthetics (Langdon 1986:39). Echoing the architectural simplicity of pre–World War II gas stations or ef-ficiency motel rooming units, the consistent look these quaint eateries ef-fectively became the Toddle House calling card. Much like latter day Waffle House restaurants, what with their resonant signage, evocative yellow/black color scheme, and signature shoebox architecture, the hallmark uniformity of Toddle House outlets served as a familiar touchstone for those traveling across midcentury America's increasingly complex road system.

According to Langdon (1986:36), "Toddle House . . . did try to locate on the 'work side' of the street—the side that people traveled when heading toward downtown jobs in the morning. On the work side of the street, a restaurant could get more people into the habit of stopping for breakfast; sales were said to be slower on the opposite side of the street."

The interiors of Toddle House locations appeared no less distinguishing than their distinctive facades. The company slogan of "Good as the Best" found expression inside the compact eateries through an open-kitchen design featuring stainless steel appliances/equipment, backless counter stools, checkerboard floors, and patented "cashier machines" that allowed customers to deposit their checks and payments on the way out through an honor system approach (Dowdy 2019:39–41). If one particular aspect characterized Toddle House's interior dining spaces during the chain's commercial heyday, it was the confined quarters and limited seating available to restaurant guests. A standard Toddle House could accommodate no more than fifteen customers at any one time (Lauderdale 2011), so employees "aimed to have the average customer in and out in twelve minutes" (Langdon 1986:37).

Although no longer an operable breakfast chain despite the short-lived mid-1980's revival mentioned in chapter 1 (Sherman 1987), architectural traces of Toddle House are still encountered in many large and midsized American cities across the South, Midwest, and East Coast. Unlike the conspicuity of new businesses occupying what was obviously once a chalet-roofed IHOP or a Pizza Hut building with the "double mansard" style roof (Tran and Cahill 2016), former Toddle House restaurants blend rather seamlessly into local cityscapes. The fact that they fail to immediately stick out is not altogether surprising considering most have been repainted and repurposed multiple times over the years, obscuring their original character. Still, city dwellers with a keen eye can usually identify a former Toddle House property based on the building's trademark dual chimneys and limited square footage.

Nowadays, Toddle House's lingering influence is more widely experienced beyond chance encounters in the architectural palimpsest of select US cities. Indeed, it is within the everyday operations of today's Waffle House where most people unknowingly confront the historical legacy of this somewhat obscure restaurant brand. Besides menu offerings centered around simple breakfast/dinner fare and restaurant layouts emphasizing open-air kitchens, counter service, and up-close customer/employee interactions, Toddle House's most far-reaching impact on the Waffle House brand remains its close ties to company cofounder Rogers.

Figure 2.2. Toddle House building, Mills Avenue, Orlando, Florida. Ty Matejowsky

Joe Rogers Sr.

In 2000, a small Georgia press, Looking Glass Books, quietly published the official autobiography of Rogers under the seemingly strange but ultimately meaningful title *Who's Looking Out for the Poor Old Cash Customer?*[3] Attracting scant public attention and little critical notice beyond some uniformly positive coverage in and around Atlanta, the book quickly faded from view, with occasional secondhand copies showing up on the resale market at prices few would find reasonable. Despite such minimal publicity upon its initial release and limited availability in the years thereafter, the memoir's value as a rare insider's look at the chain's regional rise and the personalities behind its continued success remains inestimable.

As an autobiographical account, the book works on multiple levels, providing key insights into the decades-long Forkner/Rogers relationship as well as revealing specific details about Waffle House operations, especially those regarding the chain's early years. With such recollections coming straight from a company cofounder, composed (ghostwritten?) in a decidedly folksy way—one that easily befits the unpretentious brand image so familiar to generations of southern restaurant-goers—the text engages readers with a friendly conversational tone that, however amiable, belies both a determined ambition and discernible sense of pride at what the author and his various collaborators have entrepreneurially achieved. By memoir's end, it is clear that Rogers is not shy about publicizing his myriad business accomplishments—it is after all his book—but only through more indirect ways such as using the first person plural ("we") rather than the singular pronoun ("I") to tout so many Waffle House achievements as team efforts. Anything redolent of executive braggadocio or credit-hogging would just not jibe with the brand's simple public persona.

Such positive attributes notwithstanding, the book does fall short in certain ways. As will be elaborated on in chapter 4, two passages describing Waffle House's treatment of African Americans prior to desegregation (Rogers 2000:146) and in the aftermath of Martin Luther King Jr.'s 1968 assassination (Rogers 2000:168–69) come across as rather tone-deaf, if not a bit self-congratulatory when considered in hindsight. Not quite as problematic as these accounts is how the book closely hews to the familiar tropes so often encountered in bestselling CEO or business professional memoirs, especially those documenting the experiences of white male entrepreneurs whose adolescence and young adulthood were profoundly shaped by the Great Depression and World War II (e.g., Sam Walton's 1992 autobiography *Made in America*). These tried-and-true elements include emphasis on humble beginnings, instilled values, guiding principles rooted in invaluable life lessons, service and mentorship under influential business veterans, handshake deals, cultivated professional connections, eventually blazing one's own trail, character-testing setbacks ultimately surmounted, business innovation, and finally some sort of retrospective reflection.

Readers already versed in popular accounts of how business up-and-comers move into corporate America's higher ranks, even while so many of their peers ultimately fail, would quickly recognize the familiar career arc and signpost personal events presented in Rogers's memoir. Aphorisms like the one from which the book's title is derived abound in *Who's Looking Out for the Poor Old Cash Customer?* Although not exactly Horatio Alger, the book nevertheless embraces many of the characteristics so evocative of a bootstrapping business tale in its unfolding narrative. Even as it deviates little from this proven biographical formula, certain gaps peek through Rogers's memoir, leaving an arguably incomplete portrait of an important player in US chain restaurant retailing.

Rogers was born in Jackson, Tennessee, in 1919, coming of age there during the Great Depression and graduating from Jackson High School in 1938. Brought up middle class, his mother, a housewife with a strong faith, and his father, a railroad man who lost his job in 1933, raised him to understand the value of hard work and interpersonal relationships—at least according to his autobiography—that informed his subsequent business career. During these years, Rogers held multiple jobs including work as a newspaper delivery boy, laundryman, and carhop at a local barbeque restaurant. About his father, Rogers writes, "Watching him I learned that people never get tired of having their egos built up. You tell them something good about themselves and they'll come back for more" (Rogers 2000:5).

As a gridiron standout, the future Waffle House cofounder also internalized lifelong lessons about competition while playing football. He wrote, "Our football coach would look us directly in the eye and say 'Son, we don't lose.' I have carried this thought with me through the years" (Rogers 2000:26). Declining a Union University football scholarship, Rogers worked at the local Kress's five-and-dime, where he "began to learn right off how a successful business operates" (Rogers 2000:33). More than anything, his short time there impressed upon him something that he considered to be his most important business lesson: "You never lose a satisfied customer" (Rogers 2000:33).

Rogers enlisted in the Army National Guard in 1940 before transferring to its Air Corps branch in the months leading up to Pearl Harbor. Married in 1942, he attended flight school in Texas, earning his wings in 1943. Flying B-24s and eventually achieving the rank of captain, Rogers served as a flight instructor until after World War II. He turned down an opportunity to pilot for American Airlines, deciding instead to go to work for Fred Smith at Toddle House. In the late 1940s, Rogers oversaw chain operations in New Haven and Philadelphia, regularly working the grill himself.

Rogers writes reflectively of this time: "In 1947, cooking in a short-order restaurant was something of an art—a profession. The grill men carried their own skillets and spatulas and everything, and some of them considered themselves as hosts as well as cooks" (Rogers 2000:67). Rapidly advancing through the company ranks, Rogers—by this time with two small children—was relocated to Atlanta in 1947 after accepting a promotion to serve as Toddle House's Southeast division manager. During his time in the Big Peach, he would meet and do business with various movers and shakers, most affiliated with the regional dining scene. The most influential and life-altering relationship he forged was with his realtor and Avondale Estates neighbor, Tom Forkner.

Tom Forkner

Forkner never penned a book documenting his upbringing, education, and career. Leaving no comprehensive statement of his core business philosophy much less any in-depth account of his professional triumphs and setbacks, much of Forkner's background and accomplishments in the public record remains subsumed within the broader Waffle House narrative and his successful relationship with Rogers.

Ostensibly a more behind-the-scenes and low-key personality compared with Rogers's out-front customer relations persona, Forkner primarily concerned himself with company innerworkings, always looking for ways to boost profitability (Sharpe 2017). Even until his 2017 death, a month or so after Rogers's, Forkner remained relatively mum about his own Waffle House experiences. As helpful as such personal insights would be in illuminating the Waffle House story, serving to supplement or balance Rogers's recollections, enough material has accrued over the years to provide an informative biographical profile.

Born in the small middle Georgia town of Hawkinsville in 1918, Forkner was the fifth of seven children. His family later relocated near Atlanta in the part of DeKalb County that would later become Avondale Estates. Forkner attended Young Harris Junior College, going on to attain a law degree from the John Marshall Law School in Chicago. A practicing attorney by the age of twenty-three, he spent the war years in Oak Ridge, Tennessee, working on the top-secret Manhattan Project, serving as an intelligence and security officer. Leaving the military and returning to Georgia, he took the over the family business, Forkner Realty Company, after his father passed away. It was in his capacity as a local real estate agent that Forkner crossed paths with Rogers, selling his future business partner an Avondale Estates home in 1949.

After a late 1950's health scare, Forkner incorporated more leisure activities into his lifestyle, including what become an abiding passion for golf. This love of the game proved no mere hobby; in fact, Forkner racked up an impressive array of titles and accolades over subsequent years, eventually earning him induction into the Georgia Golf Hall of Fame in 2007. According to the *Augusta Chronicle*, "Forkner won his Georgia Senior Championships in 1968, 1969, 1982, and 1986. He also teamed to win the Georgia Seniors Four-Ball championship twice (1974 and 1980); and has won the 80-over division of the World Super Seniors tournament (2004 and 2005). He also qualified for the first two U.S. Seniors Opens, in 1980 and 1981" (Westin 2007).

For many, such athletic achievements would likely represent the pinnacle of one's public life. Not so in the case of Forkner, as his business accomplishments with Rogers far overshadow his impressive feats on the links. By this point, the circumstances surrounding how the two came together to create such an enduring and successful restaurant chain appear more apocryphal than genuine. This probably has much to do with the difficulties of retrospectively reconciling how a company with some 1,990 outlets nowadays could begin modestly, with just one store in the suburban South almost seventy years ago.

Rogers and Forkner

In the summer of 1954, even as his travels for Toddle House took him across the Southeast to inspect multiple company outlets, Rogers often met with his neighbor Forkner to discuss various business and real estate matters. Among other things, the two talked about how Toddle House disallowed managers like Rogers from increasing their stake and/or connection in the brand through company stock purchases. Unable to reap additional financial benefits for his hard work and lacking incentive to invest more of himself in an organization that denied staff this kind of employee perk, Rogers found himself approaching a career crossroads of sorts. Left unremedied, he saw this policy as serious enough for him to one day leave Toddle House and venture out on his own. His growing introspection about his place in the organization, coupled with the fact that Avondale Estates lacked its own twenty-four-hour breakfast eatery of the Toddle House variety, effectively sowed the seeds of what would become the very first Waffle House.

From these chats, the broad strokes of a new business venture emerged. Conceptually, it is clear that both Rogers and Forkner envisioned their undertaking as an unpretentious eatery serving simple breakfast/dinner selections to everyday folk in and around Avondale Estates and Decatur, staying open twenty-four hours a day year-round. The original Waffle House venture initially featured a sixteen-item menu including selections of waffles, hash browns, bacon, eggs, sausage, burgers, and patty melts. Of these, waffles were purportedly most popular with customers. In fact, by most retrospective accounts, it was waffles' favored status with the dining public that emerged as the deciding factor in calling the restaurant Waffle House (Wyatt 2005). Yet assertions like these beg the obvious question: how could a new eatery have a most popular menu item much less be named after it when the restaurant had not yet opened to the public? Perhaps Roger and Forkner devised the name based on the former's experiences working for Toddle House.

The origins of the Waffle House name become even more murky when trying to ascertain which cofounder actually hit on the catchy title. At various points, both Forkner and Rogers laid claim to coming up with the name entirely on their own. In 2005, NBC and the Associated Press gave sole credit to Forkner, quoting him as saying that "it was the highest profit item you could do, so I said, 'Call it Waffle House and encourage people to eat waffles'" (Wyatt 2005). Rogers, for his part, wrote in his autobiography: "'What will we call it?' Tom asked. 'How about Waffle House' I said. Tom wasn't excited about the name. He said it didn't describe exactly what we had in mind to do. But the restaurant world was undergoing a tremendous change, and the right name was important for us. McDonald's started the same year as we did, and more and more people were going to take-out food. I want[ed] customers to know that we weren't take-out, and I figured that everybody had sense enough to know that you couldn't take a waffle out. People had to come in and sit down and eat, and that's where I wanted them" (Rogers 2000:98). Questions still linger as to how the iconic Waffle House name came to be. Yet, in fairness to each cofounder, both Forkner and Rogers were well into their golden years, when memories often prove unreliable, as these claims were publicized.

So, besides coming up with the name and menu during and after their initial summer of 1954 discussions, Rogers and Forkner still needed to complete certain tasks before their eatery could become operational. Specifically, the plan for their joint collaboration entailed a bifurcation of duties whereby Forkner was tasked with one set of obligations and Rogers entrusted with some equally important responsibilities. This sort of division of labor would go on to characterize the Forkner/Rogers dialectic for years to come, and in 1954 and 1955, it mainly entailed Forkner finding a suitable lot and commercial builder for the restaurant and Rogers taking the lead on how to run the place. The duo would eventually settle on an undeveloped site halfway between Avondale Estates and Decatur for the new eatery (Rogers 2000:97–98). According to Rogers, "That's how we started out in business together, and for the next fifty years we've never had a contract between us. Neither of us has once said to the other that we were going to do something without doing it, and neither of us has ever lied to the other. We've gone through the years working that way" (2000:97–98).

Securing a $6,000 bank loan for restaurant equipment and getting Forkner's brother, John, to purchase the designated property so they could pay him a $150 monthly lease fee without directly tying themselves to a specific piece of real estate, Forkner and Rogers used Toddle House operations as a basic template for how to launch and manage their new Waffle House facility (Rogers 2000:101–6). From a nearly identical accounting system to a preference for keeping cooks and waitstaff behind the counter as much as possible, the duo approached its inaugural restaurant venture with an "if it ain't broke, don't fix it" philosophy. Even the batter recipe used to make their signature product, waffles, came from Toddle House (Rogers 2000:136).

As with Toddle House, flashy aesthetics took a backseat to simple functionality in the new eatery's architectural design. Everything from Waffle House's distinctive building size/shape to its iconic colors followed an effective minimalist approach. The shoebox building so inextricably associated with Waffle House restaurants nowadays was something Rogers emphasized from the outset. Even while interior features would go on to change subtly and significantly in the years to come, the company would deviate little from the distinctive and easily replicable exterior sported by the very first Waffle House location. Similarly, the restaurants resonant yellow/black color scheme was something Rogers devised for simplicity. According to a 2018 *Atlanta Journal-Constitution* news story, he "picked the colors yellow and black because it reminded him of a school bus. He thought it would increase the restaurant's visibility to drivers. It's a common misconception that the founders chose the colors because Joe Rogers Junior was a Georgia Tech grad" (Guta 2018).

Interestingly, Toddle House was not the only midcentury Memphis brand from which Rogers and Forkner drew inspiration (Rogers 2000:104). Given the multiplicity of chain and mom-and-pop eateries operating in town and cities across 1950's America, creating roadside signage that visually stood apart from competitors proved a viable business strategy in attracting the attention of potential customers. During these years, perhaps no other elevated curbside marquee was more iconic and effective in showcasing what a business had to offer than the one used by motor hotel pioneer Holiday Inn (Nelson 2002). The chain's "Great Sign" featured "an emerald green curvilinear field with a big white neon 'HOLIDAY INN' done in casual script. This was affixed to a red pylon atop which a yellow star exploded its energy into the night. Meanwhile a winking Vegas-style arrow pointed tired travelers to the office while an illuminated window box below advertised rates and local gatherings" (Nelson 2002).

Forkner and Rogers modified this aesthetics by changing the color scheme and inverting the design. According to Rogers (2000:104),"We turned the arrow upside down and put it across the bottom so that the roving lights ran down the outside of the sign and underneath, pointing to our first restaurant. We put waves on the bottom of the WAFFLE HOUSE letters so that the words sort of dripped off the sign, like butter and syrup running off waffles. Soon after, blinking lights in signs were outlawed."

Waffle House Opens

Opened on Labor Day in 1955, Waffle House proved a success with local diners. Over subsequent weeks, the restaurant seemed well on its way toward achieving Rogers and Forkner's goal of pleasing "everybody who walked in the door and . . . (making) a little money, then take that money and go out and buy another restaurant" (Rogers 2000:106). Lacking a five-year plan or any type of stated benchmark goal wherein a given number of locations would be up and running within the near future, the duo approached their new venture in an exploratory and open-ended sort of way.

Waffle House's auspicious beginnings notwithstanding, the restaurant and its owners' budding partnership could not escape Toddle House's considerable shadow. Even as Rogers and Forkner cribbed many operational details and design ideas for their breakfast eatery from Toddle House, they still went to great lengths to avoid directly competing with this highly capitalized regional brand (Rogers 2000:106). In the fall of 1955, in fact, the prospect of taking on Rogers's current employer in any head-to-head fashion proved both unwise and unfeasible. Just how aware Toddle House was about one of its division manager's operating an independent breakfast eatery within its sales territory remains an open question. Yet, in a move suggesting either complete unawareness of Rogers's new sideline venture or alternatively as a way to retain his talent and knowhow, Toddle House offered Rogers a promotion, albeit one without the option of acquiring company stock, quickly upending the Forkner/Rogers partnership before it really got going.

So, approximately three months after his new coventure launched, Rogers promptly accepted a vice president position in the Toddle House organization, overseeing the established chain's operations in its newly created Central region, basically everything east of the Mississippi River, with give or take around one hundred eateries. Assuming this new leadership role not only necessitated a move back to Tennessee for Rogers and his family it also placed his obligations to both twenty-four-hour breakfast ventures at cross-purposes. Conflicted about owning Waffle House stock while his Toddle House responsibilities needed his full attention, Rogers sold Forkner his stake in the Avondale Estates undertaking in 1956, leaving his partner with no expressed commitment to one day return.

For the next four to five years, Waffle House remained under Forkner's watch even as he prioritized his real estate business over the restaurant. Forkner enjoyed the diner as a gathering spot for his Avondale Estates neighbors, but the daily grind of overseeing a fledgling 24-7 eatery began exacting a toll on him, necessitating the hiring of additional help. Through Rogers, Forkner contacted a former Toddle House manager who had just opened a new restaurant venture in Atlanta in 1957 called the Wagon Wheel on Peachtree Street (see chapter 4). Mortgaging his house, Forkner came up with cash to buy the Wagon Wheel and convert it into a second Waffle House location (Rogers 2000:116). The eventual success of this new branch led to the opening of several more Waffle Houses in and around Atlanta. By 1960, with four Waffle House restaurants up and running, the venture seemed poised for great things.

Rogers Returns

Rogers left Toddle House in 1961 just as the company was being bought out by a rival chain. Returning to Atlanta with his wife and four children, Rogers accepted Forkner's offer to rejoin Waffle House at a reduced salary and without the secretary and big office he enjoyed at Toddle House. As Waffle House continued to expand over the next several years, both Forkner and Rogers looked for ways to distinguish the restaurant from its mom-and-pop and chain competitors. According to Rogers, "We were determined not to earn a reputation that so many restaurants of that era had, that of a dingy, neglected, greasy spoon kind of place. We were going to turn the lights on bright so customers could see every inch of the place, and every inch was going to be clean. We tried globe lights and liked them, and they became one of our trademarks. You see those globe lights, and you know it's a Waffle House. We also tried to keep signs out of the window. For security reasons I want to see the cash register from the street" (2000:126–27).

Such efforts also entailed continually seeking out industry talent— many former Toddle House managers ended up at Waffle House overseeing individual stores—as well as looking for ways to enhance customer/employee interactions and improve worker efficiency by reducing the number of steps required to complete any number of tasks. For example, standard Waffle House restaurants maintain a thirty-three-seat capacity. According to Rogers, "We found that thirty-six seats required one more person behind the counter, and the return on our investment declined. Ask anybody who's run a thirty-three seat Waffle House and he'll tell you it's the most efficient moneymaker in the business" (2000:158).

Integrating feedback provided by customers, employees, designers, suppliers, and wholesalers became a hallmark of Waffle House's business model. Likewise, observing how restaurant patrons use the counter and dining areas proved helpful in this regard. Balancing how many aspects of their operations should remain in-house as opposed to purchased from vendors remained a concern for Rogers and Forkner as their number of restaurants grew throughout the 1960s (Rogers 2000:133–43). Over the years, Waffle House menus came to include products and items supplied by mainstay brands of the US food industry including Minute Maid, Kraft, and Coca-Cola (Rogers 2000:136–37).

Waffle House Expands

In June 1967, Waffle House adapted a franchising system wherein select independent operators would pay to secure the right to utilize the company brand and know-how in their restaurants. By this point, the company maintained twenty free-standing outlets of its own, generating some $2 million in annual sales (Rogers 2000:166). According to Rogers, the Waffle House traits most appreciated by its potential franchisees were its simplicity, utilization of surplus property/real estate (i.e., focusing on noncorner lots), and, finally, testing out all new ideas before requiring them of nonbranch operations (Rogers 2000:173–75). Elaborating further, he writes, "We sold our first thirteen franchises . . . for a total fee of $5,000. In light of the value of a franchise now, $385 apiece may seem terribly low to some. It was less than our daily sales average at the time. But we never set out to make money on the initial franchise fee. That money was just enough to pay for the support we offered to get them started. The return on our investment was the percentage that came back from the franchise restaurants every month through the decades" (2000:167–68).

By this point, Forkner and Rogers had expanded the chain into new territories including North and South Carolina, Florida, and Alabama. For Waffle House, "the art of selecting a site, 'buying the dirt' and building its own restaurants started in the early 1960s. Ever since then Waffle House, Inc. has built thousands of restaurants across the country. From the initial site research to buying the land to building the restaurant to installing the equipment, Waffle House and its subsidiary LaVista Equipment Supply get the restaurants ready to open for business—usually in just a few months" (Heath et al. 2005:109).

In fact, in the six years since Rogers returned (1961–67), Waffle House added sixteen eateries to its roster, bringing the total to twenty restaurants.

Rogers writes, "Through the 1960s and into the '70s, our growth strategy never changed. We built a new restaurant when we recognized the need for it, had the money to open it, and had a manager trained to run it. Without all three of those things in place, we held what we had" (Rogers 2000:159).

Around this time, Waffle House began looking to expand beyond their traditional base of operations within more densely settled towns and cities. Properties along stretches of interstate and regional expressways emerged as possible locations for their restaurants. As more and more late-night travelers took such roadways, Forkner and Rogers approached these roadside properties, however cautiously, as viable business sites. Testing the waters in Conyers, Georgia, southeast of Atlanta, they built their first roadside Waffle House along Interstate 20. Its success spawned many more company eateries of this variety over the decades, elevating the yellow/black Scrabble-tile Waffle House sign to a southern icon.

By 1970, Waffle House maintained thirty-five company-owned branches and thirty-seven franchise restaurants (Rogers 2000:182). To help oversee operations, the chain subdivided its sales area into districts administered by seasoned regional supervisors who reported back to corporate headquarters in Norcross, Georgia, twenty miles north of downtown Atlanta. This approach allowed the company to ensure adherence to their rigorous standards through a management structure. Rogers writes, "We structured lines of responsibility to give us close control and supervision of each restaurant. We decentralized our operations and ran them with a centralized policy. We taught each manager how to run a restaurant, then stepped out of the way and left him with the responsibility for sales, control, and employee satisfaction" (2000:165).

Joe "Bud" Rogers Jr. and Walter G. Ehmer

Fresh out of Harvard, Joe "Bud" Rogers Jr. (1950/1951–) came to work for his father's firm in 1971. After several years of apprenticeship, the younger Rogers assumed the company reins, serving in top leadership roles from 1973 to 2012. A brief bio in *The Waffle House Experience*—a photobook commemorating the company's fiftieth anniversary also published by Looking Glass Books, states: "To say Joe Rogers, Jr. knows Waffle House inside and out is a big understatement. Joe was the window washer at the first restaurant in 1955. From there he graduated to washing dishes, making pies, prepping hashbrowns and cooking. After college, he came back and worked his way to President in 1973, then Chairman in 1988. With more than 30 years as Waffle House CEO, Joe is the longest-serving chief executive in the restaurant industry. His leadership bridged the system from the founders dream to today's very vibrant, successful chain" (Heath et al. 2005:29).

With Rogers Jr. now calling the shots, cofounders Forkner and Rogers Sr. adopted more voluntary roles within the company. The two effectively stayed on in an advisory and ambassadorial capacity during Rogers Jr.'s tenure that proved less about everyday oversight and more about promoting the Waffle House brand, leaving them ample time to hunt, fish, golf, and enjoy other leisure pursuits throughout their semiretirement (Rogers 2000:185–98). Both Forkner and Rogers Sr. remained active with the company well into their nineties, never truly relinquishing their Waffle House affiliations even up until their passing within two months of each other in the spring of 2017.

Rogers Jr. used his four-decade stint as leader to elevate Waffle House into the regional icon and restaurant powerhouse with national repute that it is recognized as today. Under his stewardship, Waffle House's corporate footprint grew at a steady clip, deviating little from the cautious but successful formula established by Forkner and Rogers years earlier. Never one to unnecessarily borrow or leverage capital in order to expedite expansion, Rogers Jr. avoided accruing debt much like his father before him, only investing in new locations and properties when company funds were available. Also like his predecessors, Rogers Jr. did little to alter Waffle House's simple bill of fare. Proven breakfast items such as waffles, eggs, bacon, sausage, coffee, alongside lunch/dinner favorites including sandwiches, burgers, and steaks remained central to the core restaurant menu. What is more, primarily a cash-based business for most of its history, Waffle House did not begin accepting credit card payments in its company-owned branches until 2006 (Ruggles 2015).

From the 1970s on, few chains could match Waffle House in terms of numerical expansion. The company established hundreds of eateries throughout the South during these years, even moving into territories outside its regional stronghold. Part of what drove this Waffle House growth during this period was its launch of two subsidiary endeavors: LaVista Equipment Supply Co. and WHI Inc. The former mainly dealt with the design and selling of restaurant equipment while the latter enterprise was a real estate holding company also dabbling in vending machines. Unlike much of the competition, Waffle House held vast property holdings, owning much of the real estate on which its restaurants operate.

As the first decade of Rogers Jr.'s tenure drew to a close, Waffle House operated somewhere between three hundred and four hundred stores. By the end of the 1990s, this number increased almost three- or fourfold with some 1,230 restaurants operating as franchises or company-owned branches. These years of growth in the 1980s and 1990s had their share of hiccups or at the very least perceptions of company problems or stagnation. According to *FundingUniverse.com*, which provides detailed profiles of top US companies, Waffle House's franchising scheme seemed no longer financially viable by the late 1980s. Reports in the Atlanta media suggested the chain would no longer take on franchising partners and instead focus on company-owned branch operations. Whatever the veracity of such speculation, the company essentially remained mum on its franchising plans, eventually moving forward with its standard operating approach (FundingUniverse 2020).

Despite such speedbumps along the way, in anticipation of its fortieth anniversary in Avondale Estates, Waffle House effectively came full circle in January 1995, opening its one thousandth restaurant down the street from its inaugural location and what would become its namesake museum. By 2020, Waffle House was fast approaching its two thousandth outlet, significantly outpacing its primary restaurant rivals of Denny's and IHOP in sheer numbers.

Even as corporate breakfast/lunch counters such as Sambo's, Howard Johnson's, Toddle House, Steak 'n Egg Kitchen, Kettle Restaurant, and Huddle House either went out of business or significantly downscaled operations, Waffle House emerged as a prominent fixture across the US chain restaurant foodscape under Rogers Jr.'s multidecade leadership. While still retaining his office as Waffle House CEO, Rogers Jr. stepped away from his role as company president in 2006, allowing Walter G. Ehmer (1966–) to assume this leadership position. According to the *Newnan Times-Herald*, Ehmer "joined Waffle House in 1992 as a senior buyer in the purchasing department before he was promoted to director of purchasing in 1996. He was then promoted to vice president of finance in 1999, chief financial officer in 2001" (Bell 2016).

Because Waffle House has remained a closely held company all these years—with ownership of the vast majority of corporate stock kept in-house—data publicizing company sales figures and other relevant information continually prove hard to come by. In the 1980s, it was "reported that Waffle House employed 4,500 people, had a financial worth of approximately $60 million, and had total assets of about $81.2 million" (Mote and Stansell 2020). Another account "estimated in 1987 Waffle House had generated about $210 million in sales, up from about $175 million a year earlier" (Mote and Stansell 2020).

As noted, Waffle House achieved much with Rogers Jr. at the helm. His time as CEO produced financial gains and brand unity without sacrificing the customer-first ethos originally touted by Forkner and Rogers Sr. However, not everything during his years as CEO can be so positively characterized. The company experienced multiple public relations crises in the years prior to his stepping down from the CEO position in 2012. Some of these related to highly publicized cases of racial discrimination (see chapter 4) that led Waffle House to adopt a more inclusiveness stance vis-à-vis how it engages employees, clientele, and surrounding communities (e.g., "America's Place for Inclusion"). Others pertained to less savory matters, namely, a tabloid-ready seven-year legal dispute involving Rogers Jr., and his housekeeper with allegations of infidelity, sex tapes, purported blackmail/retribution, and the like (Dostal 2012).

Against this backdrop, Ehmer became Waffle House CEO in 2012 with Rogers Jr. assuming his new role as chairman of the board and director. Until the 2020 COVID-19 pandemic, which saw the company take the unprecedented step of temporarily shutting its doors at hundreds of locations nationwide, enduring significant losses in terms of sales and people laid off, Ehmer's tenure as CEO had been one of building on the gains of his predecessors. Indeed, two years after becoming CEO, Waffle House earned around "$1.044 billion in sales, up from $1.007 billion in the year prior" (Ruggles 2015). By 2017, it was estimated that company revenues approached $1.3 billion (Schenke 2019). Despite such profitability, an atmosphere of egalitarianism pervades Waffle House's Norcross corporate headquarters where "all 300 employees . . . work in cubicles, everyone from CEO Walt Ehmer to Chairman Joe Rogers, Jr." (Schenke 2019).

Moreover, it was under Ehmer that the company readily embraced social media, promoting its products and services through various platforms such as Twitter and Facebook, striving to stay current with a dining public increasingly savvy about digital technology and corporate branding. In March 2020, Waffle House boasted over 763,000 Facebook followers with the number increasing due to news stories appearing in the media related to Waffle House's coronavirus response (Russo 2020).

Similarly, utilizing the Internet and smartphone apps to streamline food ordering/delivery took off during the Ehmer years. With just a few screen swipes or keyboard strokes, customers could now access Waffle House menu items with little or no trouble, retrieving orders curbside or having them delivered via online platforms such Uber Eats and GrubHub. How far and in what ways such technological advances will affect Waffle House's ability to

Figure 2.3. Waffle House closed to indoor seating because of COVID-19, Orlando, Florida, April 2020. Ty Matejowsky

provide simple and inexpensive meals without compromising Forkner and Rogers's original vision emphasizing the human touch (i.e., "who is looking out for the poor old cash customer?") remains to be seen.

Waffle House's position within America's highly variegated foodscape appears relatively secure for the foreseeable future barring additional economic fallout from 2020's global pandemic. As the company's standing within the South's (fast-)casual restaurant scene expands or persists under Ehmer's leadership, and as Waffle House's corporate footprint extends into territories well beyond its core regional stronghold during his watch, the chain continues to embrace a public identity centered around simple fare, unpretentious ambience, and friendly counter/table service.

Also informing this popular brand image is the curated corporate history showcased in venues like the Waffle House Museum and *Who's Looking Out for the Poor Old Cash Customer?* Highly resonant, these depictions evoke many of the tropes widely encountered in mainstream business success stories. Foregrounding particular narrative elements while downplaying or ignoring others, a particular version of Waffle House's formative years and its cofounders' enduring partnership emerges, one leaving little room for the nuances and ambiguities that also inform these episodes of chain history. As noted throughout this chapter, certain details receive short shrift when it comes to how the Waffle House story is publicly recounted. The professional legacy of Rogers and Forkner, and the historical rise of Waffle House, assumes more realized distinction as information beyond the popular accepted narratives is taken into account.

Waffle House: Real and Imagined

If the one-paragraph historical marker greeting visitors filing into Waffle House's original location and namesake museum stands as the official word on the brand's historical significance and cultural relevance in today's South, then findings highlighted over previous pages suggest a less cohesive and one-dimensional storyline. Various unsung players and contradictory details relevant to the chain's regional rise remain as yet unwoven into the narrative fabric comprising popular depictions of the Waffle House story. Details explored in this chapter help render a more nuanced portrait of the chain's initial launch, regional expansion, and irrefutable staying power in America's restaurant foodscape.

From the inextricable influence of Toddle House on Waffle House operations to Rogers years-long absence from his newly launched restaurant venture with Forkner during the mid- to late 1950s, from the disputed origins of the Waffle House name to the company's persistent tight-lipped stance over its finances and figures, less publicized information such as this reflects something more textured and shaded when it comes to documenting Waffle House's formative years and its subsequent growth. Indeed, a fuller accounting of the chain takes shape as these findings are situated alongside what is typically foregrounded in mainstream profiles of Waffle House history. The nuanced renderings arising from such considerations assume particular meaning given how the restaurant is so routinely regarded nowadays as a viable part of regional iconography.

Within the gauzy light of the southern imaginary, it often becomes difficult to discern anything beyond the broad stokes emerging from the interweaving strands of narrative, imagery, and sentiment that collectively define this amorphous and sometimes conflicting assemblage of regional identity. This is certainly the case with Waffle House, or at least with how its beginnings and cofounders' enduring partnership are commonly articulated and publicly understood. As noted throughout this book, the chain's reputation has developed to the point where it seemingly precedes itself, feeling all but entrenched to even the most casual members of the dining public.

Efforts to wrest Waffle House's formative narrative away from such reductive tendencies are surely complicated given the continued sway and uncritical reflexivity invoked by the southern imaginary. This conceptual framework continues to shape ideas about regional identity across the Bible Belt and beyond. In a region long accorded underdog status, the resonant appeal of a bootstrapping business tale becomes difficult to dislodge, particularly one involving a restaurant so readily affiliated with everyday working folk.

In the case of Waffle House, it seems to tap into long-vaunted ideals about southern character and the entrepreneurial grit necessary to succeed businesswise. Waffle House's professed inclusivity and its unofficial status as the party crowd's after-hours destination of choice (see chapter 3) do much toward reinforcing such notions. With only modest efforts at crafting or publicizing its corporate history, Waffle House has long benefited from the elevation of particular sensibilities and contexts borne out of the southern imaginary's more idealized and democratizing proclivities.

3

Waffle House after Dark

Shift Happens

Today, the particular sway Waffle House holds over the South's highly corporatized foodscape in terms of sheer numbers and imaginative grip is beyond doubt. The restaurant's reputation as a venue for all kinds of criminal and/or freak flag behavior is no less indisputable, approaching an outsized presence throughout the Internet and across the pop culture landscape. However distorted or deserved, this flipside characterization of "America's Best Place to Eat" has worked its way into the popular consciousness, matching and even in some ways eclipsing the rather humdrum brand image publicly maintained by the company all these years. For patrons and nonpatrons alike, such dubious distinction casts Waffle House's daily operations, especially in its graveyard shift, in an unflattering albeit often comical light.

In this chapter, I delve into this aspect of Waffle House operations, documenting a wide range of illicit and felonious occurrences whether on-site or near company locations. These run the gamut from petty alcohol-related infractions to more serious crimes involving grave bodily harm or even loss of life. However tragic or farcical such incidents ultimately prove, they nearly always occur after sunset, adding elements of uncertainty and danger to third-shift Waffle House, particularly on weekend nights. Various explanatory considerations can illuminate why the 24-7 restaurant is so often synonymized with odd and unlawful goings-on. Yet, so as not to unnecessarily create and/or perpetuate one-sided accounts of Waffle House customer/employee behavior, I conclude this chapter by covering several accounts recently in the headlines that are a bit more uplifting in nature.

Recognized nowadays as an industry leader that provides its largely blue-collar clientele simple meals at affordable prices, much of what publicly defines Waffle House's current standing in America's chain restaurant foodscape proved well beyond the predictable horizon when the eatery first began operations in Avondale Estates so long ago. On that Labor Day weekend in 1955, Joe Rogers Sr. and Tom Forkner likely never envisioned that their newly launched Waffle House venture would achieve so much growth and success over the subsequent decades. Arguably, as with any other fledgling restaurant enterprise, such long-term considerations remained largely aspirational, subordinate to the more pressing needs of running a business day-to-day and into the near future. Despite it being anyone's guess how things would ultimately turn out, these positive outcomes are evident with benefit of nearly seventy years' hindsight.

Likely less foreseeable from Rogers's and Forkner's mid-1950s' perspective was the general public's casual embrace of Waffle House as a veritable touchstone of southern identity. Amid the Bible Belt's myriad complexities and contradictions, the brand's gradual elevation from a simple 24-7 eatery to a celebrated regional icon remains one of those rare corporate feats to which few start-up restauranteurs purposefully aspire, and fewer still go on to achieve. The various ways Waffle House encapsulates southern culture and engages the southern imaginary—with its inherent inability to consider much beyond the region's most obvious imperfections and romanticized idiosyncrasies—surely works in the company's favor on this front, especially as the chain only obliquely acknowledges or promotes this particular regional affiliation in its current marketing approach.

Perhaps most unanticipated for Rogers and Forkner's embryonic partnership was the eventual pigeonholing of Waffle House into various unflattering stereotypes, among them ones culminating in the chain's abiding caricature as a late-night venue for wide-ranging antisocial behaviors. Considered through these optics, Waffle House is a place where customer and employee conduct often treads, and sometimes abruptly transgresses, the fine line between raucous revelry and out-and-out criminality (Brown 2011). This enduring characterization remains deeply etched into the popular consciousness, abetted by multiple pop culture depictions (see chapter 5) and the collective impact of myriad print and broadcast news reports spotlighting the lurid and sensational and reinforced across the Internet on various websites trafficking in snarky headlines and blithe smirkiness (e.g., "Report: Couple Caught Having Sex in Waffle House Parking Lot. The Woman, Who Had Been Drinking, Also Tried to Wear a Cheeseburger as [a] Sandal"—*Loganville-Grayson Patch* headline from Loganville, Georgia, November 4, 2013).

As noted in the introduction and fleshed out over subsequent pages, what seems like an endless stream of extreme and cartoonish occurrences—ones usually involving some combination of intoxication, debauchery, criminality, and law enforcement intervention—has long plagued Waffle House, informing popular opinion about the brand, particularly its standing vis-à-vis other (fast-)casual chains (Brown 2011). The recurring frequency and sheer quantity of such "police blotter" activities have now reached the point where documenting them all in one volume appears nearly as unwieldy as it does repetitive.

Quite often, these Waffle House incidents and attendant coverage appear to follow one of several basic plotlines or scripts or at the very least come cut from the same general cloth. Indeed, with a backlog of transgressions, crimes, and misdeeds seemingly piling up, the accumulated effect of these frequently bizarre cases has irrevocably shaped the optics of how Waffle House is publicly perceived both regionally and nationwide. Doubtless, if the "Florida Man" Internet meme (Russell 2020:180–82) so aptly encapsulates all of the colorful black sheep behavior for which the Sunshine State, specifically, and the South, more generally, has dubiously come to be known, it also serves as a journalistic trope that conflates "the travails of the drug-addicted, mentally ill, and homeless" with some sort of state-specific "mythical hyper-weirdness" (Norman 2019). A similar kind of dynamic is applied to most Waffle House coverage wherein the weird and wacky becomes privileged above the disinterested and circumspect.

Waffle House Rap Sheet

Consider the following cases, all drawn from recent news reports from basic Web sleuthing. With no special prompt to search out extreme or bizarre Waffle House occurrences, most Google searches end up skewing in an oddball direction. News accounts ran the gamut from the cartoonish to the disturbingly criminal, all foregrounding in some way the shadow side of Waffle House, most conveying a general sense of disorder and potential danger in chain operations.

By now, this type of media slant is understandable, particularly in relation to Waffle House, given the sort of "if it bleeds, it leads" ethos driving so much local and national reporting. Add to this a rich vein of exploitable material easily hyped for its inherent comedic value and the makings of an entire subgenre of police beat journalism—"Waffle House Arrest"—cohere into something with undeniable audience allure. Replete with "truth is stranger than fiction" story angles and details that appear almost self-generated for maximum tabloid impact, reasonable questions arise as to whether this reportage would resonate in the same way if the reported incidents occurred somewhere besides Waffle House. Nowadays, it seems certain that events dubbed "newsworthy" with respect to Waffle House enjoy a different kind of media currency when compared with analogous encounters at Denny's or IHOP.

The incidents described here provide a general overview rather than an exhaustive list of the kinds of strange and sometimes deadly encounters capturing the public imagination with respect to Waffle House. With some of these accounts garnering only local attention and others making more of a national media splash, the cumulative impact bolsters the prevailing (lazy?) stereotype of Waffle House as a focal point of aberrant late-night happenings, obscuring just how infrequently such events actually occur within the day-to-day mundanity of Waffle House operations. To wit:

- Around 8:00 p.m. on Tuesday February 12, 2019, Tyrone Hamburg, twenty-six, walked into a New Orleans Waffle House, quietly donned an employee uniform, and began prepping food and taking customer orders as if he actually worked there. At some point during his charade, he removed $300 from the store register and then exited the establishment with none of the waitstaff any wiser. Hamburg was able to carry out his ruse undetected in part because Waffle House restaurants frequently bring in workers from other locations to fill in during busy dining shifts. He was eventually arrested after the police called upon the general public to provide any information that would lead to his whereabouts or apprehension (Prentzel 2019).
- On January 23, 2019, a partially naked thirty-eight-year old Florida woman, Freedom Ryder Zobrist, was arrested after allegedly blocking traffic and dancing in the parking lot of a Pensacola Waffle House. Police were called to the scene by a Waffle House employee who had earlier confronted Zobrist about her erratic behavior inside the restaurant. Initially fleeing on foot, Zobrist returned hours later seeking her abandoned possessions, which employees had deposited intact outside the Waffle House's rear exit. Zobrist refused to leave the property once she reclaimed her belongings, becoming increasingly agitated and confrontational. After verbally abusing workers and threatening to shoot everyone in the store with an unproduced firearm, Zobrist walked into the parking lot, removed her pants and underwear, and began gyrating provocatively. With her lower half exposed, she attempted to grab the genitals of the employee who had previously confronted her before licking both sides of his face and then poking

him aggressively in the chest. She then attempted to prevent customers from leaving the parking lot by dancing, still without any pants, in front of their vehicles. Zobrist was taken into custody and arraigned on a total bond of $5,000 (Phifer 2019).

- In the predawn hours of March 11, 2002, three shift workers—Christina Delarosa, Willy Absolu, and Barbara Nunn—were shot in the restaurant freezer of a Davie, Florida, Waffle House by occasional customer Gerhard Hojan, twenty-seven, as his accomplice, ex-restaurant employee Jimmy Mickel, thirty-three, robbed the store safe with a pair of bolt cutters. Delarosa and Absolu died on the scene while Nunn survived the gunshot wound inflicted to her head, calling 911 from the nearby gas station to which she crawled. Nunn provided law enforcement with the perpetrators' identity before being rushed to the hospital. Mickel ultimately received multiple life sentences for his part in the crimes, while Hojan, the triggerman, currently sits on Florida's death row awaiting his fate (Olmeda 2018).

- In 2015, some Waffle Houses still permitted tobacco use even as most restaurants remained smoke-free. This patchwork policy became a point of contention that quickly escalated into homicide, leaving a fifty-two-year-old Biloxi, Mississippi, Waffle House server dead from a gunshot wound to the head. Witnesses said that around 1:00 a.m. on Friday, November 27, 2015, ex-firefighter Johnny Max Mount, forty-five, produced a 9-mm handgun and fatally shot Julie Brightwell after she asked him to extinguish his e-cigarette. Mount was arrested on-site without incident and later pleaded not guilty to first-degree murder charges related to the slaying. Years earlier on Christmas Eve 2002, Mount had sustained multiple on-the-job injuries after being hit by a car. Friends say he suffered a traumatic brain injury that altered his personality, possibly contributing to his fatal encounter with Brightwell (Baker 2015).

- On a sweltering August night in 2011, Charles Patrick O'Bryan called the Waffle House in Panama City, Florida, where his wife waitressed, first to speak with her and then to warn everyone there that he planned to "run his truck through the building and kill everyone" (Forbes 2011). True to his word, O'Bryan showed up and intentionally crashed his 1987 Ford pickup into the restaurant, leaving his wife with minor injuries. He then tried to attack his wife and her coworkers with a knife before someone on the scene subdued him with a broken piece of metal from the building wreckage. O'Bryan was charged with attempted murder and various felony criminal mischief charges (Hijek 2011). The damaged Waffle House was located directly across the street from the Panama City Police Department.

- A pair of young men from North Texas went on an armed Waffle House crime spree in the early morning hours of March 17, 2019, robbing four separate restaurant locations within a mere eighty minutes before the Grand Prairie Police apprehended them. Justanity Johnson and Xavier Parham, both eighteen, were arrested and charged with multiple counts of aggravated assault after a stolen black Ford Mustang matching the description of the alleged getaway vehicle was pulled over and both driver and passenger peacefully surrendered (Sarder 2019).
- Career-criminal Jeffrey Willard Wooten, forty-nine, entered a Buford, Georgia, Waffle House on the night of Thursday, May 1, 2014, wearing a ski mask and white coveralls. He corralled restaurant staff into a back room using a pitchfork he brought along as a weapon. After multiple attempts at unlocking the cash register and making off with the loot proved unsuccessful, Wooten ended up lugging the register to his pick-up truck parked outside the all-night diner, dropping the pitchfork along the way. Two Waffle House employees pursued Wooten into the parking lot, retrieved the discarded pitchfork, and used it to smash Wooten's rear windshield as he sped away with the cash register in tow. Possibly injured in the confrontation, Wooten led local police on a brief high-speed chase before abandoning his vehicle and evading capture for the next week or so. By the time he was eventually apprehended, law enforcement alleged Wooten had shot and killed a man during a carjacking in Knoxville, Tennessee, leading police on a second high-speed chase that culminated when he crashed into the yard of a local house (Bernarde 2019).
- In January 2019, two Waffle House workers employed at a DeKalb County (Georgia) location were promptly fired after an Instagram video surfaced showing them victimizing an unconscious patron slumped across the customer counter. Filmed during the early morning hours, the minutes-long clip features the pair laughing and egging each other on as they dumped salt and squirted ketchup on the inebriated individual, even placing a single cheese slice atop his head. At one point, one of the workers took the unidentified male's arms and maneuvered them around as if he were a marionette's puppet. It was later revealed that the victim had gone to the Waffle House to "sober up" before passing out, leaving himself vulnerable to the employees'

prankish behavior. Once he regained consciousness, the intoxicated man purportedly ordered food, paid for his meal, and walked home completely unaware that he had been mockingly exploited in this way. According to the victim's fiancée, he only found out about the incident once it was uploaded to an Instagram account where it was briefly accessible to the public alongside other videos of customers enduring similar treatment at this particular Waffle House location. Although the victim initially filed a report with the DeKalb police, he ultimately decided not to seek prosecution (Prince 2019).

- Forty-one-year-old Craig Brewer was shot in the head multiple times by 9-mm Glock-wielding Ezekiel Hicks, twenty-five, at a Gainesville, Florida, Waffle House during the early hours of Sunday, April 8, 2019. In an act of unprompted generosity, Brewer had gone from table to table surprising guests with either small cash gifts to help defray their late-night meal costs or by picking up the checks himself. The exclusion of Hicks's party triggered a verbal argument between the two men. The two got into a heated confrontation after Hicks's female companion became upset for not being among the lucky customers to receive one of Brewer's twenty-dollar bills. Hicks exited the restaurant, armed himself with a firearm, and upon returning began physically fighting with Brewer. Hicks drew the handgun from his pants and emptied multiple rounds into Brewer's head. Alachua County Sheriff's deputies, already on their way to the Waffle House in response to a 911 call requesting assistance to disperse an overflow crowd refusing to leave, recovered the murder weapon and arrested Hicks at the scene. He was charged with first-degree murder (Molina 2019).

- Just before 6:00 a.m. on the morning of Saturday, January 19, 2019, two unidentified Waffle House employees in Hardeeville, South Carolina, got into a major physical altercation involving shouted obscenities, thrown punches, knife waving, wrestling on the floor, and eventual bloodshed. By the time the melee was over, one of the men was slightly injured and a window near the restaurant's entrance was shattered. Neither man sought medical attention or wanted to press charges against the other. A nine-minute video entitled "Knifes Out While Waffle House Employees Fight" was uploaded to YouTube depicting the two going at it with other employees and customers seemingly indifferent to the escalating confrontation. Whether either employee was fired for at-work brawling remains unclear (Ferguson 2019).

- In early November 2011, four north Georgia men—Ray H. Adams, sixty-five; Samuel J. Crump, sixty-eight; Fredrick Thomas, seventy-three; and Dan Roberts, sixty-seven—affiliated with a fringe militia group were arrested at their homes by federal agents for allegedly planning to carry out a coordinated attack involving the targeting of federal and state officials and spreading terror across the South and nationwide. According to the Department of Justice, the group hatched and developed their plot while regularly meeting at the local Waffle House in Toccoa. The group's plan was purportedly based on an online novel popular among conspiracy-minded militia groups and entailed the use of bombs, silencer-outfitted guns, and the biological toxin ricin to strike a blow against what they saw as extreme government overreach by the Obama administration. For over six months in 2011, the group discussed the attack, often over coffee and breakfast in their regular Waffle House booth, even going so far as to scout out federal buildings in nearby Atlanta as possible terrorist targets. Despite their ages and lack of previous criminal records, all four ended up doing time in federal lockup for their crimes (Cook 2014; Mencimer 2011).[1]

- Anthony Q. Warner, sixty-three, the tech-savvy loner and purported conspiracy theorist, who detonated a bomb-laden recreational vehicle on Christmas morning of 2020 in front of an AT&T building complex in downtown Nashville while blaring Petula Clark's 1964 hit "Downtown" alongside a computerized warning to local residents to clear out, reportedly had few personal contacts in the years and months leading up to his spectacularly gruesome death except for a Waffle House waitress, Crystal Deck, forty-four. As she worked the restaurant floor, he befriended and regaled Deck with tales of shape-shifting alien lizards secretly living among humans. After hearing initial reports of the devastating blast that knocked regional cellular service offline for several hours, Deck immediately suspected Warner, who had cryptically warned of something he was hatching, was behind the attack. Going on to tell the *New York Times* that she thought his "cornbread wasn't really done in the middle," Deck last encountered Warner on December 17, 2020, when he showed up to her south Nashville Waffle House to gift her his white 2007 Pontiac Vibe along with a jacket and gloves (Cavendish et al. 2021).

A Waffle House Divided

Much as a self-perpetuating, self-escalating feedback loop grows and intensifies as output circulates back to its original source, the corresponding media attention to these crimes and incidents works to both reinforce and amplify the ongoing caricature of Waffle House, depicting it as a dangerous or disreputable dining establishment. Informing public expectations about brand operations—basically showcasing Waffle House as a place where permissiveness, rowdiness, swearing, and unlawful activities are either tolerated or easily perpetrated—this "Florida Man"–type coverage undermines the chain in securing a loyal base of repeat customers just as it obscures company shortcomings in properly dealing with on-site wrongdoing whether through ineffective policies or benign neglect (see the Waffle House Rules section in this chapter).

Other low-cost chains also experience varying degrees of negative exposure—indeed, even perennial children's favorite Chuck E. Cheese boasts a well-documented history of adult brawling and other alcohol-fueled mayhem (Bhasin 2012; Holley 2016; Prior 2008)[2]—yet few brands seemingly invite as much untoward behavior and unfavorable treatment as Waffle House. In keeping with its tight-lipped stance when it comes to releasing information about company matters, Waffle House does little to publicize the number of criminal incidents that annually occur at its facilities. For better or worse, the eatery appears stuck in a perennial feedback loop in which the more adverse coverage it receives, the more it heightens public expectations about just what constitutes appropriate on-premises behavior among restaurant workers, customers, and the like.

For some, the ongoing emphasis of the brand's bizarro side offers nothing so much as an implicit license to test the limits of whatever is ultimately deemed acceptable at Waffle House properties. In many ways, this view helps to foster notions of Waffle House as a soft target for would-be criminals looking to exploit various vulnerabilities in chain operations. For others, the boundary pushing is carried out much more selectively and/or knowingly. The ironic consumption types previously mentioned in chapter 1 variously flirt with these boundaries, often bumping up against them in decidedly performative ways, looking to entertain and impress their peers while also confounding the expectations of others in real or online environments.

Such adverse or backhanded Waffle House coverage obviously predates the rapid rise of social media and digital technology in the early twenty-first century. Yet the near ubiquity of smartphones, security cameras, and other video-capturing devices as dominant features of global modernity adds new dimension and scope to this persistent stereotype, facilitating both the viral transmission and monetization of drunken and/or criminal antics. The further intrusion of digital and surveillance technologies into Waffle House dining spaces results in nothing if not an expansive dissemination of highly sensationalized content. With rare exceptions, the videos and images now so easily accessible across multiple online platforms offer little critical context and even less consideration about the human toll inflicted upon those being depicted in such unfavorable ways.

Indeed, the visceral and almost clickbait immediacy of watching uploaded images and raw footage of restaurant patrons and employees engaging in heedless acts of incivility, inebriation, vandalism, and physical violence does much to overshadow the more typical and innocuous aspects of everyday Waffle House operations. Moreover, the descriptions accompanying these exploits, whether disseminated through online news sites or other media platforms, further subvert the chain's already rather dubious image among large swaths of the dining public by highlighting as many weird and wacky details as possible.

Given the Web's capacity to both centralize and collate information, the shelf-life of these unflattering tabloid accounts can extend well into perpetuity, providing ample coverage of on-premises misconduct to anyone curious about such incidents in a "can't-avert-your-eyes" train wreck sort of way. A few simple YouTube or TikTok searches of phrases like "waffle house brawls" or "waffle house employees fighting" reveal countless graphic videos depicting various acts of on-site fisticuffs and brutal beatdowns with millions of registered views.

The mostly alcohol-fueled and profanity-laced uploads of patrons quarreling or trading blows, coupled with those of restaurant staff losing their cool with customers or fighting among themselves, bolster impressions of Waffle House as a hotbed of violent encounters and offbeat behavior. The catty if occasionally savagely funny remarks found in their corresponding comment threads add insult to injury in this regard, exposing just how unrestrained viewers can be when celebrating Waffle House less as a site of unpretentious down-home dining and more as an object of unbridled derision.

Waffle House Rules

With the dark side of Waffle House operations now firmly embedded in public thinking, questions arise as to why and how the eatery persists as such an ostensible magnet for all kinds of unsavory and illicit conduct. When meal preparation and service remain of top priority, expectations that Waffle House rigidly control the actions of its individual employees much less continually monitor its restaurant clientele and all on-premises interactions become tricky if not effectively impossible. This is especially true during peak business hours when quick order turnaround can prove quite challenging, or after the weekend party crowd shows up in droves, deep in their cups and looking to extend the festivities.

Beginning in December 2012, one Waffle House in a high-crime area of downtown Atlanta took the unusual step of adding a 20 percent surcharge to all customer bills to hire an on-site security guard to primarily work crowd control. Located in Underground Atlanta, a shopping district in the city's famous Five Points neighborhood, this particular Waffle House had not experienced any one specific crime to prompt such actions but instead opted to tack on the extra costs as a way to keep an off-duty police officer on premises to guard against potential troublemaking, considering there were some 260 major felony crimes reported in the surrounding area over the previous months. Much to some customers' dismay, this additional fee meant that meals costing five dollars at other Waffle House eateries went for six dollars there (Suggs 2013).

Such enhanced security measures are largely site-specific and would doubtless prove counterproductive if applied companywide. Indeed, approaches designed to insulate Waffle House from potential crime must not only be weighed against the financial costs of keeping salaried security guards on-site around the clock but also how the presence of armed off-duty officers would impact the chain's standing within America's prevailing restaurant foodscape. In an effort to better engage the consumer sensibilities of today's dining public and cultivate a welcoming atmosphere for everyone inside its nearly two thousand restaurant enterprises, most Waffle House locations assume a low-key and limited tack when it comes to safeguarding its employees and clientele (Sharp 2018). Rather than implement anything vaguely concrete or heavy-handed policy wise, Waffle House assumes a minimal security posture within its stores. Although everyone who enters its doors is automatically subject to various company-crafted protocols including a consent to video surveillance, most guests pay these operational formalities little heed. At all local restaurants, official efforts to get out ahead of the problems posed by ill-intentioned individuals and unruly groups mainly come in the form of a detailed code of conduct affixed to the eatery's glassed entrance as a large decal titled House Rules.

This firm but friendly set of written policies delineates in a bullet-pointed list just what Waffle House will tolerate in terms of customer behavior as well as what guests can expect in regard to employee service and hospitality. The document's left side features a series of operational ground rules, the most important elements of which are highlighted in blue (e.g.,

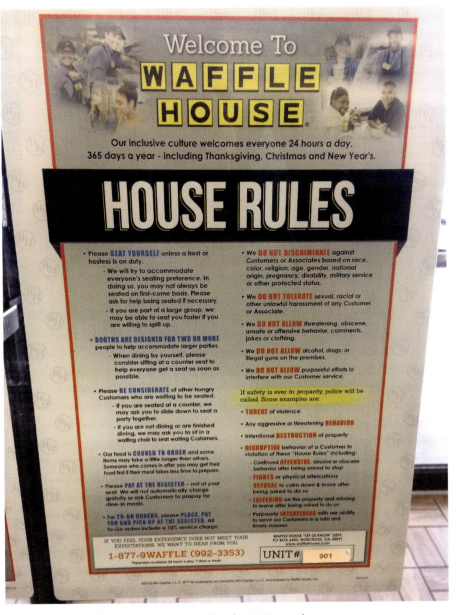

Figure 3.1. Waffle House rules, Orlando, Florida. Ty Matejowsky

"SEAT YOURSELF," "BE CONSIDERATE," "PAY AT THE REGISTER"), for diners to effectively follow. The right column, conversely, lists a series of rules that highlight sometimes in red the kind of customer actions that may lead to refusal of service, ejection, or police involvement (e.g., "We DO NOT ALLOW alcohol, drugs or illegal guns on the premises"). The House Rules even provides a toll-free number that dissatisfied patrons can call to report problems and issues to upper management. Doubtless, this carefully worded document serves as a go-to source for employees settling certain types of on-premises disputes as it lays out in no uncertain terms the kinds of behaviors that can result in customer expulsion or law enforcement notification.

Posted directly next to it is another colorfully rendered rubric known as the Full House Policy. This spells out the rules and regulations specifically pertaining to how the chain addresses matters of high customer turnout and potential dining area overflow. With a standard Waffle House eatery capable of accommodating only some thirty-three individuals at any given time, clarifying its methods for seating and serving arriving parties becomes essential, especially during late-night and early morning weekend shifts when groups of revelers show up still abuzz from a night of party going. Just how cognizant Waffle House diners actually are about the guidelines articulated in both the House Rules and Full House Policy remains questionable as each is fairly detailed and located in a high-traffic area nonconducive for comprehensive reading.

Despite the presence of codes of conduct aimed at establishing a basic set of ground rules, it seems evident that certain factors—operational or otherwise—encourage unwanted or criminal activities, or at the very least leave Waffle House vulnerable to this type of misbehavior. Whether individually or collectively, these elements work to complicate the smooth running of local Waffle House eateries, allowing episodes of sporadic disruption to punctuate operations, wielding an outsized influence over prevailing brand perceptions. Again, it bears mentioning that these conditions are not exclusive to Waffle House eateries. Other chains, particularly those with all-night breakfast/lunch counters located off of interstate highways or in more urban enclaves, similarly endure such random or unwanted incidents ranging from the merely exasperating to the murderously criminal.

For example, two of the deadliest and earliest mass shootings to grip the US popular imagination occurred at popular chain restaurants. The first—the 1984 mass shooting at a McDonald's in the San Ysidro neighborhood of San Diego, California—left twenty-one people dead and nineteen injured. The second attack, also carried out by a lone assailant, was the 1991 Luby's Cafeteria massacre in Killeen, Texas, where twenty-three individuals lost their lives, with twenty-seven wounded in the unfolding carnage. Both events presaged the April 2018 Waffle House shooting in Antioch, Tennessee, just outside of Nashville, which could have had a much higher fatality count if it were not for the heroic intervention of a restaurant patron (see introduction).

As an industry that employs millions upon millions of Americans, however, the US restaurant sector appears relatively safe when the aggregate number of on-site worker deaths is utilized as a sole metric. Though still remaining quite low, the per capita death rate for kitchen workers and servers has trended upward in recent years, thanks in part to the devastation wrought by the early twenty-first-century opioid epidemic (Sharp 2018). Recent data from the Bureau of Labor Statistics show that of the 146 reported worker deaths between 2014 and 2016 at limited-service restaurants such as Waffle House, 58, or 40 percent, were classified as homicides. The number of on-premises worker homicides grew from 14 in 2014 to 23 in 2016, a 64 percent increase. Despite this leap, rates actually fell from their 2007 high when the bureau reported 35 restaurant worker homicides in a single year (Sharp 2018).

Unlawful House

Waffle House and its chain restaurant competitors generally remain quite safe, according to the available data. Yet, just as certain abiding stereotypes popularly accepted at face value are predicated on some discernible element of truth, perceptions of Waffle House as a late-night hub of boozy impropriety and potential confrontation are grounded in long-shared perceptions of the 24-7-365 chain. With a conspicuous record of bizarre on-site and criminal encounters—ones well-documented if also sensationalized in the public sphere—efforts to dismiss prevailing views about Waffle House and its after dark operations appear rather formidable. Indeed, with such persistent notions of the restaurant as a habitual site of overnight wrongdoing that frequently runs afoul of local law enforcement, these negative conceptions will doubtless remain firmly ensconced in the cultural ether, barring some intense corporate rebranding or marketing strategy reboot.

Media accounts documenting these oft-outrageous occurrences help foster this consensus view about third-shift Waffle House, leaving ample room for brand rehabilitation. However gratuitous in tone and description such coverage appears, a strong case can also be made that it is not just the actions of individual Waffle House employees and customers that fuel this particular characterization. The company itself bears some responsibility on this front. Waffle House could take a more active role in overseeing its everyday operations, bolstering certain operational guardrails at its restaurants, and enacting various preventative measures that effectively tamp down on overly boisterous or malicious behavior.

Perhaps more by default than design, Waffle House fosters many of the conditions that allow these incidents to arise and occasionally spiral out of control. By dint of various overlapping factors—namely but not limited to Waffle House's low menu prices, around the clock operations, minimal wages, building designs, and roadside locations near heavily traveled roads and highways—the chain cultivates a particular dining environment, leaving space for various levels of acting out, troublemaking, and utter criminality not as closely associated with other eateries.

As will be elaborated, a combination of structural elements and policy considerations exert a far-reaching influence over this aspect of Waffle House operations. The public eating environment emerging from this particular confluence of factors does not always foster the best outcomes in terms of customer and employee conduct. In fact, when considering all of these policy and structural elements in concert, it becomes clear that the onus of responsibility for much of the misbehavior occurring at Waffle House cannot be placed squarely on the shoulders of restaurant staff and clientele.

So, in answering questions of why Waffle House ostensibly attracts more than its fair share of petty and felonious criminal behavior and all variety of strange on-premises encounters, a number of causal factors that work collectively to perpetuate this ongoing situation can be advanced. If any one element contributes more toward creating problematic restaurant settings—ones that undermine normative chain operations as such—it is not readily clear how to make this determination. The Waffle House that so many now recognize for its various flaws as well as its core strengths owes much of its current reputation to the interplay of multiple internal and external factors.

Cheap Meals Await All Who Enter Here

First and foremost, as an inexpensive all-night eatery, Waffle House stands as one of the few available sit-down establishments whose menu is so reasonably priced that basically anyone can eat there. Even as Waffle House adheres to the same basic social contract as its competitors—namely, the conventional understanding wherein restaurant access and service is contingent upon an individual's ability to pay for food or drink—Waffle House's bar for admission is so low that it appears practically negligible. Even those with just two or three bucks in their pockets can afford the low-cost and wide-ranging bill of fare. Its cheap breakfast, lunch, and dinner selections fill a much-needed gap within local out-to-eat foodscapes considering Waffle House remains accessible to virtually all segments of the dining public.

Figure 3.2. Waffle house customers, Orlando, Florida. Ty Matejowsky

It seems obvious that Waffle House employees would only tolerate someone hanging out on-site without ordering for so long, but with prices ranging from the inexpensive to slightly inexpensive, matters of cost never really emerge as a consistent factor in shaping what type of clientele Waffle House ultimately attracts. Nowadays, rare is the individual who cannot pay for a basic Waffle House meal, let alone afford a simple cup of coffee ($1.80), which like other 24-7 diners, comes with unlimited refills. Indeed, if ever there is another chain eatery that better embodies an antithesis of elitism and exclusivity besides Waffle House, one would surely be hard pressed to name it.

In fact, even for the acutely budget conscious, Waffle House features a Value Dollar$ Menu—introduced in 2010—whose dozen or so dishes range from one-dollar items such as the Original Angus Cheeseburger and Grilled Biscuit & Jelly to five-dollar offerings like the Pecan Waffle & Drink and Hashbrowns Scattered All the Way. For those feeling a bit more indulgent, splurging on Waffle House's high-priced menu selections including the ten-dollar-plus Papa Joe's Pork Chops & Eggs (Meat Lovers 3 Chops) or eleven-dollar T-Bone Steak (10oz.) is always an option.

No one is turned away *prima facie* except perhaps those failing to meet the company dress code (i.e., "no shoes, no shirt, no service") or any individual exhibiting obvious intoxication, although this latter point may be debatable. Indeed, it is hard to find a better example of a sit-down, all-night chain eatery that stands as welcoming to such a broad cross-section of US society than Waffle House. This extensive demographic bandwidth adds to the restaurant's ostensible charm as a microcosm of America's oft-touted democratic character, something that media figures such as Tom Junod and the late Anthony Bourdain have previously highlighted (see preface).

With so few denied a seat at the Waffle House counter, it is inevitable that along with the vast majority of reputable and easygoing diners grabbing a simple meal—perhaps themselves not all the way sober—some element of criminal types or troublemakers will frequent the eatery as well, leaving varying levels of chaos and destruction of in their wake. As argued throughout this book, their misbehavior and the resultant coverage of it tend to play an outsized role in skewing public sentiment about Waffle House away from what company higher-ups would doubtless prefer, in effect, bolstering notions of the eatery as a gathering spot for drunks and the variously ill-intentioned.

Rich or poor, Waffle House welcomes everyone and anyone who enters its doors regardless of their potential for causing problems or disruptions.

So, for clarification, this is not suggesting that those with more money are somehow better customers or that those with little or no money are the main source of Waffle House trouble. Rather, it is indicative of the fact that even marginally higher prices might play a sort of gatekeeping role in regulating Waffle House access, placing some limited constraint on just who ultimately grabs a restaurant booth or table. Just as modest tobacco taxes reduce smoking rates and other tobacco consumption behavior among youth and other groups, so too would slight price increases effectively constrain the overall breadth of Waffle House clientele.

Moreover, as Waffle House rarely scales back much less completely shuts down its operations—this infrequent occurrence typically only happens under the most extreme of circumstances such as during the leadup to or aftermath of major hurricanes, tornadoes, and other severe natural disasters or amid a sweeping public health crisis like 2020's COVID-19 global pandemic[3]—the restaurant functions as an ideal spot for those looking to cool their heels anytime. With the number of other available retail options so significantly curtailed under the cover of darkness, the twenty-four-hour eatery becomes something of a refuge for those with either no place else to go or to the mildly to severely inebriated looking to prolong the after-hours fun once local nightspots close.

In most cases, these parties may feel only subtle pressure to vacate the premises once their checks are settled. Unless it is a Friday or Saturday night with high customer turnout when restaurant seating is at a premium and the Full House Policy is enforced, after-meal lingering is permitted or, more accurately, tolerated, up to a point. Although privately owned and maintained since the mid-1950s, Waffle House approaches a public space of sorts, given how infrequently its doors close and how few price restraints it places on the dining public when it comes to accessing its facilities. However much this makes third-shift Waffle House a transitional space between public and private domains sort of like a municipal library or park that never ceases operations, it does extend the boundaries of the dining public's overall reach in terms of accessing and occupying restaurant settings almost anytime they prefer.

If anything, Waffle House represents an enduring well-lit and climate-controlled retail sanctuary, one that offers practically anyone who enters its doors—that is, anyone adequately dressed and perhaps sober enough—passable or competent service as long as they can meet the minimal cost threshold of an already reasonably priced menu. Hypothetically, no matter what else is happening or what other businesses have finally called it a night, the Waffle House light remains aglow, shining for all with the requisite means to partake of its affordable and extensive bill of fare. Such qualities inform the erroneous but widely held belief that Waffle House restaurants lack door locks, a long-standing myth that the company does little to actively dissuade seeing its restaurants as "a place where people do not lock the doors does not just mean customers can come in anytime; it also implies people are trusted" (Rawson 2013:230).

Waffle House Nocturne

There is much to commend about Waffle House's expansive parameters and indiscriminate approach in regard to engaging the dining public, yet certain drawbacks nevertheless emerge from tooling operations toward such unfettered accessibility. As one of several synchronous factors that work to shape the overall character of restaurant dining, this open-ended stance leaves Waffle House vulnerable to various problems and issues. Waffle House's beleaguered image and putative status as the "Florida Man" of restaurants (Gettys 2016) often means that the chain attracts more scrutiny than other chains even when similar incidents occur at their locations.

It seems unlikely that the misconduct and wrongdoing for which Waffle House is known falls evenly throughout the workweek, much less occurs uniformly across the various work shifts—first/morning shift (typically between 7:00 a.m.–3:00 p.m. or 8:00 a.m.–4:00 p.m.), second/afternoon shift (usually between 3:00 p.m.–11:00 p.m. or 4:00 p.m.–12:00 a.m.), and third/night shift (normally between 11:00 p.m.–7:00 a.m. or 12:00 a.m.–8:00 a.m.)—that comprise the restaurant industry's standard business day. Most anecdotal evidence situates these unusual and dicey encounters within the late-night and early morning hours of the eatery's notorious graveyard shift.

As other stores, restaurants, and retailers call it a day, Waffle House stands among that select handful of commercial brands, including Walmart, Walgreen's, and 7-Eleven, that still offers their clientele most of the perks of full customer service. The restaurant's illuminated Scrabble-tile signage, elevated and shining beacon-like above so many highway offramps, remains a familiar fixture to all those long haul truckers, law enforcement officers, and sleepless wanderers out and about in the dead of night.

Establishments offering table service throughout the sometimes chaotic but mostly monotonous graveyard shift meet a real need for the highway travelers, night owls, and others seeking sustenance when most everyone else is asleep. Yet, no matter how convenient the dining public finds

Waffle House and its competitors, these ventures remain subject to certain levels of criminality and disruption by virtue of the fact that while other businesses shutter for the evening they stay fully operational.

Although not implying that the sort of crimes and transgressions commonly associated with Waffle House—namely, disorderly conduct, public intoxication, aggravated assault, robbery, and murder—occur exclusively during third-shift operations, a lingering association between these overnight hours and activities of this type still exists across large swaths of public thinking. Such assumptions appear more than speculative considering that most of the off-kilter Waffle House encounters and on-premises fisticuffs captured by bystanders as shaky cellphone footage and uploaded to the Internet take place at night. This observation, coupled with the fact that fewer opportunities for individual concealment are available in broad daylight, particularly for those up to no good, provides this line of reasoning with some additional heft.

It is useful to consider how such commonplace assumptions square with available data. Recent statistics from ten major US cities—Austin, San Francisco, Fort Lauderdale, Dallas, Cincinnati, Los Angeles, Boston, Seattle, Pittsburgh, and Washington, DC—paint a more complex portrait of when and what types of crime take place within a twenty-four-hour cycle. Critically unpacking these findings helps elucidate just how robust presumptive links between criminality and nighttime hours actually are.

A comprehensive study funded by the *Sleep Judge* (2019; 2020), a mainstream website dedicated to all things sleep-related, examines over 840,000 incidents recorded by local police in the aforementioned cities in 2017. Even though not looking at crime per se but rather the number, type, and time of police incident reports across a cross-section of American cities, this research provides a useful resource for better understanding the character, breadth, and scope of local US crime. Findings reveal that most police incident reports (55 percent) occur during daylight hours (7:00 a.m.–6:59 p.m.), suggesting that a little more than half of all locally reported crimes in the United States happen in daytime.

Study results become more nuanced, however, when the type of crime (violent versus nonviolent) documented in the examined police incident reports and time of the week (weekday versus weekend) in which the police reports occur are considered. Perhaps unsurprisingly, the more serious and violent offenses such as rape/sexual assault, murder, robbery, aggravated assault, and driving while impaired that take place at night (7:00 p.m.–6:59 a.m.). Less personally injurious crimes including larceny/theft, simple assault, drug violations, and property damage are predominately noted in those police incident reports from daylight hours.

Tellingly, this crude sort of bifurcation between serious/violent and less serious/nonviolent crimes really only pertains for weekday (7:00 p.m. Sunday–6:59 p.m. Friday) police incident reports. During the weekend (7:00 p.m. Friday–6:59 p.m. Sunday) the majority of all police incident reports—whether detailing serious/violent or less serious/nonviolent offenses—occur at night, suggesting that most weekend crimes happen after dark. As a corollary, the three nights of the week with the highest number of police incident reports taken are Friday (597.3 per 10,000 police incidents), Sunday (639.3 per 10,000 police incidents), and Saturday (646 per 10,000 police incidents). Such findings nicely dovetail with prevailing anecdotal assertions correlating Waffle House crimes and misdeeds with weekend nighttime settings.

All in all, this study provides some helpful insights for understanding the type of crimes to which third-shift Waffle House and other inexpensive all-night diners are primarily subject. Again, the severity and utter strangeness of some the incidents that have befallen Waffle House over the years have captured an outsized share of mainstream attention, but such factors have also done much to obscure just how uneventful most overnight shiftwork actually is. As restaurant operations unfold across late-night and early morning hours, little occurs that anyone would find all that exciting much less significantly newsworthy.

Nighthawks at the Waffle House

The nocturnal tones and caffeinated rhythms of third-shift Waffle House create an overall ambience somewhat at odds with what typically transpires during the rest of the day. The liminality frequently encountered between dusk and dawn in venues like Waffle House works to reshape prevailing social relations, often relaxing the behavioral inhibitions and/or flattening hierarchical differences that hold sway during daylight hours (Melbin 1987). However subtle, graveyard-shift interactions skew away from normative patterns typically experienced in daytime settings. Although such altered arrangements do not always engender negative outcomes—they sometimes cultivate more egalitarian environments where orientation toward inclusivity intensify (Rawson 2013)—such shifts quite commonly establish conditions favorable to messy and chaotic encounters.

In the 2013 work "'America's Place for Inclusion': Stories of Labor, Food, and Equality at the Waffle House," Katie Rawson highlights the theoretical work of sociologist Murray Melbin regarding nighttime behavior in public contexts across Western developed society. His *Night as Frontier: Colonizing the World after Dark* (1987) proves revelatory when it comes to understanding the mutability of social frameworks in places like third-shift Waffle House thanks to, among other things, the increasingly stark realities of wage-labor capitalism, extended transportation nodes, and ubiquity of artificial light. Rawson notes that

> Melbin compares late-night experience to a geographical frontier, positing that late at night, interactions change, creating a space with fewer social constraints, more lawlessness and violence, but also more frequent positive social interaction. The lower population density of late-night hours disrupts hierarchies, giving marginalized people more freedom with fewer people to enforce both organizational rules and social norms. Putting more power into individuals' hands, with less of a guarantee of authoritative involvement, leads to several outcomes. First, it widens acceptable patterns of behavior. Second, because there are fewer people, individuals are more likely to engage in human interaction—to converse with a stranger, for example. Finally, because social pressures are changed by lower population density, people are more likely to engage in longer, less direct conversation. These changes in interaction correlate to ideas of inclusion: a greater diversity is accepted, and people are more likely to interact outside of their normal sphere.
>
> Of course, this theory of night behavior also posits higher rates of lawlessness, so that while behavioral differences can support feelings of inclusion, Waffle House also sees its share of violence and crime. (Rawson 2013:231)

Waffle House's low-cost bill of fare and 24-7-365 accessibility—the so-called myth of lockless doors (Rawson 2013:231)—contribute to an eating environment where the line between private and public space significantly blurs, particularly during its third shift. During the morning and afternoon shifts, however, this line of demarcation stands more clearly defined, altering how guests use Waffle House as a public space. Indeed, it does so differently from Starbucks and other quick-service chains that allow for extended socializing, schoolwork, or de facto offices where typing away on laptops or loudly taking business calls proves the norm.

Instead, Waffle House adheres to a more traditional restaurant model where tasks unrelated to meal consumption generally meet with disapproval, particularly during daylight hours after checks have been settled.

According to journalist Andrew Knowlton (2015), "the goal is to have every table in and out in 20 minutes." Anonymized cellphone location data from April 2019 and presented in the *New York Times* (Baicker et al. 2020) underscore Waffle House's success in meeting this objective. Of the twenty or so sit-down chain eateries considered, visits to daytime Waffle House are by far the shortest in duration—around twenty to twenty-five minutes—but highest in weekly numbers. Unsurprisingly, one of its competitors, Huddle House, had the next shortest restaurant visits—around thirty-five to forty minutes—with Chuck E. Cheese topping the list with visit durations somewhere between fifty-five and sixty minutes.

Within the less time permissive circumstances of Waffle House, guest behavior such as conducting personal business on-site, completing school projects, or any other customer action that transgresses the prescribed dimensions of the social contract by which most restaurants operate raises the prospects of a worn-out welcome or invitation to leave. Quite simply, in regard to customer utilization of Waffle House facilities over a twenty-four-hour span, daytime Waffle House differs both subtly and significantly from overnight Waffle House.

As anyone who has ever made a 3:00 a.m. weekend visit to Waffle House can attest, a latent volatility imbues the restaurant's dining area, especially when operations approach full capacity. The muted possibility that things could easily go awry with the slightest of provocations never feels so close as when overextended Waffle House personnel scramble to meet the demands of a clientele partly sober and partly under the influence of alcohol and who knows what else. As boisterous conversations invariably overlap, amplifying one another into a cacophonous din, ordering becomes difficult. Under these circumstances, the guardrails that typically constrain social interactions feel less entrenched, heightening potential confrontation inside the eatery's confined quarters. Although not a powder keg per se, the lack of ample restaurant space—where bumping against fellow diners at neighboring tables or vying for servers' attention with other counter customers proves all too easy—intensifies an atmosphere already unconducive to swift conflict resolution, should disputes arise.

Presumably, most guests strive to avoid confrontations while visiting third-shift Waffle House, or any other twenty-four-hour eatery, for that matter. Few patrons would prefer enduring the unpleasantries of witnessing such conflicts and even more so directly participating in them. Surely, nothing casts a pall over mealtime experiences quite like an escalating verbal row at a nearby table or a potentially violent encounter born out of some drunken brouhaha. Even if the likelihood of encountering such incidents, let alone seeing them spiral out control, is low, in the case of Waffle House, such prospects still retain enough plausibility so as not to be readily dismissed. With a reputation that effectively precedes itself, Waffle House stands as a late-night eatery where expectations of experiencing anything from the mind-numbingly boring to the utterly bonkers are never beyond the realms of possibility.

In reality, the vast majority of today's dining public concern themselves little with things that could conceivably go wrong while eating at Waffle House, but for others, decisions to patronize this popular chain or not are informed by matters not wholly related to reasonable prices and down-home cooking. Indeed, for some, the mere prospect of ending up in such uncomfortable situations is more than enough to make them seriously weigh the pros and cons of ever visiting the chain in the dead of night. Recent alcohol consumption or overwhelming hunger may help blunt this type of anxiety, eventually leading these Waffle House averse to abandon previous safety concerns in the quest for cheap grub and/or ongoing companionship with friends and peers inside the fluorescent-lit dining area.

For still others, the potential for late-night Waffle House trouble is something that adds a perverse bit of novelty to the restaurant's overall graveyard-shift appeal. If such thrill seeking remains peripheral to more immediate concerns like finding inexpensive comfort food or choosing from a select number of sit-down eateries still open for business, it nevertheless factors into equations about where to go when almost everything else is closed. However remote the possibility of encountering something bizarre, injurious, or downright criminal, it is often enough to sway dining decisions toward Waffle House. Among the social media savvy of this more adventurous sector of today's dining public, in fact, third-shift Waffle House is more than just a site of potential hullabaloo. For them, it serves as a viable backdrop for either staging outrageous incidents or randomly recording events that can later be posted online to varying degrees of acclaim or notoriety should they go viral. Unsurprisingly, restaurant staff and other guests are not always portrayed in the most flattering of lights in these clips.

The case of South Carolinian Alex Bowen cooking himself breakfast at a nearly deserted Waffle House in December 2017 and then promptly uploading his exploits on to Facebook while the restaurant's lone shift worker slept head down on a tabletop (see preface) comes to mind in this regard. No less illustrative of this practice are the dozens upon dozens of YouTube and TikTok videos featuring on-site brawling between and among Waffle

House personnel and customers, as well as the aforementioned January 2019 case, wherein two Waffle House employees got fired for Instagram posts showing them dousing an inebriated patron with condiments and kitchen ingredients.

Whistling Past the Graveyard Shift

As noted, a combination of inexpensive menu items, twenty-four-hour business, and particular interior design leaves Waffle House vulnerable to various levels of criminality and misbehavior. Exacerbating these factors is the dearth of emotional investment on the part of some restaurant personnel sufficient to fully engage diners with friendly and efficient service. By no means exclusive to Waffle House, lackluster restaurant service remains a pervasive problem across the quick-service industry, particularly among those low-end fast-casual and fast-food chains paying insufficient hourly wages for sometimes high-pressure work. Chains often tout exceptional service and amiability on the part of their crew members (Rogers 2000), but the reality of the situation frequently suggests otherwise.

The satirical newspaper *The Onion* alludes to this disjuncture in a fake article published as COVID-19 raged across America in the spring of 2020

Figure 3.3. Waffle House employees, Orlando, Florida. Ty Matejowsky

with the tongue-in-cheek headline "Undaunted Texas Waffle House Waitress Has Been Expecting to Die There Everyday for the Past 20 Years Anyway." Additionally, one former Waffle House cook describes working the post–last call restaurant rush as a hard-won "badge of honor," stating, "It's like the Marines who serve a four-year tour of duty and hate it at the time but brag about it later. If you can work a double-shift on New Year's Eve when the bars let out, with a cook sick out and only two waitresses, you've accomplished something. You dread dealing with drunks, but they usually leave good tips" (Dyer 2008:170).

At around-the-clock eateries such as Waffle House, a case can be made that those working late-night and early morning hours experience much less incentive compared with dayshift employees to go above and beyond when it comes to customer interactions. The fact that Waffle House offers its graveyard-shift workers little in terms of commensurate salary and benefits (Editorial Board 2020) in return for long hours of tedium punctuated by unenviable bouts of dealing with drunk and occasionally oddball characters whose strange or boorish behavior can test the limits of even the most patient of individuals does not bode well for top-notch dining experiences. For reasons both directly and indirectly related to such workplace victimization, chains like Waffle House may face challenges in attracting top third-shift talent.[4] So, perhaps to guard against ill treatment from intoxicated customers or send a clear message to the overly chatty that a near-empty restaurant does not equal an invitation for long-winded conversations, some night-shift personnel may come across as rather off-putting.

Tack onto this the reasonable fear that interceding in customer disputes or clashes involving other crew members will exact some kind of physical and/or legal cost, it becomes increasingly clear as to why third-shift Waffle House workers regularly appear so aloof and disinterested. Taking a bullet for the company, so to speak, is just not in the cards for most who don the black apron and blue shirt of the Waffle House uniform. Anecdotally, few of the customer fight videos posted online actually show Waffle House employees stepping into the ruckus to break apart those brawling. Many simply depict workers off to the side going about their duties or behind the counter ignoring the fracas altogether.

Admittedly, it is hard to imagine anyone stuck working the graveyard shift as being overly motivated in demeanor and actions or consistently earning high customer service marks, especially when drawing a Waffle House server's hourly wages, which incidentally do not include large gratuities (Peterson 2014). Speaking to the *Atlanta Journal-Constitution*, Joe

Rogers Sr. problematically described restaurant staff as follows: "Most of our waitresses have hard lives. A lot of them have a bunch of kids at home, and maybe their husbands don't have good jobs" (Osinski 2004). By now, employee inattention or passivity at chain twenty-four-hour eateries should not elicit much outrage on the part of the dining public. As part and parcel of the realities encountered on this rung of today's service economy, less than optimal waitstaff interactions are certainly common enough. Still, it is probably no exaggeration that some of the late-night altercations erupting at Waffle House are, if not triggered by real or perceived incidents of lackluster service, then certainly informed by them.

Yet, to the credit of Waffle House executives and in an apparent show of solidarity with everyday restaurant wage earners, no one in the organization receives time off for holidays. Upper management are expected to work on Thanksgiving, Christmas, and New Year's just as their grill and kitchen counterparts do. In 2012, company executive Dave Rickell told an Atlanta television station, "We don't feel that it is right to ask our employees and managers to work holidays if executives aren't" (Leslie 2012). Likewise, many if not most company executives lack personal offices within Waffle House's Norcross, Georgia, corporate headquarters. Most spend their days in the field overseeing individual restaurant operations, making sure Waffle House practices and policies are being followed. Rickell further noted: "I don't have an office. We have a corporate office, but I don't have an office there. We like our operations people to be in the field every day. It's pretty hard to manage a restaurant from an office. It's a special part of the culture where we're all in this together" (Leslie 2012).

Waffle (Money) Maker

The convenience, affordability, and accessibility for which the Waffle House brand is now recognized does much to bolster its standing both within the (fast-)casual retailscape and among various segments of the US dining public. That Waffle House continues to rely extensively on cash transactions while other industry players increasingly embrace credit cards, mobile apps, and digital wallets as primary modes of payment speaks volumes about the restaurant's blue-collar roots and ostensible cachet.[5] Clearly, such practices are problematic when considered against the operational backdrop of Waffle House restaurants. To thwart potential employee or customer theft, the chain limits the amount of paper and coin currency accessible within its counter registers at any one time, and it also relies on protective measures such as drop safes and money dispensers to control how cash is handled on a daily basis. Despite such safeguards, notions of Waffle House as a cash-friendly business remain pervasive.

Location, Location, Location

Again, with so many Waffle House eateries situated along interstate highways or near offramp exits, it is unsurprising that the company enjoys considerable popularity among budget-conscious families, truck drivers, or others traveling long distances, seeking quick and inexpensive meals while on the go. Utilizing commercial real estate that either runs parallel or stands adjacent to heavily traveled stretches of roadway is doubtless smart business for just about any retail chain. This time-tested tactic not only allows establishments to operate in spatial proximity to a steady flow of vehicles that runs throughout the day and into the night—ones presumably containing scores of potentially hungry customers—it also streamlines the logistics of running a commercial eatery by facilitating the bulk delivery of wholesale food items and ingredients. Supply-laden 18-wheelers from restaurant distribution centers or kitchen commissaries can unload their wares and get back on the road with less hassle.

Since the late 1960s, when Rogers and Forkner launched the first roadside Waffle House location along Interstate 20 near Conyers, Georgia (see chapter 2), the securing and operating of properties near busy roadways have remained vital components of company expansion plans. The ability to entice those journeying down the highway to activate their turn signal, cross lanes of traffic, and exit toward the Waffle House parking lot becomes easier when drivers know that merging back into traffic afterward will present little or no trouble.

Anyone traveling on the interstate through the Carolinas or states like Florida and Georgia for the first time cannot help but recognize Waffle House's roadside ubiquity and strategic placement along so many readily accessible spots on the regional highway system. As the miles tick by, the elevated yellow/black restaurant sign appears on the horizon with such recurring frequency that it effectively punctuates the landscape, rivalling perhaps billboards for South Carolina's iconic South of the Border tourist attraction, or Lion's Den Adult Superstore, and those "FORGIVE MY SINS JESUS SAVE MY SOUL" advertisements, in outdoor marketing reach.

This ease of access also represents an Achilles' heel of sorts. It translates into high numbers of transient groups and individuals who, however cool-headed and composed, are not subject to the same type of social pressures as frequent and repeat customers, particularly with regard to mealtime interactions with restaurant staff and fellow diners. To wit, these one-time visitors can breeze through a roadside Waffle House secure in the understanding that any discourtesy or acting out on their part will likely invite no serious sanction. With prospects of return visits essentially nil, the implicit checks on behavior that restaurant regulars face (e.g., improved future service and/or continued restaurant admittance) do not readily apply to those just passing through. Given Waffle House's reputation as a site of after-hours revelry, it is evident, again, that alcohol plays a role in informing this dynamic.

Granted, a sizable representation of highway travelers and others for whom the chain's accessibility predominates when making dining decisions only goes so far in explaining Waffle House customer misconduct and occasional criminality. When considered alongside some of the other factors presented in this chapter, however, its underlying role in cultivating a permissive kind of retail environment assumes sharper clarity.

Highway Robbery

Waffle House's roadside accessibility plays a significant role in leaving the eatery susceptible to serious types of lawbreaking. As a security weakness variously exploited in crimes hinging on quick getaways, location is particularly relevant to persons planning and carrying out armed robberies. Waffle House restaurants continually fall into the crosshairs of those looking to make off with daily store earnings, especially in the dead of night. Easy to reach and comparatively free from parking lot congestion, with no drive-through lanes, Waffle House eateries present few real challenges to anyone entering or exiting its facilities whether for innocent or nefarious purposes.

Indeed, the company's longtime strategy of locating so many of its branches and franchises within close proximity to major interstates, expressways, and arterial roads makes Waffle House a soft target for would-be and repeat felons. For armed perpetrators, in fact, this kind of accessibility confers a freedom of movement that makes for speedy escapes once registers are cleared out. Criminals can be back out on the road within minutes of a holdup, racing down the freeway, blending into the anonymity of fast-moving traffic, and increasing their odds of evading apprehension.

With so many of its eateries situated within miles of each other along consecutive stretches of interstate highway, especially within and between southern cities, Waffle House stands exposed to repeat victimization by different perpetrators over an extended period of time and also by the same offenders in the midst of an ongoing crime spree. Whether through word of mouth or continual media reports, roadside locations have gained notoriety for lax security that make them convenient targets for armed robbery. Whether planned or opportunistic, the case mentioned earlier in this chapter involving Justanity Johnson and Xavier Parham robbing four different Texas Waffle House locations in under eighty minutes comes to mind.

If such ease of access is not enticing enough, Waffle House's twenty-four-hour operations and cash-friendly leanings enhance the restaurant's attractiveness to enterprising criminals. Like many all-night convenience stores, chain locations not only deal in high amounts of hard currency, they also commonly remain understaffed and minimally occupied for much of the workweek, notwithstanding the sometimes boisterous weekend graveyard shifts. Near-empty restaurants with only one or two employees overseeing operations stand as an open invitation to armed assailants.

Fewer on-site customers during third-shift hours, coupled with a reduction in the number of passers-by and police making the rounds outside, diminishes opportunities for external intervention in thwarting Waffle House crimes underway. Exacerbating these on-site vulnerabilities are the large posters and other promotional displays often affixed to restaurant windows. Robberies in progress become difficult to detect for anyone walking or driving past—particularly from a distance. Odds that eyewitnesses or good Samaritans emerge to call 911 and report Waffle House holdups effectively dwindle. Although not necessarily a pervasive problem for Waffle House, insufficient or improperly working exterior lighting can also compromise potential help from informal nighttime surveillance.

Waffle House and Routine Activity Theory

Within today's (fast-)casual foodscape, Waffle House is routinely elevated as an exemplar of a restaurant chain perennially in the public eye for negative reasons. As other brands earn popular distinction for things like launching new products or modes of service, mentions of Waffle House invariably seem rooted in various types of "police blotter" activities that invariably foreground the sensational over nuance. By now, delinking Waffle House's beleaguered public image from myriad incidents of on-site wrongdoing proves quite the challenge given the proliferation of online and traditional media coverage devoted to the brand's seamier side.

Information in this chapter does much to dispel notions that Waffle House crimes and misconduct are strictly born out of the actions of ill-intentioned individuals who randomly select the chain to carry out their malfeasance. The assorted mayhem, fights, and robberies that punctuate normative restaurant operations emerge not just out of bad actor behavior but also arise from a confluence of structural and operational elements working concomitantly to create a dining milieu sometimes unsuited for blunting antisocial behavior. Although nothing directly compels people to act out at Waffle House, criminally or otherwise, current company policies and operational practices establish a basic set of parameters wherein the incidence and scope of adverse occurrences are much greater than would otherwise be the case. Of course, all of this is subsumed within the much broader and complex socioeconomic landscape of early twenty-first century America, where a hyperdrive mode of shareholder-first capitalism holds sway over practically all aspects of daily life.

In fully appreciating the breadth and frequency of problematic Waffle House encounters, it is instructive to briefly consider the routine activity theory (RAT) developed and popularized by criminologists Lawrence Cohen and Marcus Felson (1979). Without much deference to subtlety or nuance, RAT posits that crime physically emerges in time and space when three factors—a "potential offender, a suitable target, and the absence of a capable guardian" (Bottoms and Wiles 2004:620)—intersect in a three-circled Venn diagram. Current Waffle House operations lend themselves readily to this schema's underlying logic, as all three spheres find overlap in and around restaurant facilities. Untangling the interplay among these constituent elements, much less assigning them hierarchal rank, proves difficult as the convergence of all three gives RAT its conceptual power.

A continually accruing record of on-premises crime and misbehavior demonstrates that, when it comes to Waffle House, there is no shortage of individuals willing to risk possible sanction and arrest, as well as court grievous bodily harm, in the commission of serious if not sometimes highly original antisocial acts (e.g., 2014's Waffle House pitchfork robbery). Within the context of RAT—where humans are presumptively rational actors—the benefits of engaging in such activities outweigh whatever downsides they pose.

In terms of targetability, Waffle House eateries occupy a fairly vulnerable position within today's (fast-)casual restaurant scene for many of the reasons just outlined. Viewed in the framework of RAT, these features cumulatively conspire to enhance Waffle House's attractiveness to would-be and repeat criminals, however opportunistic or calculated these individuals may be. Again, for armed robbers, in particular, Waffle House holds special appeal given that its 24-7 operations, roadside locations, and receptiveness to paper currency provide perpetrators easy access to daily store earnings and viable escape routes to abet their nighttime getaways.

Finally, a look at security efforts at most Waffle House eateries reveals a string of deficiencies that warrant reevaluation to better anticipate and deter on-site crime and misconduct. Even though stores are well illuminated and employ a clear set of policies regarding customer conduct (i.e., House Rules), these features go only so far in guarding Waffle House properties and employees against repeat victimization, especially third-shift armed holdups. Without on-premises security guards, regular drive-by police patrols, or other visible or recognized protective measures in place—ones that unequivocally transmit messages of serious repercussions if broached—Waffle House will remain in the sights of various ill-intentioned individuals and groups.

For Waffle House and other budget-brand retailers (e.g., Dollar General, Family Dollar), preemptive steps to further safeguard its employees and customers are typically weighed against estimates of incidence and cost before implementation (MacGillis 2020). Yet, barring the embrace of more rigorous and conspicuous security measures, the capable guardianship identified by Cohen and Felson as so essential for foiling motivated individuals from criminally exploiting suitable targets like Waffle House will persist.

Sunnyside Up

Much as a photonegative rendering of a familiar image reverses its colorful vibrancies, recasting them into starker tones of black and gray, the shadow side of Waffle House explored in this chapter subverts brand efforts at projecting, however offhandedly, a quaint down-home image. Providing a resonant counternarrative to the company's official marketing stance just as it reveals much about the darker inclinations of today's dining public, the implications of this flip-side characterization are significant and far-reaching. Within the context of the southern imaginary, it becomes just another aspect of regional life that invites easy caricature and dismissal from non-southerners and elitist gourmand types.

Despite the resonant and sensationalized characterizations of Waffle House that have held sway in the popular imagination for so long, rays of light occasionally pierce the gloomy darkness. Allowing in just enough warmth and illumination to seem less like the organic responses of everyday restaurant folk and more like clever marketing ploys devised by advertising executives looking to flip the script on ingrained public thinking. A number of chance occurrences have added new wrinkles to Waffle House's oft-maligned and underdog image. Indeed, it is important to both recognize and foreground some less adverse Waffle House encounters to better situate the chain in a more complete and realistic light. Besides the feel-good story from March 2018 of Texas City Waffle House waitress Evoni Williams mentioned in the introduction, other incidents of employee kindness and customer altruism have taken place at various branch and franchise locations over the years.

Indeed, it is probably fair to suggest that such on-site magnanimity occurs more frequently than it attracts public mention. The kind of person-to-person encounters that reaffirm basic human decency arguably happen all the time but rarely seem newsworthy enough for mainstream audience expectations for a Waffle House story. Owing to their poignant storylines and heartwarming sentiments, these good-natured incidents typically only receive brief notice from national and regional media outlets. Possibly due to this limited shelf-life and fleeting impact, they seemingly fall short in swaying popular sentiments about Waffle House away from long-held public preconceptions.

Some of the uplifting stories that have garnered recent press include the following:

- Right before Travis Jeffrey Reinking shot four people with an AR-15 at an Antioch, Tennessee, Waffle House in April 2018 (see introduction), a waitress, Virginia Stanley, had asked customers sitting at the counter, including Michael Davis, to switch seats to prevent him from getting wet as she washed dishes nearby. Davis's compliance may have ultimately saved his life because he ended up farther away from the gunman when he sprayed the open-air kitchen with semiautomatic fire. Later, Davis's mother, Vickie Davis, unsuccessfully tried to track down the waitress to thank her for saving her son. Davis left her contact information with the Waffle House manager and awaited word from Stanley. About a month later, Davis was put in touch with Stanley's fiancé. In an appreciative gesture, Davis coordinated with a local bridal shop that donates wedding dresses to military women and first responders, Glitz Nashville, to ensure the bride-to-be was properly attired for her big day (KARE staff 2018).
- A scheduling snafu at a Birmingham, Alabama, Waffle House in early November 2019 left an unsuspecting worker whose nametag read "Ben" scrambling to cover an entire Saturday night/Sunday graveyard shift by himself. As service ground to a halt and tempers frayed among a clientele of thirty or so mostly sober customers, several sympathetic guests, noticing something was amiss, rolled up their sleeves and one by one sprang into action. Without being asked, a few

donned aprons and began busing tables, stacking cups, or washing dishes, leaving Ben free to prioritize how to best handle payments, food orders, and meal preparation. Sliding behind the counter, an unidentified young woman in high heels and sequined cocktail attire learned how to operate the store coffeemaker on the fly, going on to clear away debris and try to fill an order or two. What minutes before was a collection of strangers crossing paths at a 24-7 chain eatery quickly morphed into a volunteer restaurant crew doing their utmost to assist a wage earner backed into a very tight corner. According to eyewitness Ethan Crispo, without these good Samaritans stepping in, things easily could have escalated into an ugly confrontation between "Ben" and his unattended customers, possibly even prompting the lone Waffle House associate to up and quit his job. For their part, most visitors simply rolled with the novelty of the situation, happy to get whatever third-shift service they could. Even though company officials later appreciatively but firmly noted their preference for only having employees behind the counter, for Crispo that night's events stand as an object lesson in how everyday people can rise to the occasion, illustrating humanity at its best (Klein 2019; Specker 2019).

• A thirty-five-second clip entitled "Georgia Waffle House Customers Volunteer to Help Due to January 2014 Snow Storm" was uploaded to YouTube by one Bob Wells on January 29, 2014. The cellphone footage depicts a bustling Waffle House restaurant struggling to handle an overflow of guests dressed in heavy winterwear and lined up out of the door. Mixed among the blue-shirted and black-aproned associates behind the counter are various customers moving about, refilling coffee mugs, and delivering meals to other hungry customers. The so-called Snowmageddon cold wave gripped much of the East and Southeast, shutting down scores of businesses throughout much of the Bible Belt with the notable exception of Waffle House (Oxford 2014). The description reads: "Waffle House on Mansell Road in Alpharetta, GA is inundated with travelers trapped on the road due to the snow storm. Customers volunteer to help the two Waffle House employees feed and take care of people that have been stuck in their car for hours without food or something to drink. Milk was also taken outside to a mother with a baby stuck in a car. This is the true Southern Spirit" (Wells 2014). Company representatives have recently alluded to this incident when speaking about Waffle House's "special sense of community" (Prior 2019).

- Timothy Harrison, an eighteen-year-old Woodlawn High School senior and Waffle House employee in Center Point, Alabama, showed up for his 7:00 a.m. restaurant shift on May 27, 2021, the day he was scheduled to walk across the stage and receive his graduation diploma. Coworkers were surprised to see Harrison as he previously had requested the day off to attend the ceremony with family members at a large venue in nearby Birmingham, about an hour away from his house. When these plans fell through because of conflicting family work schedules, compounded by a lack of a ride, Harrison opted to go to Waffle House to try to pick up his regular shift hours. After telling colleagues about his situation, the store manager, Cedric Hampton, flew into action, coordinating with friends, family, and off-duty coworkers to get Harrison fully ready for the 3:00 p.m. ceremony. Among other things, this entailed chipping in cash to buy Harrison some dress clothes, driving to the school to pick up graduation tickets and cap and gown regalia, and transporting Harrison to the venue for the ceremony with only minutes to spare. Harrison told local media that although the day started out on a disappointing note it shaped up to be the best day of his life. Hampton, a father of three, told reporters, "We are one big family at my Waffle House. We are all about supporting our people." Soon after this heartwarming story received public notice, Harrison was offered a full scholarship along with books at the nearby Lawson State College. Both Harrison and Hampton got to tour the campus on June 10, 2021, with Harrison telling reporters that before this unexpected and fortuitous development, he had not expected to attend college but rather join the military. He further added that he intended on studying business and computer science (Page 2021).

The light and dark aspects of Waffle House do much to shape prevailing notions about the eatery, its clientele, and the geographical region with which it remains so closely affiliated. Few other restaurant brands of a similar size and scope contend with such a beleaguered reputation while at the same time enjoying the accolades that go along with so many unselfish acts of human kindness. As the accounts documented within this chapter suggest, Waffle House's public image encapsulates both the best and worst of what it means to be an American at this particular historical juncture.

4

Waffle House and Race

Any consideration of Waffle House as a putative southern icon and regional restaurant mainstay must inevitably grapple with America's shameful legacy of racial discrimination and exclusion. Given that the company's historical roots extend well back into the Jim Crow era, and that its corporate footprint covers the entirety of what is colloquially known as Dixie—a real and imagined place whose mercurial and subjective geographies remain inextricably affiliated with the Antebellum South and Confederate States of America (Garreau 1981)—such reconciliation is both necessary and vital. Despite touting itself as "America's Place for Inclusion" and taking important steps toward fostering a more equitable workplace and dining environment in the past two decades, Waffle House continues to come up short when it comes to effectively tackling issues of racism among its employees, managers, and clientele. Problems confronted in this chapter are not exclusive to Waffle House, but they take on special resonance given the way the chain is so widely embraced and regularly showcased as a veritable symbol of today's South.

America 2020

Amid a tanking economy with tens of millions of Americans out of work and a surging global pandemic disproportionately impacting people of color—especially in southern US states with Trump-aligned Republican governors including Georgia, Florida, Texas, Mississippi, and Alabama who prematurely rescinded stay-at-home and lockdown orders going against the advice of public health experts and unleashing a second more deadly wave of COVID-19—the killing of George Floyd (1973–2020) by Minneapolis police on May 25, 2020, triggered a mass wave of social protest not seen in the United States for generations.

For many, the forty-six-year-old African American's death was not just a tragic loss of life but a combustive spark igniting a powder keg of pent-up frustration at the status quo of racial injustice and extrajudicial killings of unarmed Black males, evoking the cases of Emmett Till (1941–55), Trevon Martin (1995–2012), and Elijah McClain (1996–2019), among others.[1] In a cathartic release of collective anger at institutional structures and arrangements that historically bestow material and institutional advantages to some while continually disenfranchising and victimizing others, communities nationwide took to the street, giving full vent to this urgent mixture of sadness and exasperation at no small risk to their physical health or material well-being. Over subsequent days and weeks, much of the previous inertia that had characterized efforts toward effecting positive social change and bringing about racial justice and police accountability effectively vanished, not only in the United States but also around the world.

Besides reinvigorating the oft-vilified Black Lives Matter (BLM) movement and speeding calls for real and meaningful reform of America's military, prison, and law enforcement apparatus, Floyd's untimely death, alongside those of Ahmaud Arbery (1995–2020) and Breonna Taylor (1994–2020), spurred considerable soul-searching on the part of so many everyday white Americans about how to address and dismantle the presumed certainties inherent to white privilege and structural racism. Among city and state governments, popular corporations, professional sports leagues, and media conglomerates, this sort of introspection prompted internal and external appeals for a prompt remedial response. For a plurality of Americans, in fact, business as usual no longer seemed sufficient, particularly when it came to confronting the growing number of Black people—mostly men and often unarmed—killed or injured during law enforcement encounters.

For really the first time in recent memory, many white Americans appeared waking up to the fact that people of color face notably different circumstances and challenges when going about their daily lives. Their daily lives are rooted in historical and structural inequalities that inform everything from interpersonal interactions to the prevailing symbolic landscape that provides meaning across time, place, and context. As the record of African American deaths following law enforcement encounters—as well as the unequal effects of overpolicing and mass incarceration in the War on Drugs era (1971 until now) on Black communities make clear—the realities confronted by nonwhite people can often prove matters of life or death even as similar situations rarely elicit such dire outcomes for their white counterparts. Because of their skin color, white people—especially cisgender white males—enjoy more leeway when it comes to opportunities, freedom of movement, second chances, and benefits of the doubt than do people of color.

Accompanying this ostensible awakening to the plight of minority groups was a growing receptiveness by some white Americans to finally acknowledge their own complicity and favored status within a hegemonic order that touts equal protection under the law but, in reality, continues to privilege some while marginalizing or mistreating others. As this recognition of historical and contemporary culpability gained traction in 2020, newfound urgency informed efforts toward consciously deconstructing the structural oppression of marginalized peoples and providing equitable opportunities for all, irrespective of anyone's individual and systemic background.

Reimagining the Southern Imaginary

If circumstances necessitated actionable redress from individuals and organizations in the summer of 2020, the United States, in general, and South, specifically, did not lack for potential targets. With frustrations boiling over, it did not take long for the course of events in May and June to overtake any inclinations toward passivity or hedging when it came to immediate responses. Seemingly in one fell swoop, many iconic symbols related to the southern imaginary or white European hegemony were either forcibly removed from their privileged positions within the real and imagined public squares of American life or voluntarily taken down in response to mounting public pressure in the weeks following Floyd's death.

These symbols had come to divide Americans over recent decades, generating a familiar kind of Red and Blue State polarization that cleaves to well-established lines of early twenty-first-century political partisanship and tribalism. The "heritage, not hate" or "pride, not prejudice" rationales employed by many white defenders of a decades-long embrace of trappings affiliated with the southern imaginary and antebellum and postbellum America no longer enjoyed as much widespread currency with communities nationwide. Although some of the symbols considered in this chapter elicit more vigorous debate and fierce resistance than others, all convey a limited and distorted view of history, one that invariably elevates white perspectives and experiences above others.

For those working toward a more racially just and inclusive society, probably nothing evokes as much long-standing antipathy as the Confederate monuments and memorials so prominently featured in town squares and school campuses nationwide. With their three-dimensional public foregrounding, aura of historical permanence, and blatant legitimization of Lost Cause mythologies, these ornamental reminders of past events and personalities physically manifest—often in larger than life ways—the varied emotions and passions still stirred by events that very nearly tore the United States asunder over 150 years ago.

Along with the Confederate battle flag, which even in the early twenty-first century many southern states still either officially displayed on public grounds or incorporated into their state insignia and flags, which by virtue of their near ubiquity were widely encountered day in and day out by white and nonwhites citizens alike—the statues, cenotaphs, monuments, plaques, and memorials dotting towns, cities, and campuses across the South and other parts of America no longer enjoy the sort of consensus view that informed dominant narratives about their establishment and preservation. Given their increased use during the Trump era as rallying points for the Alt-Right, Proud Boys, and various other extremist groups (e.g., August 2017's Unite the Right rally in Charlottesville, Virginia), they became some of the first symbols in the summer of 2020 to be vandalized, defaced, decapitated, set ablaze, or even pulled down from their highly visible public stations.

The removal of plaques and toppling or dismantling of statues venerating Confederate leaders such as Robert E. Lee, Jefferson Davis, and Stonewall Jackson as well as those honoring rank-and-file servicemen fighting against the Union during the Civil War (1861–65) put up by the likes of the United Daughters of the Confederacy beginning in the late nineteenth century, and later ones established in the 1950s and 1960s in a barely veiled display of white supremacy against an ascendant Civil Rights Movement, was lauded by many as welcome and long-overdue steps toward achieving the "more perfect Union" articulated in the Constitution's preamble. Of the 1,800 public Confederate memorials documented by the Southern Poverty Law Center in early June 2020, 775 (43 percent) were monuments or statues, with the remaining examples being highways, parks, government buildings, or military bases (Hoff 2020).

Official instances of Confederate statue removal—usually done in the dead of night and on short notice to minimize or preclude counterprotests—had achieved some measured success over previous years in cities like New Orleans and Austin, but these earlier efforts are nothing on the scale of what occurred in the wake of Floyd's death. Even less common was the deliberate toppling of Confederate monuments and memorials by protestors as typified by 2018's controversial felling of the "Silent Sam" statue on the campus of the University of North Carolina at Chapel Hill.[2] Before the summer of 2020, the revanchist reverence for Confederate emblems across the Bible Belt remained so deeply entrenched that only high-profile incidents like 2015's Charleston church shooting (see introduction) could move the needle toward action for their complete removal or relocation to less visible locales.

Among throngs of cheering and mostly nonviolent protestors in June 2020, the toppling of dozens of Confederate statues, as well as memorials paying tribute to key figures associated with the genocide of indigenous peoples in the Americas including Christopher Columbus and Junípero Serra,[3] exemplified a renewed push to seriously confront the moonlight and magnolias romanticism that has long informed public discourse about the South and to more expansively dismantle all overt and implicit expressions of institutional racism in everyday life. As visible signifiers of ideologies and regimes no longer widely embraced beyond select segments—namely, white Evangelicals and residents of small-town or rural America who see their privileges, values, and way of life as under assault by myriad outside groups and forces—of the United States' increasingly variegated demographic tapestry, time seemed to be running out for their continued public foregrounding.

In a matter of weeks beginning in late May 2020, a wave of purposeful change swept across institutional and corporate America, one that surprisingly elicited buy-in from operations long resistant to vigorously tackling aspects of their public profiles previously identified as racially insensitive to African Americans, Native Americans, and other nonwhite groups. Although not yet getting at the root causes of persistent structural asymmetries within America's political and socioeconomic fabric—such as endemic poverty, inadequate healthcare, underfunded public schools, shareholder-first economic policy, overpolicing, and expansive incarceration—these initial efforts at righting wrongs entailed steps including apologizing for past complicity in the preservation of systems that protect and nurture white privilege as well as making commitments to enact antiracist policies moving forward.

These measures involved steps such as the dropping of controversial names, mascots, iconography, and symbols that held public currency for decades. To wit, the US Army not only changed its policy regarding the use of Confederate symbols at its installations, banning the display of Confederate flags and related paraphernalia, it more ambitiously reversed its long-held stance about keeping ten military bases named in honor of prominent Confederate military figures including Fort Bragg, Fort Hood, and Fort Gordon.[4] Located throughout the South—three in Virginia, two in Louisiana, two in Georgia, and one each in Texas, North Carolina, and

Alabama—the official titles of these installations date back to World War I and had remained despite the fact this military branch is now around 20 percent African American.

Army officials resisted calls to rename these facilities for decades. Even as recently as February 2020, the Pentagon defended the names as reflecting the spirit of reconciliation that restored the Union to a whole in the mid-1860s. After Floyd's death and the ensuing calls for reform, the army promptly backtracked on its earlier rationale, generating overwhelming bipartisan support for finding less divisive base names from the Pentagon and Congress. Surprisingly, many Republican senators and house members backed this push despite the charged atmosphere of 2020 election year politics and President Trump's vocal opposition to both name changes and Confederate statue removal.

Perhaps less newsworthy was the traction gained on changing local school names. Student, parent, and alumni outcry spotlighted the dozens upon dozens of public and private institutes named after Confederate luminaries or other figures with documented racist pasts. Primarily located in the South, these primary and secondary schools often have majority nonwhite student bodies. Corey Mitchell, writing in *Education Week* (2020), notes: "At the beginning of June 2020, at least 208 schools in 18 states were named for men with ties to the Confederacy, an Education Week analysis of federal data found. Since June 29, 10 of the Confederate-named schools have changed names. Currently, 53 schools are named for (Robert E.) Lee and more than a dozen each honor Stonewall Jackson and Sidney Lanier, a poet and private in the Confederate Army. Countless other schools bear the names of individuals with racist histories, including 22 that are named after politicians who signed the Southern Manifesto opposing school integration after the 1954 *Brown v. Board* Supreme Court decision."

Texas leads the pack with the dubious distinction of having forty-five Confederate-named schools locally operating. The two states with the next highest numbers of schools bearing such titles are Virginia with twenty-six and Georgia with twenty-three. Even distant states like California and Washington have one or two schools named in this fashion. The ensuing public shaming from various groups was enough to prompt some districts and oversight bodies to announce or explore immediate name changes.

Beyond America's military and educational apparatus, others trafficking in problematic symbols of the southern imaginary and related domains came to recognize the moment's historical gravity, committing themselves to making meaningful changes in how they engaged mainstream audiences moving forward. Turning a deaf ear to growing calls for social justice proved risky, if no longer tenable, given the groundswell of support for swift action on matters of ongoing racial inequality. The threat of consumer boycotts and withdrawal of sponsorship from major advertisers further incentivized entities to move in this.

As the summer of 2020 unfolded, many embraced a newfound wokeness, even going so far as to completely overhaul their public images. Such changes initially appeared more cosmetic than substantive, yet they still represent an important shift in national conversations about race, white privilege, structural inequality, and law enforcement accountability, especially considering that earlier public outcry about problematic aspects of various corporations, brands, institutions, and others met with notable resistance, inaction, or outright backlash. Amid the tumult and turmoil of nationwide protests calling for ending police brutality and racial injustice, multiple players in American life began implementing various operational changes.

Some pertinent examples warrant consideration here given how the use of symbols and imagery grounded in the southern imaginary's overdetermined expressions of plantation-era America do much to elevate an iconography that effectively obscures the traumatic and dehumanizing experiences endured by so many in the antebellum and postbellum South. Those behind various well-known and enduring brands and enterprises announced significant changes in the summer of 2020 that involved either abandoning any direct affiliation with these toxic aspects or significantly retooling or historically contextualizing their use going forward. Whether these were food conglomerates such as Quaker Oats and Mars, Inc., dropping or retooling mascots associated with some of their major product lines such as Aunt Jemima or Uncle Ben's[5] or popular musical groups including the Dixie Chicks, Lady Antebellum, and Lynch Mob shortening or retiring their band names altogether,[6] an invigorated push to recalibrate public personas gained momentum in the summer of 2020.

In like manner, the front offices of various sports organizations such as NASCAR and the National Football League (NFL), particularly its Washington Redskins franchise, made commitments to significantly alter their operations,[7] taking steps toward increased inclusivity at events and eliminating divisive symbols as this wave of racial awareness and reforms continued after nationwide Floyd protests. Considering that both professional football and stockcar racing attract a devoted fanbase of working-class white southerners (Daniel 2000), efforts to confront and redress contested aspects of their operations represent a significant breakthrough.

About this time, the popular streaming service HBO Max revealed plans to revamp the presentation of select classic movies on its platform. Sensitive to growing national outrage about structural racism, in general, and Floyd's death, specifically, company higher-ups decided that some of its film library warranted either temporary removal or historical contextualization. For instance, the racially insensitive depictions of African Americans in *Gone with the Wind* (1939), where the atrocities of human slavery are sanitized by portrayals of an idyllic antebellum South wherein Black people enjoy relatively content and dutiful lives as subordinates to their benevolent white superiors, was enough for HBO to suspend its foreseeable availability. Similarly, the of-its-time satire and widespread use of the N-word in Mel Brook's *Blazing Saddles* (1974) resulted in future iterations of the film being streamed with a contextual preface that adds commentary and/or denouncements of events portrayed.[8]

Likewise, Disney announced that its Splash Mountain attractions in Florida and California would immediately close to undergo a major retheming. Characters, songs, and imagery from its once-cherished but now rarely seen much less ever acknowledged film *Song of the South* (1946),which like *Gone with the Wind* has invited criticism not only for its depictions of enslaved life during the plantation-era but also for the Black vernacular widely spoken by live-action and animated characters, would all be replaced on the new rides with content from *The Princess and the Frog* (2009), a pioneering Disney animated feature also set in the South but with African American characters in the lead roles.

As to how fast-food and fast-casual brands responded to the BLM movement and the untimely deaths of Floyd, Taylor, Arbery, and other unarmed African Americans killed during police encounters or other questionable circumstances, several operators including McDonald's, Wendy's, Taco Bell, Ben & Jerry's, and Starbucks either issued statements of support for racial justices causes—some of which veer decidedly into platitudinous territory (Crowley 2020)—or made more meaningful gestures like financially contributing to antiracism organizations (e.g., Ben & Jerry's) or holding in-house dialogues with company employees and management (e.g., Starbucks). Whether heartfelt support or simple public relations, these steps reflect a new level of corporate buy-in from America's restaurant industry, a retail sector not really known for weighing in on political matters. Among the numerous restaurant brands effectively absent from these conversations about race and social justice in the summer of 2020 was Waffle House.

"Regardless of Race, Creed, Color"

Waffle House's shying away from directly engaging or even publicly commenting on the issues at the heart of the summer of 2020's BLM protests does not mean these matters are irrelevant to its employees or clientele. With corporate roots dating back to Jim Crow's waning years when an ascendant Civil Rights Movement made significant gains in altering America's sociopolitical landscape, Waffle House stands as an enduring southern brand that, partly because of the formative mid-twentieth-century geohistorical milieu from which it emerged and partly because of the power dynamics still shaping company culture at multiple levels, often struggles to live up to its self-billing as "America's Place for Inclusion."

As is the case with other chain eateries whose pedigrees date back to the postwar era (Langdon 1986:119; Romano 2017), Waffle House's regional rise cannot be readily divorced from various controversies and troubling incidents at its myriad locations across the South and elsewhere. With company operations embedded within broader structural arrangements that confer systemic advantages to white diners while historically disadvantaging peoples of color, such problematic occurrences can hardly be unforeseeable, particularly in light of the restaurant's reputation (discussed in chapter 3) as an after-hours gathering spot for so many revelers no longer compelled to abide by conventional social norms.

As chronicled throughout this book, popular narratives about Waffle House as an inclusive space where, in the words of Anthony Bourdain, "everybody regardless of race, creed, color or degree of inebriation is welcome" (see introduction) resonate in subtle and significant ways. Perhaps such democratic tendencies are best showcased during those late-night shifts when a diverse mix of party people converge on Waffle House, breaking bread among one another, free from hassle and confrontation. At least that is the image so often foregrounded in public thinking when it comes to Waffle House's more endearing qualities. In striving to delineate a more detailed and accurate portrait of today's Waffle House, however, these favorable assessments must also be weighed against other characterizations that have emerged in recent decades. Even in the last few years, the twenty-four-hour chain has come under criticism for not always treating everyone equitably let alone decently at its approximately 1,990 eateries.

In a number of instances, at its various restaurants nationwide, Waffle House has drawn scrutiny for its discriminatory treatment of African Americans and other minority groups. Besides the two high-profile cases involving police intervention mentioned in the introduction—cellphone footage of the violent arrests of Anthony Wall and Chikesia Clemons, along with Jacinda Mitchell's refusal of service, all within days of each other in the spring of 2018, which spurred widespread outrage and calls for a national boycott by Bernice King, daughter of Martin Luther King Jr.—a spate of other Waffle House encounters have gained media attention as of late, some leading to multimillion-dollar lawsuits or other types of restitutive actions (see Waffle House among the Competition section in this chapter).

Much like calls for resisting law enforcement accountability, portraying these Waffle House episodes simply as isolated incidents perpetrated by a few bad apples belies larger patterns of discrimination or intimidation against people of color at company facilities. Even as the company takes steps to cultivate a more welcoming and inclusive atmosphere inside its eateries for employees and customers alike (see Waffle House's Southern Strategy section this chapter), Waffle House has not yet fully escaped the tarnish of racism that, however overtly or implicitly conveyed, still informs darker expressions of the southern imaginary in the popular consciousness.

Waffle House among the Competition

Waffle House is neither the only fast-casual operator subject to criticism for its treatment of African Americans nor likely the worst offender in this regard. If official sanction and financial penalties levied by the Justice Department provide some of the best indicators of determining which corporate eateries most egregiously discriminate against Black and nonwhite clientele, Waffle House may not even be among the top culprits. Given the number of restaurant brands facing similar or even more serious allegations of racial bias over the years (see sections on individual companies in this section), such issues appear more of an industrywide problem than an issue specific to one company (Kwate 2019).[9]

Several other chains have earned notoriety for subjecting African Americans and other segments of today's dining public to assorted unlawful and demeaning practices at their outlets. Allegations of prolonged wait times, preferential white seating practices, requesting upfront payments, overcharging for food, using racial slurs, and outright refusal of service have been levied against some of America's top (fast-)casual brands, many of which directly compete with Waffle House for a share of the all-night breakfast chain market. Individually and collectively, these instances of restaurant mistreatment and discrimination shine a harsh light on the unfinished work that still lies ahead before any meaningful racial reconciliation in the American experiment can take place.

Denny's

Allegations of racial bias and discrimination have long dogged top American breakfast chain and perennial Waffle House rival Denny's. With nearly 1,700 locations spread around the world and across all fifty states, Denny's considerable corporate footprint does little to convince many African Americans and other people of color that their patronage is actually welcomed at the twenty-four-hour eatery. Whether through inferior service, overpricing of orders, or denying accommodation to Black customers, the company has repeatedly faced legal and public relations fallout for how its employees selectively treat African Americans and other minority groups at its restaurant locations nationwide.

Going back several decades, these discrimination claims reached a critical mass in the mid-1990s with a much-reported multimillion-dollar settlement agreed upon, with the Justice Department's help, to resolve a federal class-action lawsuit filed by thousands of African American customers in California, Maryland, and elsewhere involving allegations of unfair treatment including denial of service, prolonged wait times, racist comments, and charging higher prices compared with those of white patrons. This 1994 agreement awarded plaintiffs some $54.4 million. At the time, this decision was "the largest and broadest settlement under Federal public-accommodation laws" that were passed in the mid-1960s "to end segregation in restaurants and other places that serve the public" (Labaton 1994).

In the wake of this landmark case, Denny's has tried, albeit sometimes unsuccessfully, to rehabilitate its brand image by implementing racial sensitivity training for its work staff and engaging in various types of public outreach. Among the latter was mid- to late 1990s and early 2000s television advertising showcasing African American clientele as well as popular commercials featuring Sherman Hemsley and Isabel Sanford, the two lead actors from the long-running CBS sitcom *The Jeffersons* about a hardworking and newly affluent Black couple living in a Manhattan high rise. Such measures garnered recognition for Denny's, including prominent listings on *Fortune* magazine's "Best Companies for Minorities" in 2001 and *Black Enterprise* magazine's "Best Companies for Diversity" in 2006 (Denny's 2020) even as the chain occasionally still faces public opprobrium for its employees' bias and inhospitality toward people of color (*Seattle Times* Staff 2018).

IHOP

Perhaps less so than Denny's, IHOP, Waffle House's other primary twenty-four-hour competitor, has endured bad press stemming from alleged and documented instances of employee ill-treatment of African Americans. With 1,840 locations at home and abroad, IHOP's history of racial discrimination dates back decades, echoing the kind of practices that landed its various restaurant rivals in such hot water over the years.[10] For instance, in 1992, the company reached an out-of-court settlement with a group of Black customers who were refused service and locked out of a Milwaukee IHOP. As part of this agreement, a share of funds was set aside for a minority scholarship (AP News 1992).

Similarly, in May 2018, an Auburn, Maine, IHOP was temporarily closed for employee training after a server allegedly asked for upfront payment from a party of Black teens. IHOP's front office released a statement noting the company has "zero tolerance" when it comes to customer discrimination (Sharon 2018). That same month an IHOP near Kansas City made news after one of its employees printed the N-word on the receipt of a local Black teen's takeout order. Upset at her daughter's treatment, the girl's mother called the restaurant to complain, leading to the firing of the guilty server. Franchise management acted swiftly in this regard, but their failure to inform the family about the termination, coupled with the teen receiving a ten-dollar IHOP gift card in the mail as a token of apology—much like what happened to Waffle House customer Jacinda Mitchell in 2018 (see introduction)—resulted in an angry Facebook post, which, in turn, garnered national attention for the case (Randle 2018).

This sort of behavior is not always directed at Black IHOP customers. Reports of patrons subjecting restaurant staff to racist abuse sometimes make the news. For example, a day or so before New Year's Day 2018, an African American waitress working at an IHOP location in Sherman, Texas, returned to a table where she had just been serving four high school kids wearing letter jackets to find someone in the party had deliberately cut their pancakes into the letters "KKK." Upset, the waitress photographed the plate with the offending message and posted it on Snapchat and Facebook. Adding insult to injury, the server noted that another customer had called one of her colleagues the N-word during this same shift (Gettys 2018).

Cracker Barrel

Causal restaurant and giftshop hybrid Cracker Barrel—another Waffle House rival known for its down-home cooking and embrace of the southern imaginary—has gotten mired in various legal proceedings over its five-decade history related to the ill-treatment of Black patrons and employees at its 650 US locations. In 2001, the company made headlines for the $100 million lawsuit lodged against it by approximately twenty customers and backed by the NAACP alleging all types of discriminatory practices including serving Black diners food out of the trash and refusing to issue gift cards to Black customers who complained about poor service (Tamen 2001). Although the case never went to trial, Cracker Barrel agreed to an $8.7 million settlement to all NAACP-affiliated litigation in 2004 (*Seattle Times* 2018).

Against this backdrop, the Justice Department determined in 2004 that Cracker Barrel had knowingly discriminated against African Americans at multiple locations in seven states (Schmit and Copeland 2004). Reported offenses included racially segregating customers, seating white diners ahead of Black patrons, offering inferior service, and allowing waitstaff to refuse service to Black clientele. So egregious were these violations of federal public-accommodation laws, in fact, that Cracker Barrel ended up signing a five-year agreement with the Justice Department to implement an array of nondiscriminatory policies and procedures subject to outside audit to ensure compliance (Schmit and Copeland 2004).

Two years later, the brand made headlines again, this time for a $2 million settlement that ended a lawsuit based on racial and sexual discrimination at three of its Illinois restaurants (Pallasch 2006). Out of these proceedings, Cracker Barrel not only began prominently displaying its nondiscrimination policy on its store entrances but also listing this information on its website and menus alongside details about filing customer complaints (DuPlessis 2006). Moreover, the company began implementing outreach efforts to attract a more diverse workforce as well as cultivating ties with the NAACP (French 2005).

Waffle House

Waffle House has been sued multiple times in recent decades over allegations of racially discriminating against people of color (Mohdin 2018). According to the *Atlanta Business Chronicle* (2005), by 2004, nearly two dozen "federal cases have already been filed against Waffle House and its franchisees" for such reasons. Part of the impetus for the 2007 launch of the company's very own in-house publication *Inc* was, in fact, to mitigate the fallout from numerous legal proceedings lodged by nonwhite restaurant staff and clientele claiming inequitable treatment in its eateries, by helping Waffle House craft a more welcoming and inclusive public image going forward (Rawson 2013:221). Some of these cases ended quietly out of court; others went to trial with rulings unfavorably adjudicated against the chain (Mohdin 2018; Rawson 2013:230).

Over the years, Waffle House has endured a run of bad publicity as incidents involving restaurant discrimination and racial bias directed at minority customers resulted in both high-profile lawsuits and adverse media coverage (see introduction). For example, in 2001, members of a gospel group, the Heavenly Sons, filed a federal civil rights lawsuit, alleging workers at a Monroe, North Carolina, Waffle House made the singers vacate their counter seats so that white patrons could have them (Frazier 2001). The men allege that they were then forced to leave the restaurant amid verbal taunts and arrival of local police (*Charlotte Observer* 2001).

Four years later, a group of Black patrons from Alabama, North Carolina, Virginia, and Georgia sued Waffle House in federal court. Filing multiple suits, some of which involved the NAACP, plaintiffs provide troubling details of their experiences. Among other things, the lawsuits "describe incidents including servers who allegedly announced they did not have to serve African-American customers; allegedly serving unsanitary, fly-infested food to African-Americans and other minority patrons; allegedly ignored African-Americans while white patrons were seated and provided service; allegedly directed racial epithets at African-American patrons; and allegedly became verbally abusive when asked to wait on African-Americans" (*Atlanta Business Chronicle* 2005).

Two years before the controversial 2018 Wall and Clemons arrests and somewhat reminiscent of Mitchell's contemporaneous denial of service at an Alabama location amid threats of physical violence (see introduction), another episode of racial discrimination threw Waffle House into the spotlight.

In 2016, a Black couple sued Waffle House for $2 million, alleging denial of service by a white waitress at its Baytown, Texas, location, and intimidation after a white customer wearing the regalia of an area motorcycle gang, the Banditos, displayed a knife to the couple's party in the parking lot. The African American diners stated they were made to vacate a table so that a group of white bikers including the waitress's father could use it. Once the bikers arrived and chatted with the waitress, they sat directly behind the plaintiffs, making the customers feel uncomfortable, even following them out of the restaurant as the waitress insulted them (George 2015).

As with other chains, some legal proceedings brought against Waffle House come from employees. In fact, some of the earliest documented discrimination lawsuits against the company come from its restaurant servers. To wit, a white employee fired from her waitressing job at a Georgia Waffle House sued Waffle House in 1984, alleging that her marriage to a Black man was at the root of her dismissal (*Gresham v. Waffle House, Inc.* 1984).

Similarly, in 2014, an African American employee brought a lawsuit against the chain, claiming he was subject to both discrimination and retaliation before being fired from his job (*Ferguson v. Waffle House, Inc.* 2014). For these and other incidents of alleged employee or customer mistreatment, Waffle House usually responds with a carefully worded statement expressing both general concern for those involved while still vigorously upholding the company's stance of treating everyone at its eateries fairly and equally.

Waffle House in Black and White

Waffle House persists, even as claims that it sometimes fails to maintain settings free from customer or employee discrimination make the news. Part of the chain's ability to weather such allegations is predicated on its brand equity, a marketing term describing the commercial and social value that consumers invest not just in a brand's products and services but more so in the brand as an entity in and of itself. The collective goodwill already invested in the Waffle House brand name partly derives from a popular image that readily aligns with idealized versions of down-home regional hospitality (Szczesiul 2017).

These sentiments assume particular dimension when considered through the prismatic optics of today's southern imaginary (Baker 2011). This collectively experienced and intersubjective American mythos—variously reinforced through resonant depictions in film, television, literature, music, and the like—regularly foregrounds a down-to-earth friendliness of regular folk doing their best in the face of circumstances frequently beyond their control. Quite often, portrayals of Black and white people amiably interacting with each other amid quaint or quirky surroundings find expression in this amorphous constellation of interpenetrative narrative, imagery, and sentiment that continues to hold sway over so much popular thinking and popular culture (e.g., *Forrest Gump, Hap and Leonard, Driving Miss Daisy, Green Book*).

With the notable exception of Cracker Barrel (Tolentino 2016), another chain eatery trafficking in idyllic expressions of regional identity that privileges both openness and warmth in social interactions, public perceptions of Waffle House are easily informed by prevailing notions of unfeigned southern charm as exemplified through patient and mannered friendliness along with a general reluctance in expressing opinions and/or judgments about others (Szczesiul 2017). Even with its limited marketing bandwidth in America's prevailing restaurant scene, Waffle House finds ways to advantageously leverage its unpretentious southern image when engaging consumer sensibilities or confronting public fallout from alleged discrimination at its myriad facilities (see Waffle House's Southern Strategy section in this chapter).

Although practically all US eateries strive to maintain inviting and hospitable retail environments, brands like Waffle House and Cracker Barrel have a leg up, so to speak, considering how their respective operations evoke so many of the southern imaginary's more favorable qualities. The restaurants' simple countrified fare, unassuming or even rustic aesthetics, and affable everyday workers and clientele have come to define so much about both eateries in the popular consciousness. At the very least, such regional affiliations and presumed receptiveness toward all segments of the dining public confer a benefit of the doubt, however tentatively, whenever troubling allegations arise at their restaurants. Conversely, popular chains such as Denny's and IHOP stand somewhat apart in this regard, seeing as their operations lack a kind of go-to geocultural reference point that necessarily elicits expectations of friendly and responsive service.

Waffle House does not openly embrace its southern affiliations, and it eschews traditional advertising approaches such as radio and television marketing in favor of more indirect modes of promotion, but the chain does work to showcase its proven track record of hiring African Americans and people of color at its hundreds of locations nationwide. A quick perusal of Waffle House's social media postings on Facebook, Instagram, and Twitter promptly dispels any notions that the firm discriminates in hiring at local venues. These online platforms prominently feature photos of restaurant staff from all types of backgrounds serving and interacting with a multiethnic clientele, representing a veritable cross-section of today's dining public.

Such publicized depictions notwithstanding, ascertaining the demographic breakdown of Waffle House employees in reality proves challenging. Even if the firm keeps track of such non-job-related data, which is unlikely as this information has no bearing on work qualifications, all Waffle House workforce figures remain largely hidden from public view because it is a private company. Without much to go by except perhaps a few rough observational calculations or anecdotal evidence, some recent ballpark estimates have come to the fore hinting at Waffle House's demographic makeup.

Findings from North Carolina visual artist Micah Cash offer some indication of just how many Waffle House personnel are of African descent. His rather poignant photo essay "Waffle House Vistas," published in the *Bitter Southerner* and later turned into a glossy coffee table book, documents the interplay of retail commerce and the regional built environment from the window-seat perspective of multiple Waffle House restaurants across the Bible Belt. Cash chronicles his travels across nearly a dozen southern states through snapshots and commentary, using Waffle House window-panes as framing devices both literally and figuratively for understanding the banality (?) and beauty (?) of everyday life that plays out against the South's street-level commercial fabric. After traveling hundreds of miles during his two-year journey, visiting dozens of Waffle House eateries, interacting with waitstaff, and capturing countless digital images, he provides some demographic insights about the chain. He notes, "Throughout this project, I would estimate that 60 percent of the Waffle House staff that I encountered and 55 percent of the clientele were African American. There was a 50/50 breakdown between women and men, and no obvious age range" (Cash 2019).

Without overestimating the value of these guesstimates, his figures seem to align with prevailing public sentiments suggesting that Waffle House not only attracts sizable numbers of Black patrons, it also serves as a top industry employer for people of color, especially for African American women working as waitstaff. Cash's estimations do appear to reaffirm some of Joe Rogers Sr.'s rather ham-handed comments about Waffle House servers quoted in chapter 3. It seems indisputable that a wide array of working-class Americans irrespective of skin color end up sporting the Waffle House uniform nowadays.

Waffle House 2020

Against this backdrop, Waffle House's virtual silence following George Floyd's death initially appears both notable and conspicuous. It was notable not just because other chains lent their voice to a national outpouring of grief and condemnation but also because Waffle House had assumed a more inclusive public posture beginning in the mid-2000s, right around the time it launched its in-house company magazine, *Inc.* It was conspicuous considering that, throughout the summer of 2020, as global protests against police brutality and structural racism dominated public discourse, Waffle House pretty much kept its focus on operational matters, at least judging by its social media postings and contemporaneous news accounts. Of utmost concern for the company during this tumultuous time was Waffle House's handling of COVID-19's impacts on local restaurants and customer/employee well-being (Sorvino 2020).

Even as Waffle House's lack of urgency in acknowledging much less vocally supporting social justice issues may seem out of step with the 2020 zeitgeist—especially with a diverse labor force and plenty of nonwhite patrons frequenting its eateries—on reflection, this disengagement makes sense when considered in light of the brand's by now well-established paradoxical position in the South's chain restaurant foodscape and wider sociocultural milieu. Variously echoing what Patterson Hood termed "the duality of the Southern thing" (see introduction), Waffle House's oft-conflicted status within popular thinking finds expression in this ostensible hesitancy to engage issues highlighted by the BLM movement in any meaningful way.

The duality that imbues so many aspects of the brand's operational and symbolic character, just as it evokes the complexities and incongruities of contemporary southern identity, informs the sometimes contradictory entanglements between Waffle House and its sizable nonwhite clientele. Indeed, the chain appears caught on the horns of a public relations dilemma. On the one hand, the brand enjoys widespread cachet across multiple segments of today's dining public, even from those for whom such allegiance would seem an odd fit nowadays. To wit, when BLM and other demonstrators descended on downtown Atlanta for consecutive nights of sporadically unruly protests in May 2020—leaving behind considerable property damage even to popular area attractions including the iconic CNN Center—the nearby Waffle House restaurant was conspicuously spared their anger. Cellphone video from that night originally posted to Twitter and later publicized in the *New York Post* actually shows groups of roaming protestors chanting, "Not the Waffle House! Not the Waffle House!" (Levine 2020). Such random occurrences hint at widespread brand support among everyday African Americans, perhaps signaling to company higher-ups that there is no real need to publicly favor social justice and police reform causes.

On the other hand, even in the twenty-first century's third decade, Waffle House seems unable to decisively shake its reputation as a chain not always accommodating to African Americans or other people of color (Lamour 2020). Even though Bernice King's May 2018 call for a nationwide Waffle House boycott fell short of achieving any meaningful grassroots impact—bearing in mind her push against Waffle House occurred soon after the Antioch shooting when the company enjoyed an outpouring of public sympathy and support—it did generate its share of bad publicity, once again adding to perceptions of persistent problems of racial discrimination and customer ill-treatment.

Other chains with similarly beleaguered reputations as Waffle House (e.g., Starbucks) used the events of the summer of 2020 either as opportunities for employee and staff teachable moments or as occasions to chart new directions in their public outreach by offering support and actionable efforts to better their operations vis-à-vis all segments of American society.[11] Perhaps the perceived risks of alienating too many Red State working-class white people also informed Waffle House's final calculus about how to best respond if at all to BLM-related concerns.

Waffle House's Southern Strategy

As argued throughout this book, when it comes to matters of race—among other relevant issues—a dichotomous tension becomes discernible within Waffle House's public profile as well as in its daily operations, albeit probably to a lesser extent. Variously arising out of this dualistic schema is a distinctive restaurant characterization that both reflects and reifies a resonant version of the southern United States. Indeed, the lingering contradictions at the heart of Waffle House's popular image discussed throughout this book are but one example of the still unresolved regional dialectic that animates so much of the socioeconomic and political life across large swaths of this part of Red State America.

Sorting out the ironies, intricacies, and inconsistencies lurking beneath southern identity and then relating them to the dissonance between ongoing intolerance, including racial injustice; and enduring and supposedly welcoming regional institutions, such as the Evangelical church (Wilson 2004; Jones 2020) or southern hospitality (Szczesiul 2017), proves instructive for unpacking some of the core conundrums of Waffle House's split-screen status among everyday diners. Company efforts at addressing its real or perceived deficits in treating everyone equitably at its hundreds of US outlets entail efforts like foregrounding people of color in its marketing outreach across multiple platforms and contexts as well as deploying a resonant corporate narrative that evokes many of the southern imaginary's more evocative tropes.

Anthony Bourdain was not exaggerating in 2015 when he noted the veritable cross-section of (mostly sober?) Americans who end up frequenting Waffle House at all hours of the day and night. Such observations echo those of years earlier from Grammy-winning singer-songwriter and current Dead & Company guitarist, John Mayer. When asked how he felt about Waffle House's place in his then-adopted home of Atlanta, Mayer responded in part: "Love it! Martin Luther King had a dream, and I think Waffle House was in it. It's a supernova of cultures—the most diverse room in all of Atlanta at any given moment is a Waffle House. It's where, at the end of the night, different cultures, viewpoints, and appetites all come together to enjoy the same lowest-common-denominator meal" (Raub 2006).

Over the years, journalists and others covering Waffle House have gotten a lot of mileage out of both Bourdain's and Mayer's quotes whether writing puff pieces for popular magazines or more critical accounts of the eatery for scholarly journals (Rawson 2013). Each soundbite exemplifies the emerging flipside characterization of Waffle House that looks past, if also conspicuously winks at, the beleaguered side of the chain's popular persona, emphasizing the eatery's role as a convergence point where Americans of all stripes harmoniously gather to enjoy simple breakfast counter fare amid unpretentious surroundings.

This sort of benevolent characterization readily conforms to Waffle House's go-to approach in devising, implementing, and reinforcing a resonant corporate narrative. Efforts to shape this public image of warmth and inclusivity have met some success in recent years even though the company's executive board still lacks significant representation of women and people of color (Comparably 2020), and stories of the restaurant's struggles with equitable treatment for all at its myriad locations—never mind the seemingly endless stream of Waffle House police blotter activities—regularly make the news (*Atlanta Business Chronicle* 2005).

Corporate narratives—which according to Rawson (2013:218) not only "form and influence company discourse and decisions, both of which affect customer and worker interests" but also "respond to a broad range of cultural pressures, particularly ones that relate to profitability"—have emerged as vital aspects of doing business in early twenty-first-century America. Providing consumers reliable goods and services no longer seems to suffice for retailers and other commercial operations looking to earn and retain a place at the table of US market capitalism, especially in today's hypercompetitive corporate dining scene.

Developing and occasionally refining things like an appealing company back story, mission statement, motto, logo, and brand theme, among other relevant features, prove all but essential nowadays for enterprises seeking to craft a coherent corporate narrative. Chain restaurants pursue such efforts not only to retain loyalty from their traditional base of repeat customers but also to gain an edge over competitors in attracting those nominally brand adverse. With so many out-to-eat options from which to choose, sometimes other factors inform dining decisions besides price or menu selections. In America's highly variegated restaurant foodscape, in fact, eating sit-down meals outside of the home often includes expectations of enjoying comprehensive consumer experiences where food and drink are neither the only nor necessarily the most important aspect of what customers get for their retail dollars.

Indeed, unlike in the past, today's consumers often expect more from their favorite retailers in terms of products and services and how they treat various segments of the dining public or weigh in on relevant and/or timely social issues. This appears particularly true for major players in the US restaurant industry. For example, Atlanta-based fast-food giant and one-time Waffle House partner Chick-fil-A became a culture war lightning rod when news surfaced in 2012 that its chairman, president, and CEO Dan T. Cathy had donated millions of charitable dollars to organizations actively opposing marriage equality. LGBQT community calls for a company boycott and the resulting social conservative and Evangelical Christian backlash to such anti–Chick-fil-A efforts embroiled the brand in controversy for years, only to quietly be resolved when its 2018 tax filings revealed Chick-fil-A had finally ceased all such controversial donations (Taylor 2019).

Against such a backdrop, Waffle House began bolstering its corporate image by prominently featuring African Americans and other people of color—whether as uniformed employees or loyal brand customers—in its company social media posts. From the mid-2000s onward, Waffle House keenly recognized that most Americans do not want to associate with much less financially support brands whose operations are perceived as un-friendly to minorities.

For Waffle House, conveying messages of inclusivity is now interwo-ven into the company narrative, though the eatery does not always live up to such aspirational sentiments in its everyday operations (*Atlanta Business Chronicle* 2005). Indeed, Waffle House, like other US chain restaurants, could do more for its hourly workers, by paying them actual living wages or by implementing more robust sick leave policies so that falling ill or caring for ailing loved ones does not jeopardize job status.

Despite the conspicuous reach of Waffle House's various Facebook, In-stagram, and Twitter postings, even before the chain developed an online presence, the company's unfolding public narrative sometimes included de-pictions of Black patrons, servers, and kitchen staff. Such mentioning or celebrating is certainly as warranted now as it was then given the sizable representation of African Americans within the US dining public and Waf-fle House workforce. As the eatery continues to invest time and effort in crafting a more welcoming brand image—one that resonates with every-day restaurant diners as much as other segments of American society—it is essential that Waffle House play to its demographic profile as the company strives for historical accuracy in its evolving corporate story.

Smothered, Covered, and Inclusive

By most available Waffle House accounts, matters of race, discrimination, and inclusive restaurant spaces first appeared on the company's radar about midway through the civil rights era, soon after the nonviolent Greensboro lunch counter protests (see chapter1). In excerpts from *Who's Looking Out for the Poor Old Cash Customer?* (Rogers 2000) and elsewhere (Osinski 2004; Dyer 2008:168), the chain, or at least those in its upper management, appeared largely oblivious to the day-to-day realities faced by people of color, particularly African Americans, when it came to accessing the same basic goods and services as their white peers prior to the passage of federal legislation in the mid-1960s that officially outlawed restaurant segregation (Plunkett-Powell 1999:163).

For many white southerners of the time—particularly the not overtly racist or KKK-sympathetic segments of society—such inaccessibility was largely understood through the optics of the "separate but equal" legal doctrine that held sway in political life before the mid-1960s. Within this abandoned schema, racial segregation across public domains was deemed both constitutional and legitimate so long as equivalent facilities were accessible to all groups. Such reasoning seems to find expression in the Waffle House accounts documented in this chapter. To wit, the given rationale as to why Black southerners only started patronizing Waffle House eateries around this time bears no relation to entrenched Jim Crow dining practices but instead is related to the fact that heretofore "Black person(s) never asked to be served at a Waffle House" (Rogers 2000:146).

The two main Waffle House anecdotes chronicling how the chain confronted the sweeping changes transforming America's sociopolitical fabric in the 1960s—the first purportedly takes place in 1961 or close thereafter, a version of which Katie Rawson incisively covers in her essay "'America's Place for Inclusion': Stories of Food, Labor, and Equality at the Waffle House" (2013:227–30) and the second occurring in 1968 amid the tumult and turmoil immediately following Martin Luther King Jr.'s assassination[12]—are recounted from Joe Rogers Sr.'s perspective several decades after the fact. However much this time lag clouds his descriptions' reliability, both episodes—as currently written—are now viewed as both legitimate and definitive within Waffle House's overarching corporate narrative.

Indeed, retrospectively detailing events from so many years back proves a dicey proposition for anyone striving to accurately report events as they occurred. Such efforts can result in imprecise accounts that inadvertently fudge basic facts related to time, date, or location just as they end up stretching readers' credulity given the human propensity to take very complex social encounters and render them into concise and cohesive narratives largely divorced from the Rashomon nature of most human interactions.

As detailed here, two potentially volatile situations that brought Jim Crow–era injustices directly into Atlanta-area Waffle House facilities are not only expeditiously handled with minimal fuss or complication by company personnel but also both find swift resolution with outcomes that prove more or less agreeable to all parties involved. Truth be told, one can be forgiven for wondering if Waffle House ever again needed to address matters of on-site inequality after reading these accounts.

Waffle House Integrates—1961 or 1964?

Rogers's first anecdote offers an established restauranteur's take on the attempts by civil rights protestors to leverage the era's segregated dining spaces to their advantage by drawing attention to their cause and ultimately effecting meaningful change. According to Rogers (2000:146) in *Who's Looking Out for the Poor Old Cash Customer?*,

> When I came back to Atlanta in 1961, students at Atlanta's black colleges had begun their sit-ins to force integration of restaurants and were drawing national publicity with their actions. We anticipated they would come to our restaurants, and we were ready. Ready to serve them, that is. We saw no reason to turn a customer away, and if black people wanted to eat with us, we were happy to serve them.
>
> In the segregated South, of course, people made certain assumptions, one of them being that black people didn't eat in "white" restaurants. So up to that point, no black person had asked to be served at a Waffle House.
>
> A group of students came to [Waffle House] #2 on Peachtree and Tenth streets [formerly the Wagon Wheel restaurant; purchased by Tom Forkner in 1957], with police and reporters and television cameras, expecting to make news by being turned away. Randy Chavers [former Toddle House manager hired by Tom Forkner in mid-1950s] and I drove out to the restaurant when they arrived, not sure what to expect but confident in our position.
>
> I told the students, "If you're here to eat, please come inside and eat, but if you're here to cause trouble, please leave."

They came in and we served them, then they moved on down to the next restaurant on Peachtree Street.

This account is problematic for several reasons. It apparently misconstrues the protestors' main intent in seeking Waffle House service. Rather than view demonstrators as out to peacefully highlight the systemic and multigenerational racism holding sway over American life—abetted by the US restaurant industry—Rogers characterizes them as seemingly out to cause "trouble" or pull a fast one on Waffle House personnel. Perhaps from an early 1960's mainstream perspective, Black people seeking equal treatment as their white counterparts constituted "trouble" but to hold such views some four decades later when writing one's autobiography remains something of a headscratcher. Similarly, ideas of asking customers how they planned to behave prior to being served seems as disconcerting in the 1960s as it does in the 2020s. No less troubling are suggestions that Waffle House eateries in the Jim Crow South were always accessible to local Black college students and other African Americans if only they had simply "asked" for service. This defies logical explanation let alone historical reality.

Notions that individual choice or general preference ultimately determined who ended up patronizing so-called white restaurants, rather than a two-tiered American caste system wherein transgressions of established legal and cultural norms by nonwhite people, particularly in southern states, often yielded real physical violence, makes for a particularly muddled reading of prevailing social arrangements before, during, and after the civil rights era. Finally, insinuating that those working for Waffle House somehow turned the tables on protestors or beat them at their own game by immediately serving them instead of making them leave or refusing them accommodation smacks of a not-so-subtle white paternalism, however unintended. Indeed, it suggests that the college students' entire intent hinged on pulling off a gotcha publicity stunt in front of print and broadcast media reporters specifically designed to publicly shame Waffle House rather than to participate in a social movement aimed at effecting positive social change.

Equally problematic is the juxtaposition of this first autobiographical passage from Rogers's book with a local newspaper account published on January 16, 1964 (*Atlanta Daily World* 1964 as partly quoted in Rawson 2013:228–29), which states that

a demonstration at a restaurant Tuesday evening resulted in [12 people] being served. The sit-in demonstration took place at the Waffle House at

972 Peachtree St. N.W. The demonstrators sat without service for about an hour before the manager, Randolph Chavers, entered the restaurant and told his head waiter to serve the young people. Up until this time the head waiter stated that the establishment was closed and he wasn't serving anyone. He said he was sending for the manager who would have to make a decision. . . . When asked if it was the policy to everyone, the manager replied, "as long as they come in orderly and not cause any disturbance, they will be served."

Reconciling the obvious tension between this newspaper piece and what Rogers describes in 2000 raises issues that warrant some critical unpacking. Indeed, if the 1964 reportage serves as the primary source for historical accuracy, which is very likely since its publication occurred immediately after the events described and not years after the fact, it seems that Rogers takes a bit of authorial license by not only shoehorning himself into this pivotal episode of Waffle House's corporate narrative but also by moving events back by two or three years. According to the *Atlanta Daily World* (1964), it was Chavers and not Rogers who negotiated the resolution that ultimately allowed demonstrators full restaurant access.

Nothing from Rawson's excerpt (2013:228–29) or the full 1964 newspaper account places Rogers at the scene, but there is some indication that Waffle House management had some advanced knowledge that a coordinated protest was a possibility. Clearly, Rogers's status as a company executive overseeing multiple locations makes his presence coinciding with a protest at this particular store unlikely. Yet, seeing as various college-aged adults affiliated with the Student Nonviolent Coordinating Committee—a national organization launched in 1960 and dedicated to addressing the exclusion of African-Americans from US civic and political life through direct-action initiatives including restaurant sit-ins (Carson 1995)—had been arrested over the previous days for peacefully demonstrating at some of this Waffle House's nearby competitors (*Atlanta Daily World* 1964), such anticipations were not entirely out of the question. The fact that "police were on the scene all the while to see that order was kept" (*Atlanta Daily World* 1964) adds credence to this presumption.

Similarly, although the Greensboro lunch counter protestors were local college students, no definitive newspaper evidence emerges—although it is probably a safe bet—that college students were involved in this Waffle House case. They were simply described by the *Atlanta Daily World* as either "young persons associated with the Student Nonviolent Coordinating Committee" or "demonstrators [who] sat for about an hour without service." In much the same vein and as this newspaper coverage seemingly corroborates, service for these demonstrators—even restaurant service contingent upon them not causing "trouble"—was never actually a foregone conclusion despite what Rogers's autobiography implies. The head waiter's initial contention that the Waffle House was closed and no longer serving diners, coupled with the prolonged wait time and then apparent need to seek Chavers's advice, belies Rogers's claims in *Who's Looking Out for the Poor Old Cash Customer?*

Rogers's 2000 portrayal of this potential sit-in demonstration appears more straightforward in delineating exactly who were the protagonists and antagonists in this case, and how conflict was ultimately avoided, yet the contemporaneous *Atlanta Daily World* account from 1964 portrays things as a bit less cut and dried and unfavorable to Waffle House's popular reputation. Despite Rawson's efforts at highlighting these newspaper findings in her 2013 work, it is Rogers's more accessible and upbeat telling of events that ultimately ends up a part of the Waffle House corporate narrative because few readers would likely seek out scholarly writings on the chain, much less original print media news sources.[13] A lengthy quote from Rawson (2013:229–30) helps elucidate the discrepancies between these two different tellings of very similar Waffle House accounts:

> These stories have the same general outcome: when asked, all people would be served. However, reconfiguring the placement and the players in the incident (not to mention the three-year gap between 1961 and 1964) shifts the power of this incident dramatically. It removes the struggle and waiting from the Civil Rights protest, the local variation in the struggle (the waiter deciding to close entirely), and the lower-level labor and management, replacing them with the ownership. It places Waffle House squarely on the side of social progress, instead of addressing the contentious negotiations of public space in Atlanta restaurants in the 1960s. Developing from the theory that social and individual memory is formed around contemporary needs, we can look at how Waffle House's current relationship to charges of discrimination provides some impetus for positively repositioning its relationship to integration. This is not to say that Rogers's story is a deliberate fabrication, rather, it offers a response to changing social contexts (i.e., attitudes toward integration and race in America).

When considered altogether, it seems given the choice between embracing a decisive and favorable narrative (i.e., Rogers's 1961 account) rather than the one characterized by nuance and ambiguity (i.e., the 1964 *Atlanta Daily World* newspaper account), Waffle House unsurprisingly opted for the ostensibly older anecdote.

Waffle House Keeps the Peace, 1968

Cut from the same basic cloth as his first autobiographical account, the next selection from *Who's Looking Out for the Poor Old Cash Customer?* entails Rogers and company grappling with potential "trouble" from local Black Atlantans immediately following the 1968 King assassination. While the previous passage primarily focuses on African Americans' access to Waffle House service and facilities several years earlier, the following excerpt mainly deals with company efforts at coordinating and maintaining operational viability amid an unfolding crisis situation, something that would become a hallmark brand feature over the years to come (e.g., Waffle House Index).

Unlike the preceding 1961 example, however, no corresponding and/ or contemporaneous news story emerges to readily corroborate or dispute Rogers's telling of the 1968 occurrence. Accordingly, if what the 1964 *Atlanta Daily World* newspaper piece reveals about some of his assertions concerning Waffle House's purported integration in 1961 are accurate, the subsequent autobiographical account from 1968 should probably also be taken with a grain of salt. Whatever the following passage lacks in documentable veracity, however, it more than makes up for in immediacy and panache, making its inclusion as part of the Waffle House corporate narrative pretty much a sure bet. Writing in 2000, Rogers (2000:168–69) notes:

> In April 1968 riots and looting broke out across the country following the assassination of the Rev. Martin Luther King, Jr. Some Atlanta business people expected the same kind of trouble here, and many closed their doors. We talked with Richard Rich, of Rich's department store, and Howard Stark, who was running all the C&S banks in Atlanta. We also talked with Davis Brothers and Huddle House. Everybody was on the phone asking, "What are you gonna do?"
>
> I said, "Well, we served black people on Peachtree Street [Waffle House Unit #2 formerly the Wagon Wheel restaurant] before a lot of other people did. We don't have anything to run from."
>
> We would stay open twenty-four hours, as usual while everyone else closed.
>
> That afternoon I spoke with all our district managers and said, "Now, boys, we may have trouble and we may not. I don't know. But here's the

plan. I'm going to assign each one of you a territory. You go cover it, and we'll meet back here in two hours to see how we're doing."

We didn't have car telephones, of course, so we kept one of the secretaries at the office all night. I told the boys, "If you've got any trouble, call the office. We'll all keep in touch."

Somewhere along about midnight, Ronnie [a Waffle House manager] said, "When this is over we need to retreat somewhere to find someplace to rest."

They'd been talking about a houseboat, so I said. "I tell you what I'll do. We get through tonight without any problems, and we'll buy a houseboat on Lake Lanier [a manmade reservoir northeast of Atlanta]."

By 4 a.m. we had no problems at any of our restaurants, and nobody much was out by then, so I sent everybody home.

In the days that immediately followed, we received calls from several black leaders who thanked us for staying open. And by summertime we were out on the boat at Lake Lanier.

This account—like its 1961 predecessor—is problematic for reasons both obvious and opaque. Again, conflating the collective outrage expressed after the assassination of the contemporary figure most readily associated with racial equality and nonviolent protest as "trouble" reveals a kind of ahistorical understanding of the country's African American experience, one that elevates immediate business concerns over long-standing issues of racial injustice and exclusion. While rioting and looting occurred in the aftermath of King's killing in places like Washington DC, Detroit, Chicago, and Baltimore, his hometown of Atlanta remained relatively calm during this time, even hosting King's funeral on April 9, 1968, with tens of thousands peacefully attending (Burns 2012). Although the atmosphere was undeniably tense throughout this period, characterizing Black Atlantans upset about his slaying as trouble seekers places Waffle House's late 1960's priorities somewhat at odds with the inclusive brand reputation the company strove to foster.

Of equal note is both the foregrounding of Waffle House as the Atlanta business community's putative linchpin for responding to potential civil unrest—remaining audaciously open while other businesses temporarily shuttered—as well as the touting of its alleged lead in spearheading restaurant integration at the local level, something the 1964 *Atlanta Daily World* story throws a bit of cold water on. The all-night mobilization of company managers patrolling their respective Waffle House territories coupled with a houseboat purchase, lake vacation, and reported acclaim from local Black leaders for staying open make for a curious, congratulatory take on one of the civil right era's worst tragedies.

A Waffle House Lodestar

Before Waffle House fully embraced the Internet in the mid-2000s, it mainly went about highlighting its record of employee diversity in laudatory albeit selective ways. For instance, *Who's Looking Out for the Poor Old Cash Customer?* (Rogers 2000:117–18) and *The Waffle House Experience* (Heath et al. 2005:24–25) devote attention to Waffle House's longest-serving hourly associate, Lucy Shelton (1925–2012), a.k.a. "Miss Lucy," whose portrait hangs in the corporate office and signature farewell to departing customers, "we'll see you next time," is posted on the door of all Waffle House locations (Berrios 2012).

Shelton began her Waffle House career at the chain's second unit, the former Wagon Wheel restaurant that Tom Forkner mortgaged his house to purchase in 1957 (see chapter 2) as well as the site of the 1961/1964 integration story previously discussed. In fact, she even waitressed at the Wagon Wheel location before its Waffle House conversion, working there until the late 1960s, before moving to another Atlanta-area Waffle House where she worked first as a server and then later as a greeter before retiring in 2004. All in all, Shelton stayed with Waffle House for some forty-seven years.

Her upbeat demeanor and her longevity with the company were recognized by customers and Waffle House higher-ups. So well cherished was Shelton, in fact, that in the latter part of her career, the branch where she worked brought in extra employees on her birthday to deal with the overflow crowds (Berrios 2012). Writing a dozen or so years before her passing, Rogers Sr. (2000:117–18) states: "I wish they could all be like Lucy Shelton. She's kept that attitude for almost fifty years with us. We still celebrate her birthday and anniversary every year, and a large portrait of her hangs in the general office. She is a legend, and we all love her."

Doubtless, Rogers is thoroughly genuine in this praise of Shelton just as when he expressed gratitude throughout his public life to all the thousands of rank-and-file Waffle House employees who individually and collectively contributed to the restaurant's remarkable success (Osinski 2004). In his autobiography and numerous interviews (Rogers 2000), Rogers often made plain that he, his son, and Tom Forkner placed considerable value on the people who, regardless of skin color, donned the black apron and blue shirt of the Waffle House uniform or frequented the chain as loyal customers.

Over the years, Waffle House has done much to celebrate Lucy Shelton the person just as they showcase Lucy Shelton the de facto company lodestar. Perhaps a cynic would view this pronounced foregrounding as a kind of public relations ploy verging on tokenism given the, until recently, lack of upper-management and corporate office diversity. All the same, Shelton has not only come to embody the "Poor Old Cash Customer" ethos long central to the company's core business philosophy (see chapter 2) but has also emerged as something of the public face for all of the hourly shift workers whose sweat and toil allow the restaurant to thrive. Foregrounding Shelton's story within the Waffle House narrative also bolsters a forward-leaning brand image. It is one where Waffle House stands relatively ahead of the curve when it comes to embracing inclusion for employees and customers alike. To wit, in the 2012 *Atlanta Journal-Constitution* obituary for Shelton, her time waitressing at both the original Wagon Wheel restaurant and later at its Waffle House incarnation receives particular comment: "During those days it was unusual for an African-American to find work on Peachtree Street because of racial segregation. Mrs. Shelton was often asked to take restaurant earnings to the bank for change, another responsibility not often entrusted to an African-American worker during that time" (Berrios 2012).

If such details seemingly cast all involved in a positive light—of course with the obvious exception of the general Peachtree Street business community—they do so only in a bittersweet kind of way. Shelton's well-deserved place in the Waffle House story resonates partially because it highlights some of the best of what the chain and by extension the American South represents to the country as a whole, namely, friendliness, honesty, loyalty, unpretentiousness, and steadfastness. Yet, when considered against matters discussed throughout this chapter, it also comes tinged with a bit of woe, evoking not only Jim Crow–era injustices but also the continued discrimination and ill-treatment experienced by people of color at today's Waffle Houses.

———

Appreciating Waffle House's place within the South's material and sociocultural foodscape entails the various ways race informs understanding of its everyday operations as well as the symbolic potency it wields as both a putative microcosm of regional identity and as a sometimes beloved, sometimes beleaguered, iconic restaurant brand. With the chain's origins rooted in the mid-1950s—essentially right at the cusp of a transformative time in US history when the events and personalities of the Civil Rights Movement cohered into an irrepressible force of sociopolitical change that worked to dismantle the Jim Crow era's prevailing cultural and legal strictures through nonviolence and civil disobedience—many presumptions about the social order and racial arrangements became imprinted on Waffle House, at least initially.

The company's efforts over the years to cultivate a more welcoming and inclusive popular image have not always aligned with lived experiences for Black Americans and other people of color within Waffle House restaurant spaces, as the individual cases documented throughout this book attest. Waffle House may not be among the worst offenders when it comes to paying fines or settling disputes rooted in discriminatory practices against employees and customers, but it has faced the harsh media glare and public relations fallout that comes with allegations of racism and maltreatment at its myriad facilities.

For Waffle House, the events of the summer of 2020 represent something of a missed opportunity not only to demonstrate industry leadership but also to improve customer outreach, particularly to its sizable African American clientele and staff. As a resurgent BLM movement spurred a considerable amount of introspection on the part of so many white Americans about their historical complicity and privileged status within US society after George Floyd's extrajudicial killing, real and demanded change came to the fore in national discourse as many hallmark features of the southern imaginary were either forcibly removed from their elevated roosts in the built and symbolic landscapes of today's America or significantly rethought or ridiculed as relics of an undesirable bygone era. However US race relations unfold over the near and distant future, it seems all but certain Waffle House will endure, given the dining public's demonstrated record of both embracing and shaming this iconic roadside brand.

5

Waffle House in Popular Culture

Waffle House has enjoyed—or perhaps more accurately en-
dured—a secondary existence as a topic of mainstream entertainment for
quite some time. Whether celebrated or derided in music, television, film,
fiction, stand-up comedy, or professional and college sports, Waffle House
holds an undeniable viability within this highly mediated realm, especially
when refracted through the kaleidoscopic lens of the southern imaginary.
As examples documented in the pages that follow make clear, Waffle House
frequently serves as an easy analogue for the American South, where very
few regional virtues or imperfections remain concealed from public appraisal. Understanding this varied pop culture resonance as it relates to
Waffle House is important in that it both helps shape and reinforce prevailing notions about the brand whether for good or ill.

Few Americans living outside of the Bible Belt are unfamiliar with
Waffle House the restaurant brand or celebrated regional icon. Even as the
chain lacks a retail presence in over two dozen states and does not advertise
either regionally or nationally, most nonsoutherners know about the eatery
if not from traveling through this part of Red State America then certainly
thanks to its myriad depictions across multiple genres of US popular culture. Over the years, numerous portrayals and mentions of Waffle House—
some company sanctioned, others not—have cropped up in select movies,
television shows, stand-up comedy routines, book passages, professional
and collegiate athletics, and popular music. Waffle House has enjoyed noted
visibility if also notoriety within these highly mediated domains whether
foregrounded as primary subject-matter or employed as a reliable backdrop where narrative action takes place. Surely, no other southern-affiliated
corporate eatery approaches Waffle House nowadays when it comes to pop
culture salience.

Part of what accounts for Waffle House's ongoing entertainment value
relates to its widely accepted status as both a reflection and manifestation of

messy southern modernity. The inclusion of Waffle House in so many expressions of popular culture largely hinges on its capacity to serve as both a semiotic signifier of Bible Belt lifeways and a dog whistle identifier of the *Hillbilly Elegy* (Vance 2016) variety. As examples presented over subsequent pages attest, Waffle House provides a convenient shorthand for those wanting to capitalize upon or convey something about the American South: everything from its persistent and largely racialized socioeconomic hierarchies to the prevailing geocultural and political identities that continue to animate so much of its public life. When considered vis-à-vis the feedback loop tendencies of the southern imaginary, where ingrained perceptions and sensibilities—some of which are not all that affirmatory—are continually reinforced and perpetuated, it is surely unsurprising that the Waffle House characterizations considered herein rarely deviate from stereotypical notions about the eatery and region.

Beyond these geographically based connotations, purveyors of popular media and entertainment content also traffic in Waffle House imagery and allusions when striving to delineate a particular kind of blue-collar authenticity, one that ostensibly eludes those southerners and nonsoutherners whose socioeconomic and educational status insulates them from the oft-harsh realities of workaday life. Apparently, few other corporate dining establishments pack as much resonant punch as Waffle House when it comes to evoking working-class lives and tastes within popular culture contexts. Whether these references and representations leave audiences with less than charitable impressions of the brand and/or region, their multigenre versatility and undeniable staying power suggests a winning pop culture formula. This successful recipe persists not so much for highlighting the Waffle House name within today's entertainment mediascape but more as a way to effectively capture public attention by pigeonholing the eatery mostly in one of two ways.

Waffle House thrives as a familiar roadside eatery and putative southern institution and also as a pop cultural phenomenon. With these different aspects of Waffle House variously overlapping and influencing each other, a deep dive into the chain's parallel existence as a regular fixture in mainstream American entertainment, as well as its abiding presence in the US sports world, is surely warranted. Such critical consideration serves as a means for cataloging the chain's impressive array of recurring popular depictions. It also helps render Waffle House's contradictory public persona increasingly palatable to southerners and nonsoutherners alike. By examining Waffle House's expansive reach beyond its core operational focus, findings presented below speak to the diverse ways the restaurant engages the US imagination as both an evocative trope and enduring emblem of regional and class affiliation.

What follows is a brief synopsis of Waffle House appearances across various genres of American popular culture. While always striving to identify and categorize as many possible examples within film, television, publishing, standup comedy, sports, and music, the coverage is not exhaustive. However, the examples in this chapter likely constitute the most exhaustive and detailed overview of Waffle House pop culture appearances thus far compiled.

Film

Since the mid-1990s, Hollywood moviemakers have embraced Waffle House, using the 24-7 chain as a setting for a growing number of motion pictures—many of which are American road films—whose plots typically center on the lives of everyday working folk doing their best to get by under sometimes comedic or harrowing circumstances. Locating scenes at Waffle House adds a veneer of authenticity to characters' situations as narrative action unfolds, letting viewers know in no uncertain terms that what they are seeing onscreen is taking place in the US South. Indeed, the restaurant and those working and eating there offer a particularly realistic backdrop for scripted exchanges between or among film characters, propelling story plots forward. When uttered over coffee or plates of greasy breakfast fare, this dialogue—especially the well-written and competently delivered variety—hones down the on-camera artificiality of moviemaking for actors and audiences alike.

In acknowledging Waffle House's onscreen cachet, a few salient points are worth mentioning. First, for a brand so widely associated with down-market retail dining, Waffle House has certainly attracted its share of attention from top-tier studio talent. Both Clint Eastwood and the Coen brothers—Joel and Ethan—have utilized Waffle House or analogues thereof in big-budget productions, directing memorable scenes amid the restaurant's well-known globe lighting and vinyl laminate tabletops. Second, Oscar winners such as Tom Hanks, J. K. Simmons, and Kevin Costner have used Waffle House facilities as backdrops to showcase their acting chops. Their performances often subtly draw on Waffle House's down-home nature to evoke a level of realism, however playful or humorously tinged, that elicits their southern and/or working-class characters' current predicaments and limited prospects. Last, Waffle House's various movie moments effectively transcend established film genres, making appearances in serious dramas, lighthearted comedies, coming-of-age stories, road movies, and inspirational feelgood tales that strive to reaffirm the better angels of our collective character.

Consider the following examples dating back some twenty-five years to the chain's first big marquee moment on the silver screen:

- *Tin Cup*, a 1996 golf comedy directed by Ron Shelton and starring Kevin Costner, Renee Russo, Don Johnson, and Cheech Marin, examines the quixotic quest and romantic entanglements of a former west Texas golf prodigy—Roy "Tin Cup" McAvoy—trying to clinch a berth in the US Open to win the heart of the woman whom he loves. Against the odds, the Winnebago-driving McAvoy makes it all the way to a top three spot in the tournament's final round, only to lose while making a spectacular hole-in-one shot that cements his reputation as an all-time underdog golfing legend. McAvoy's restaurant of choice is Waffle House, where he and his lovable blue-collar golf friends frequently gather while in Texas or on the road. In a scene near the movie's end, the date of McAvoy's caddy suggests that they leave Waffle House and go someplace "fancy" to celebrate. McAvoy responds, "Nothing to celebrate yet. Plus, these are my people. I am a Waffle House guy—gotta stay in touch with that." After pressing her request again, she is summarily set straight by his rough-around-the-edges Texas friends. One states, "This is the *Waffle House*," as another adds "Hell, I been dreaming of waffles for 1,800 miles." Across the table from them, one golf buddy marvels aloud, "They got a Waffle House in Odessa just about like this," only to be corrected: "Odessa? It's in Midland, ain't it?"
- *Crossroads*, a 2002 coming-of-age road film starring pop princess Britney Spears in her first major acting role, follows the travails of three Louisiana friends leaving the Pelican State to embark on a cross-country journey of self-discovery. On the way to California in a muscle car convertible, Spears, her two female friends, and her potential love interest stop at a Waffle House to discuss how to stretch their already limited budget of just under $500 all the way to the West Coast.
- *The Ladykillers*, a 2004 Coen brothers comedy caper starring Tom Hanks, J. K. Simmons, and Marlon Wayans, features a group of hapless lawbreakers planning the perfect riverboat casino heist at the local "Waffle Hut," an obvious Waffle House stand-in. Perhaps what audiences remember most about the film is the fight that ensues

between Wayans's character, a hotheaded casino janitor, and Simmons's character, an overtalkative demolitions expert who suffers from irritable bowel syndrome, after the former repeatedly asks the latter in outright disbelief, "You brought your bitch to the Waffle Hut?"

- *ATL*, a 2006 coming-of-age hip-hop dramedy set in Atlanta starring rappers T.I. and Big Boi, details the formative experiences of a group of local teens striving to realize their dreams in the Big Peach. For this circle of friends, Waffle House is more than just a 24-7 eatery for consuming plates of food and sweet iced tea. It also a regular hangout to discuss their trials and tribulations as well as scope out the opposite sex.

- *Due Date*, a 2010 black comedy–cum–road film starring Robert Downey Jr. and Zach Galifinakis and directed by *The Hangover* (2009) and *Joker* (2019) filmmaker Todd Phillips,[1] documents the misadventures of an odd couple forced to share an Atlanta to Los Angeles car trip after both inadvertently end up on the US government's No Fly List. At a Waffle House stop toward the journey's beginning, Downey's straight-man character confronts Galifinakis's badly permed aspiring actor character about the latter's unwise decision of transporting his dead father's ashes in a tin coffee can. Upset by such reprimand, he becomes stricken by a sneezing fit, saying "We shouldn't have come here. I'm allergic to waffles."

- *The Good Lie*, a 2014 American drama starring Reese Witherspoon as a nervy Kansas City employment counselor of the *Erin Brockovich* mold who befriends three Sudanese refugees, tells the story of her efforts to help these "Lost Boys" adjust to their strange new midwestern environs. When one of the young men snags a Waffle House job interview with her help, he is chirpily asked by the restaurant manager what brought him to America. He deadpans much to the lady's discomfort, "My parents were killed in a civil war and my sisters were taken as slaves."

- *Love, Simon*, a 2018 coming-of-age and coming-out box office hit, is the story of a closeted high school boy who falls in love with an anonymous online suitor amid his efforts to balance family, school, and friends with someone's online attempts to perhaps publicly expose his hidden sexuality. More feel-good affirmation of contemporary teen life than some sensationalized cinematic misfire, the Atlanta-based *Love, Simon* stars Nick Robinson as the titular character who regularly hangs out with friends at the local Waffle House. One of his female friends is coaxed into standing up in a restaurant booth and proclaim her self-confidence after an encounter with a flirtatious Waffle House waiter.

- *The Mule*, a 2018 crime drama featuring Bradley Cooper and starring Clint Eastwood who also produced and directed the film, tells the story of a down on his luck midwestern horticulturalist and Korean War veteran who falls into drug running to stave off economic ruin during his final years. His improbable work smuggling contraband for a Mexican cartel—abetted by his status as an elderly white man with no criminal history—allows him to regain financial solvency as well as help those around him. Eastwood's character becomes increasingly scrutinized by his cartel bosses and DEA agents who close in on him as he pauses a final drug run to make amends with his dying, long-estranged wife. It is at a roadside Waffle House where he crosses paths with the DEA agent played by Cooper. The understated tension of their restaurant encounter is palpable as neither realizes the other's true identity.

- *The Secret: Dare to Dream*, a 2020 romantic drama starring Katie Holmes and Josh Lucas, is based on the Oprah-approved megaselling 2006 self-help book *The Secret* by Rhonda Byrne that posits the dubious claim that positive thinking attracts personal success. Holmes plays a Louisiana widow deep in debt who has a fender-bender meet-cute with Lucas's mysterious character who not only fixes her car but also repairs her roof following some intense hurricane damage. Later, after it is revealed that he came to town to give her the proceeds of an invention created by her late husband, the couple share their first date at Waffle House, kissing in the parking lot amid the glow of the iconic restaurant sign.

- *The Mitchells vs. The Machines*, a 2021 computer animated feature with a cast including Danny McBride, Maya Rudolph, and Abbi Jacobson, centers on a family road trip for a film school bound daughter often at odds with her well-meaning but bumbling father. At one point, she tricks him into kissing the family dog on film outside of a Waffle House. Their differences are finally resolved after coming together to put down a dangerous robot rebellion.

These synopses all demonstrate Waffle House's onscreen viability whether used as a backdrop for coming-of-age narratives (*Crossroads*, *ATL*, and *Love, Simon*) or as a convenient locale in cinematic cross-country road trips (*Tin*

Cup, Crossroads, Due Date, and *Connected*). Moreover, the brand's multiple film appearances also demonstrate its capacity to convey both a sense of regional place (*The Ladykillers, The Mule,* and *The Secret: Dare to Dream*)—that is, letting audiences know that what they are seeing takes place in the South—and a resonant working-class identity (*The Good Lie* and *The Mule*). For a company long adverse to traditional advertising approaches, this kind of product placement is an effective way to increase brand visibility and reinforce its status as a putative blue-collar touchstone.

Television

Beyond its growing filmography, Waffle House has also made some small-screen appearances, usually earning mention in stray bits of dialogue in select prime-time dramas or late-night comedy shows. Since the early 2000s, television scriptwriters have variously integrated Waffle House into certain episodes and series either as a way to evoke a particular kind of regional setting or when striving to convey something about a character's working-class or southern background. Unlike their big-screen counterparts, instances of Waffle House making a splash on network and cable television rarely include overt depictions of restaurant facilities much less those of its iconic yellow/black corporate signage.

To be sure, the chain seems downright resistant to allowing production companies to feature Waffle House eateries and employees on screen however innocuous or favorable such portrayals are originally conceived. When it comes to protecting its brand image, Waffle House apparently sees little upside in permitting mainstream television programming to include actual depictions of its properties and personnel. For this and other reasons, most of Waffle House's intersections with the small screen entail some kind of offhand restaurant reference or casual mention. To wit:

- In episode five of the third season of A&E's hit crime series *Breaking Bad* (2008–13) entitled "Más," Waffle House gets a mention after Jesse Pinkman (Aaron Paul) is dispatched to El Paso with a huge bankroll by former schoolteacher turned violent drug lord Walter White (Bryan Cranston) to purchase an RV to expand their illegal narcotics operation. Rather than follow White's instructions, Pinkman and some of his compatriots spend most of the money on a substance-fueled night at a local strip club. Upon exiting the adult establishment at first light, Skinny Pete (Charles Baker) states, "That was . . . [vomits] awesome, bro later" before stumbling away through the parking lot. Distraught at his glaring mistake, Pinkman tries to explain his dire predicament to Combo Ortega (Rodney Rush), who only responds, "Waffle House . . . ?"

- In the ninth episode of season two of ABC's popular series *Lost* (2004–10)—"What Kate Did"—Waffle House earns a brief mention ostensibly as a way to evoke a bit of regional authenticity. In a flashback sequence, the US marshal relentlessly pursuing one of the series leads, Kate Austen (Evangeline Lilly), who is on the run for her father's murder, tracks her down to a remote bus station as she buys a ticket to Tallahassee. Overhearing her destination, he quips, "Tallahassee? I spent a week in Tallahassee in one night. It's all strip malls and Waffle Houses."

- CBS's long-running late-night talk show, *The Late Show with Stephen Colbert* (2015), featured a Waffle House bit in a July 2016 episode replete with a musical number entitled "No Shirt, No Shoes, No Knuckleheads." For the segment, Colbert recounts how his teenage years growing up in South Carolina often entailed after-hours visits with friends to the local Waffle House. Noting how the restaurant's picture menu makes it easy for inebriated customers to order, he also admits recently learning that all store jukeboxes feature Waffle House–themed songs (see Popular Music in this chapter). With a new lifegoal of adding another selection to this highly specialized collection of tunes, Colbert enlisted the help of alt-country singer-songwriter and Grammy winner Sturgill Simpson to craft the perfect Waffle House tribute, one that customers could play anytime they visited the chain. To verify that the song was now available at all store locations, he returned to his childhood Waffle House with Simpson to film a segment that included the duo interacting with customers and employees as well as the "world jukebox premiere" of the song. After cutting the red ribbon draped across the touchscreen music machine and breaking a fake bottle across its bow, the song plays as a gag-filled montage of Waffle House insanity unfolds.

- A season 43 episode of *Saturday Night Live* that aired in March 2018, soon after the Marjorie Stoneman Douglas High School shooting, features an Oval Office cold open with Alec Baldwin as President Trump. In the sketch, Trump talks about gun control and mental health issues amid ongoing White House turmoil and turnover, stating, "I said I was going to run this country like a business, and that business is a Waffle House at 2 am. Crazies everywhere, staff walking out in the middle of their shifts, managers taking money out of the cash register to pay off the Russian mob." This line delivered the biggest laugh, based on audience hoots and hollers, of the entire skit.

- On the January 15, 2021, episode of HBO's *Real Time with Bill Maher*, host Bill Maher refers to the domestic terrorists, QAnon believers, white supremacists, and Evangelical Trump supporters who stormed the US Capitol on January 6, 2021, to disrupt and overturn Trump's clear defeat in the 2020 presidential election as the "Waffle House brigade."

Waffle House's scant but memorable television appearances serve as yet another reminder of the chain's pop cultural viability. Whether utilized as resonant signifiers of its prevailing blue-collar identity or as an effective shorthand for placing narrative action in southern contexts, Waffle House references do much to key audiences in on what scriptwriters deem important about places and people when moving their stories forward.

Popular Music

The entertainment genre with the deepest and more varied ties with Waffle House is likely popular music. As a perennial fixture in the touring lifestyle of professional musicians, particularly those traveling through the South, Waffle House holds a special place in today's music scene for reasons both material and aesthetic. Frequently visited as a between-show highway stop and regularly incorporated in songwriting material, Waffle House's embrace by emerging and top-name country, rock, and hip-hop acts is perhaps driven more by circumstance than any sort of abiding brand affinity. Whatever the case may be, Waffle House continues to intersect with the lives of recording and performing musicians in ways subtle and significant.

Given that most professional musicians nowadays maintain a fairly active social media presence as a way to stay connected with their devoted fanbases, it is not uncommon for Waffle House to crop up in their online postings whether visually or as some kind of resonant signifier. In a sense, these Waffle House Web appearances allow performers to effectively humanize themselves, projecting some semblance of the common touch even as their profession usually evokes images of glitz and glamour. In popular genres such as mainstream country music—where an aw-shucks humility and not getting above one's raising are all but expected from up-and-coming and established artists—publicizing Waffle House visits and affiliations appears nothing if not a fairly shrewd career move. Walker Hayes, William

Michael Morgan, and Justin Moore are just but some of the country singers who have tweeted or Instagrammed about Waffle House in recent years.

For R&B and hip-hop artists as well, there is a definite amount of street cred that goes along with referencing Waffle House in song lyrics or otherwise depicting the brand in music videos and social media postings. Arguably, few things convey "keeping it real" quite like a predawn visit to Waffle House. For example, the night before 2015's Super Bowl XLIX in Glendale, Arizona, Grammy winner John Legend and wife, Chrissy Teigen, posted to Instagram photos of their "epic" double date with rap superstar and future presidential candidate Kanye West and his former wife, Kim Kardashian, at a local Waffle House. The postings went on to receive over 1.2 million likes (Yamato 2017). Beyond this highwater mark of celebrity approval, other hip-hop and R&B artists have highlighted their Waffle House visits online including Big Boi, André 3000, Fetty Wap, Busta Rhymes, and DJ Khaled (Hill 2015).

These celebrated moments of Waffle House affirmation notwithstanding, many hip-hop artists—among other musical performers—embrace the restaurant as lyrical fodder or artistic inspiration. Indeed, for those rappers living in the "Dirty South," the all-night eatery becomes something of an after-hours hangout, a twenty-four-hour establishment that jibes well with their club-hopping and possibly illicit lifestyle. According to a 2013 *Gawker* piece,

> Lil' Wayne, 2 Chainz, Gucci Mane, Cam'Ron, Yelawolf, and Jean Rae are among the many lyricists who've acknowledged the always-open makeshift community center. Even lifelong New Yorker Jay-Z used the grub joint as a four-in-the-morning pit-stop before taking the girl from the club home in his 1999 single "Do It Again (Put Ya Hands Up)." The brand's creative influence extends beyond hip-hop: Chisel, the beloved college rock band and DIY saint, Ted Leo named a song "Waffle House."
>
> On iTunes alone there are "Sex in the Waffle House" from joke-funk group Mr. Tibbs and "Waffle House Murders" from Floridian stoner-metal band Junior Bruce. Country-rapper Colt Ford cast the restaurant as a cuckolded counseling center in "Waffle House," a gruff wail in which the narrator finds out his wife's been unfaithful and begs a friend to meet him there with a gun before he kills somebody. Half-Asian Alabama emcee Jackie Chain pretty much equates the place with scurrilous activities (trading "hoes," "smoking bomb dank," and sipping liquor) in his 2008 track "Waffle House Pimpin'" (Dodero 2013).

Waffle House stands out among a limited array of dining options for bands and solo artists on the road seeing as it jibes well with limited budgets and tight touring schedules. The familiarity, consistency, and 24-7 ubiquity of Waffle House further serves as a source of stability for those playing live shows across the South for weeks and months at a time. When untethered from the domestic normalcy of conventional homelife, anything that adds a sense of predictability and comfort holds particular allure. This sort of affirmation, coupled with the fact that per-diem food allowances go quite a way at Waffle House, helps bolsters the chain's standing among emergent and veteran road acts. In the short piece *"Scattered, Smothered, Covered, and Chunked: Fifty Years of the Waffle House,"* Atlanta-based writer Candice Dyer quotes Marshall Tucker Band guitarist Chris Hicks who states, "For us Southern boys, that glowing yellow sign is a comforting beacon. We live on the road, and when we see a Waffle House, we know that we're at least within five hundred miles of home" (2008:168).

Beyond the comfort, cuisine, and consistency Waffle House offers touring acts, the restaurant itself has developed a distinct musical cachet over the years, one that effectively sets the brand apart from other similarly capitalized corporate eateries. Indeed, practically all Waffle House locations feature digital touchscreen jukeboxes as standard dining room amenities. These brightly colored music players, manufactured by industry leader TouchTunes, prominently feature the Waffle House logo underneath where patrons pay for their song selections. Although offering on-site jukeboxes is, in and of itself, not all that remarkable, what does warrant comment is that many, if not most, of the available tunes are Waffle House–themed songs penned especially for the eatery.

The in-store play of company-sanctioned songs is nothing new for Waffle House. In fact, its first flirtation with recorded music dates back several decades to 1982 when the chain launched its very own music label—Waffle Records—to facilitate the recording of brand-inspired tunes by mostly country artists but also other music genres including bluegrass, R&B, doo-wop, and hip-hop (Campbell-Schmitt 2020). Each year, customers play tens of millions of songs at Waffle House representing various types of popular music beyond these notable Waffle Records releases. With titles such as "There Are Raisins in My Toast," "Waffle House Steaks," and "Waffle House for You and Me," the popularity of such jukebox selections over the years, coupled with the increased press coverage of Waffle House's in-house label Waffle Records (Locker 2017 ["10 Best Songs"]), spurred the next stage of the chain's musical dalliance, the Tunie Awards.

Every November since 2018, Waffle House livestreams an awards show cosponsored by TouchTunes where the most popular artists and songs played on store jukeboxes over the previous twelve months compete for special recognition. The virtual event features both live and recorded performances with nominees vying to go home with Tunie Awards in various categories including Song of the Year, Scattered, Smothered, and Discovered Artist of the Year, and the Waffle House Jukebox Legend Award. Among other recent Tunie Award winners are heartland rockers Imagine Dragons, who clinched the 2018 trophy for most-played rock song for their autotune inflected hit "Thunder"; Beyoncé, who captured the 2018 Best R&B/Hip-Hop Artist award, and southern rock legends Lynyrd Skynyrd who took away the 2018 Best Rock Artist award.

In an effort to boost brand prominence and burnish its musical bona fides within today's corporate retail foodscape, the Tunie Awards is yet another way Waffle House bucks convention when it comes to restaurant promotion. The fact that so few chains nowadays offer their clientele on-site jukeboxes is leveraged to Waffle House's distinct marketing advantage in this novel blending of mainstream music and outside-of-the-box advertising. Because Tunie Award consideration is mainly based on how many times paying customers play certain artists or songs in a given year, nominees and winners have a real way to gauge their success among ordinary working folk. For Waffle House and music industry insiders, then, the Tunie Awards represent a real win-win situation as artists earn meaningful fan recognition while the company receives some relatively low-cost publicity right before the busy US holiday travel season when millions of Americans hit the highways and quite possibly decide to visit the roadside eatery for some comfort grub and a few plays on the jukebox.

Here, in no particular order, are some selections of Waffle House finding expression within contemporary music contexts:

- By far the most notable and notorious Waffle House music figure is rap-rock pioneer, unapologetic Republican, COVID superspreader, and Confederate battle flag enthusiast, Kid Rock. Born into privilege although still claiming to be "straight out the trailer," the Detroit-bred Kid Rock revels in the blue-collar persona he created and has variously indulged over the years in part by wearing John Deere trucker hats and wifebeater muscle shirts. Against this backdrop, it is unsurprising that his musical career occasionally intersects with Waffle House in ways that garner sometimes sensationalized press attention.

In October 2007, Rock and his entourage were involved in a late-night altercation at an Atlanta-area Waffle House following one of his concerts. According to media reports (Ziegbe 2010), the self-described "American Badass" and his companions exchanged words and then blows with another restaurant patron, Harlen Akins, who recognized a female member of Rock's dining party. As the confrontation spilled into the parking lot, Akins broke a restaurant window. Rock and his entourage fled the scene in his tour bus only to be stopped by law enforcement and taken into custody a mile or so from the Waffle House for simple battery. Injured, Akins sued Rock and his entourage, eventually receiving a $40,000 jury award in 2010. Some eight years later, Rock lost his gig as the grand marshal of the Nashville Christmas Parade following a 2018 *Fox & Friends* appearance where he stated that "people need to calm down, get a little less politically correct and I would say you know, love everybody. Except screw that [*The View* cohost] Joy Behar bitch." James Shaw Jr., the hero customer of the Antioch Waffle House shooting, replaced Rock as the grand marshal (see introduction). Finally, and somewhat fittingly, Rock won the Waffle House Legend Award at the 2020 Tunie Awards.

- In the music video for the 2019 hit "Lovin' on You," country singer Luke Combs sports a Waffle House camouflage cap.
- In 2013, Waffle House sent a cease and desist letter to Nashville rapper JellyRoll who released a free twenty-one-track mixtape called "Whiskey, Weed & Waffle House," celebrating his love of the breakfast chain (Dodero 2013). With some ten thousand compact discs produced for a marketing street-team giveaway, it was the controversial album cover blatantly featuring a mock Waffle House menu on one side and a marijuana leaf, Crown Royal bottle, and Waffle House sign on the other that spurred company legal action. JellyRoll ultimately changed the mixtape's title to "Whiskey, Weed & Women" to lessen his legal exposure. Ironically, tracks on the tape include collaborations with Grizz, an unknown local tattooed rapper, who JellyRoll encountered while the amateur emcee manned the grill behind the counter at Waffle House (Dodero 2013).
- Drivin' N Cryin', an Atlanta-based rock band dating back to the 1980s, sell a Waffle House-themed T-shirt and hoodie on their merchandise web page. Both garments feature the band's name spelled out with yellow/black tiles made famous by Waffle House over the motto "Good Music Loud Since 1985."

- Central Florida rapper and vocal Trump supporter Bezz Believe released his song "Waffle House Stories" in 2017. With help from fellow hip-hop artist Starlito, Believe recounts the hardships of making it in the rap game, boasting in the track's chorus, about how he is working at 4:30 a.m. at the restaurant.
- Mega-selling roots rock band Hootie & the Blowfish, which hails from Columbia, South Carolina, released a covers album in 2000 entitled "Scattered, Smothered, and Covered." After their mid-1990s popularity waned and lead singer Darius Rucker went solo, enjoying tremendous solo success as a country artist in the 2000s and 2010s, the group went on a lengthy hiatus, before finally reforming in 2019 for a reunion tour. Notably, the stage set for the band's forty-four-city "Group Therapy Tour" was a life-size Waffle House eatery. For audience members, it appeared as if the band was playing in the restaurant's parking lot.
- Travis Porter, a hip-hop trio from Decatur, Georgia, released their track "Waffle House" in 2010. The song's lyrics and accompanying music video chronicle the group's on-site and under the influence Waffle House antics.
- American hip-hop/horrorcore pioneers Insane Clown Posse put out a 2012 covers album entitled "Smothered, Covered and Chunked." The disc's cover features an over-the-top rendering of a waffle smothered in ham and cheese next to a crushed can of Faygo soda, the band's signature drink. Perhaps this memorable artwork and catchy title represent a more than casual nod to the time the grease-painted duo was arrested for battery after a beating an eighteen-year-old boy at an Indiana Waffle House following a 1998 Indianapolis gig (MTV News Staff 1998).
- In a 2008 *Los Angeles Times* profile of singer-songwriter James McMurtry, the artist describes how Waffle House influenced the star-crossed lovers in his song "Ruby and Carlos." Reportedly, "the song was sparked by an incident when McMurtry's trio realized that the Waffle House waitresses in the North could understand their central Texas accents but the ones in the South couldn't. Tim Holt, the band's soundman, made a crack about crossing 'that Mason-Dixon Dumbass Line,' and McMurtry knew the comment would make a perfect lyric" (Himes 2008).
- In 2015, the late rapper DMX visited Waffle House after a night out at the local strip club. Finishing his meal, the "Party Up (Up in Here)" artist helped his starstruck waiter complete some restaurant cleanup duties (Hill 2015).

- According to *Rolling Stone* (Greene 2013), punk legends Iggy and the Stooges named the title track of their 2013 release, *Ready to Die*, after the Georgia pensioners who were arrested for their antigovernment plot (see chapter 3). Iggy Pop tells the magazine:

  > There were three old dudes there, about the ages of the Stooges. They were all pensioners with John Deere caps and flannel shirts and everything. They would sit around the Waffle House there plotting to blow up government offices. The waitress who brought them their pancakes overheard it and called the Feds. I thought it was so poignant, but also funny. They wanted some meaning in their life. I started writing and even had a line about "'get off my lawn!'" But it didn't hold water when I went to record it because it was too much of a cheap shot at these people. We kept the chorus that goes "I'm shooting for the sky because I'm ready to die." It's basically about how depressed and lonesome you get dealing with modern life.

- In 2017, Bruno Mars tweeted his unofficial video release party for his hit "Versace on the Floor" at an Indianapolis Waffle House. Besides an exterior clip of him dancing in front of the illuminated yellow/black roadside sign, Mars also included a photo of himself sitting in a restaurant booth perusing a menu.

- The Floozies, a funk-infused electronic duo, played months of shows in 2018, naming their trek the "Smothered, Covered, Funked, and Diced Tour." The logo was a play on the iconic yellow/black Waffle House sign.

- The American pop-indie band Never Shout Never includes a Waffle House shout-out in their 2010 song "Coffee and Cigarettes."

- Miami rapper Plies took to Instagram in 2015 to post a brief clip of him expressing his love for Waffle House while also chastising the chain for its lackluster hiring practices. He claims the restaurant gives "any person off of the street" a job, even those with "teeth missing" and looking "like they have a cold" (Hill 2015).

- American blues musician and cult southern comedian Reverend Billy C. Wirtz released a novelty song called "Waffle House Fire" in 1990. Over the sad strains of steel guitar, Wirtz talk-sings a sad tale about a Waffle House waitress named Peggy who burns down her workplace with a lighter and can of Final Net hairspray.

- In 2015, Waffle House in conjunction with food delivery app Roadie issued Grammy-winning rapper Ludacris a gift card that entitles him to free waffles for life (Hill 2015).

Clearly, Waffle House maintains a real and varied presence in today's music scene. Both as a mainstay of the touring lifestyle and as viable material for songwriting and lyrical composition, Waffle House looms large in the minds of many recording artists and performers, especially those of the hip-hop and country music genres. Indeed, it is hard to think of another restaurant chain that asserts such an abiding draw in the collective imagination and traveling regimen of contemporary musicians.

Stand-up Comedy

Given Waffle House's often beleaguered image and increasing salience as the de facto "Florida Man" of chain eateries, it is unsurprising that many stand-up comedians have exploited the brand as reliable fodder. Like touring musicians, professional comics spend considerable time on the road, sometimes necessitating late-night after-gig restaurant visits. For observational comics, Waffle House appears rife with possibilities not only for its varied menu selections but also the kind of folk who frequent the chain at all hours of the day and night. Here are some examples of big-name funnymen riffing on Waffle House:

- The late legendary stand-up comic and native Texan Bill Hicks delivered an incendiary Waffle House bit from a 1990 set recorded live at New York City's Village Gate. Hicks, never one to ease up on the idiocrasies and indignities endured by a professional funnyman while working the South's club circuit, held nothing back on either the chain or its southern clientele and employees:

    Last week I was in Nashville, Tennessee. After the show I went to a waffle house. I'm not proud of it, but I was hungry[,] . . . and I'm sitting there, and I'm eating, and I'm reading a book, right? I'm alone. I don't know anybody, I'm eating, and I'm reading a book. Fine. Right? Waitress comes over to me: [*chewing*]: "What you readin' for?" I said, "Wow, I've never been asked that. Goddang it, you stumped me. Not what am I *reading*, but what am I reading *for*? I guess I read for a lot of reasons, but one of the main ones . . . is so I don't end up being a fucking waffle waitress. Yeah, that'd be pretty high on the list." Then this trucker in the next booth gets up, stands over me and goes, "Weell, looks like we got ourselves a reader." What the fuck is going on here? It's like I walked into a clan rally in a Boy George costume or something, you know? This is a book. I read. Am I stepping out of some intellectual *closet* here? There, I said it. I feel better. (Hicks 2004:19)

- Beloved comic and CBS *This Morning* commentator Jim Gaffigan similarly takes Waffle House to task albeit without the frequent dropping F-bombs from his 2009 comedy album *King Baby* recorded live at Austin's Paramount Theater.

  > Speaking of diapers I went to Waffle House last night. I thought the IHOP was a dump until I went into Waffle House. Well, they're not even trying in there. Here's something you'll never hear in a Waffle House, "Nice job cleaning up." So, if you've never been to a Waffle House just imagine a gas station bathroom that sells waffles. You've been to a Waffle House. I love Waffle House, and not just 'cause watching someone fry an egg while smoking reminds me of my dad. The people in there, it's like a white trash convention, or for me a family reunion. It's so white trash in there it makes the IHOP appear international. I've seen a gun five times in my life. Three of them have been at Waffle House. There's definitely a dangerous feel to them. Even the Waffle House sign looks like a ransom note. There's always a letter out. Occasionally it's the W. So it'll read "awful house." "Hey that's where I want to go at 2am." That's when everyone goes. Their slogan should be "Its 2am. There's still time to make one more bad decision." You go in there and everyone's drunk. You know everyone's drunk at Waffle House 'cause they've got pictures of food on the menu. How drunk do you have to be to not remember what a waffle looks like? "Oh yeah, it's like a plaid pancake. I'll have 12 of those for a nickel." You ever go into Waffle House during the day? That's weird. "This place looks familiar. I think I threw up in here [pause] there it is." (Gaffigan 2013)

- The Blue Collar Comedy Tour—a troupe of working-class yucksters popular in the South and Midwest comprised of Jeff "You Might Be a Redneck" Foxworthy, Bill "Here's Your Sign" Engvall, Larry "Git-R-Done!" the Cable Guy (Daniel Lawrence Wright), and Ron "Tater Salad" White—included a Waffle House scene in the end credits of their second stand-up concert movie, 2004's direct-to-video *Blue Collar Comedy Tour Rides Again*. Over a Chris Cagle cover version of Lynyrd Skynyrd's "Don't Ask Me No Questions," Foxworthy and Engvall regale a lunchtime table of Waffle House customers with an anecdote about their crazy fans.

Clearly, Waffle House has real standup viability that comics variously exploit and integrate into their acts. In a way, Waffle House's beleaguered reputation makes the chain something of a low-hanging fruit for comedians looking to deliver laughs to club and arena audiences. The fact that many comics maintain similar touring regimens as musicians grounds their Waffle House comedy bits in experienced firsthand realities.

Print

Depictions of Waffle House occasionally crop up in the work of esteemed and lesser-known American writers, what with the considerable ironies and idiosyncrasies baked into the South's long, rich, and varied literary heritage. Drawing on the chain's symbolic resonance as viable shorthand for folksy regional identity and working-class character, Waffle House makes it into the work of various southern and nonsouthern authors sometimes as an unmistakable regional backdrop or sometimes as a viable signifier of their characters' reduced circumstances. More often, however, it receives fleeting mention in the text sort of like the illuminated yellow/black restaurant signage that nighttime drivers suddenly spot on the horizon before quickly whizzing past.

- In terms of contemporary regional writers, it probably does not get much more southern or grit lit than Larry Brown. A native of Oxford, Mississippi, Brown rose to prominence in the 1980s with short stories and novels depicting the grim, if often tragicomic, realities of blue-collar life in the bars and backroads of his home state. Two of his later works, *The Rabbit Factory* (2003:250) and the posthumous *A Miracle of Catfish* (2007:256), include Waffle House mentions, adding fine-grain detail to his narratives' sense of place.
- Legendary outlaw journalist Hunter S. Thompson includes a predawn letter he penned after eating at a Mobile, Alabama, Waffle House in December 1981 to fellow counterculture icon Ken Kesey in his volume of collected works *Songs of the Doomed: More Notes on the Death of the American Dream* (1990). Thompson praises the *One Flew over the Cuckoo's Nest* author for a magazine piece Kesey published in the January/February 1982 issue of *Running* about the First International Beijing Marathon. Thompson writes (1990:234–35), "If you thought the air was bad in China, you should smell Mobile in the rain at four-thirty on a cold Saturday morning. I just got back from the Waffle House across the bay, where I spent two hours eating steakburgers and reading your Beijing piece in *Running* . . . and drinking a hell of a lot of coffee, because a man with no hair and short pants can't just

hang around a Waffle House on the edge of Mobile Bay at four o'clock in the morning without running up a tab, especially when he's laughing a lot and ducking outside in the rain every once in a while to hunker down in a big red Cadillac car for a drink of good whisky and a few whacks of rotten cocaine."

He continues: "The parking lot of a Waffle House on Interstate 10 is a bad place to get weird, and it's even worse if you keep coming back inside and reading the same goddamn magazine and making the waitress jumpy by laughing out loud every few minutes and smacking orange countertop and smoking Dunhill cigarettes in a holder."

- Mary Miller's novel *The Last Days of California: A Novel* (2014) is a coming-of-age story set in a preapocalyptic America. The book's protagonist, fifteen-year-old Jess, is on a family road trip across the Bible Belt to California, handing out Evangelical tracts at all of the rest stops, gas stations, and Waffle Houses along the way. Her father makes frequent stops at the roadside eatery along the way.
- Scottish poet Harry Josephine Giles's "Waffle House Crush" from his collection *Tonguit* (2015) is a lyrical ode to what makes this perennial southern restaurant fare so mouthwatering delicious.

These examples are but only a smattering of Waffle House's appearances in contemporary literature, leaving readers with the certain knowledge that the narrative action unfolding on the page is in the American South.

Sports

Over the years, Waffle House has encroached into the US sports world in concrete and abstract ways. As a venue for quick low-cost meals, it is hard to beat what Waffle House offers those fans and players en route to athletic competitions. Like touring musicians and professional comedians, those involved with amateur and collegiate sports find themselves on the road quite a bit, traveling to or from away games or competing in meets and tournaments that necessitate overnight stays or long-distance highway travel.

With these frequent trips away from home an inextricable part of the amateur athletic lifestyle, especially at the high school and college level or in geographically diffuse states like Texas, individual competitors and multiplayer teams are often compelled to dine out at odd hours or choose among a limited number of restaurant options, ones that generally lie in close proximity to overnight lodging or readily align with per diem budget constraints. Under these circumstances, it is unsurprising that Waffle House variously intersects with American athletics, serving as a reliable place to grab a simple meal without breaking the bank or delaying the all-important need to make good travel time.

Even in the more rarefied echelons of professional sports, Waffle House occasionally gains expression whether employed as a southern signifier or as a talismanic touchstone embraced for the purported success it confers. That Waffle House sponsors its own NASCAR race team (see introduction) is surely unsurprising given stockcar racing's widespread popularity in this part of the United States. The restaurant brand's conspicuity in other sports is probably a bit more revelatory, especially in a seemingly elitist pastime like golf. Indeed, of all its entanglements with the sports, perhaps none is more of an initial headscratcher than Waffle House's golf affiliations. As a popular pursuit more commonly associated with leisure-class affluence than any sort of significant working-class participation—what with all of the time and expenses involved in securing equipment and green fees and the established traditions of spiffy dress codes and country club etiquette— Waffle House attains visibility within golf in multiple ways.

Waffle House's fairway associations may just reflect a shared Peach State heritage. Indeed, Georgia not only boasts the country's most Waffle House locations, it is also home to both Waffle House headquarters and the storied Augusta National Golf Club, the site of professional golf's premiere annual event, the Masters Tournament. Moreover, Waffle House cofounder Tom Forkner earned considerable recognition for his remarkable achievements on the links, winning numerous seniors titles over a multidecade career beginning in the 1960s. In fact, he eventually became a Georgia Golf Hall of Fame inductee in 2007 (see chapter 2). As notable is the story of country rapper and Athens, Georgia, native Colt Ford (James Farris Brown). Years before he released his 2008 mega-hit "Waffle House," he pursued a successful golf career, playing on the professional circuit throughout the 1990s.

Other instances of Waffle House attracting attention in the golf world include the following:

- After winning the fabled green jacket for the second time in 2014, golfer Gerry Lester "Bubba" Watson Jr. celebrated his second Masters's title by going out to eat at a nearby Augusta Waffle House. He not only posted a selfie of his victory dinner—a double grilled cheese with scattered and smothered hash browns—but also left the waiter a $148 tip (Manfred 2014).
- Ladies Professional Golf Association (LPGA) member Brooke

Pancake inked a Waffle House endorsement deal in 2015. Cleverly trading in on her distinctive last name, the Waffle House–Pancake partnership entailed her touring local store franchises while on the tournament circuit as well as sporting a yellow/black golf bag emblazoned with the company logo and tagline "Scattered, Smothered, and Covered" (Zak 2015).

Beyond professional golf, Waffle House also figures into the off the field lifestyles of NFL players and fans. Members of the Carolina Panthers attributed their remarkable game-winning success to frequent Waffle House visits throughout the 2015 regular season where they went 15–1 and into the 2015–16 playoffs where they clenched a National Football Conference (NFC) championship. In fact, in the lead up to their Super Bowl L appearance against the Denver Broncos, the *Wall Street Journal* ran a story under the following headline: "The Carolina Panthers' Secret Weapon: Waffle House. Players See Proximity to the Popular 24-Hour Restaurant Chain of the South as a Homefield Advantage" (Clark 2016). At the time, some twenty Waffle House restaurants operated within a twenty-five-mile radius of their homefield Bank of America Stadium. Panther players praise the chain for its inexpensive and calorically dense meals that allow them to fuel up whenever their unusual schedules demand food. Some Panthers are so fond of Waffle House, in fact, that they posted a lighthearted late-night video of themselves singing the Temptations' 1971 hit "Just My Imagination (Running Away with Me)" to YouTube filmed after practice at a local Waffle House during summer training camp (Clark 2016).

Along similar lines, Tennessee Titans wide receiver Julio Jones garnered the nickname "Waffle House" when he entered the NFL in 2011 as a draft pick for the Atlanta Falcons. The future Hall of Famer earned the colorful sobriquet for the fact that, like Waffle House, he is "always open" (Moraitis 2021). Adding a bit of preseason flair to his 2021 workout attire, Jones donned some special Waffle House cleats during the Titans training camp in Nashville (Moraitis 2021).

Beyond the players themselves, Waffle House and their special brand of southern cooking has intersected with the NFL in other ways. *Maxim* magazine hosted a pre–Super Bowl XXXVI party in Atlanta the Saturday night before the New England Patriots defeated the Los Angeles Rams 20–17. The January 2019 shindig was catered exclusively by Waffle House and featured musical performances by top R&B and hip-hop artists including Jamie Foxx, Diplo, and Future. The corporate food truck dished a hacked menu with servings of hash browns, waffles, lemon squares, biscuit and gravy cups, and coffee. Tickets for the red-carpet event were expensive, ranging from $750 for general admission to a truly staggering $75,000 for onstage seats (Underhill 2019).

Somewhat less celebratory was the plight of NFL fan and fantasy football aficionado Lee Sanderlin, 25, who upon finishing last among his league competitors was forced to spend twenty-four-hours at his local Waffle House in Brandon, Mississippi, as punishment. Documenting his self-imposed sentence on Twitter, Sanderlin enjoyed the option of subtracting an hour from his term for each waffle he consumed. Online audiences were riveted by his hard-earned observations on the overnight tedium and gastronomical distress he endured over consecutive hours starting on Thursday June 17, 2021. By the next morning he downed some nine waffles, finishing his time there in some fifteen hours. Upon completing this grueling quest, Sanderlin—who generously tipped Waffle House waitstaff—sarcastically tweeted, "This was horrible and I recommend no one ever do this" (Victor 2021).

Like their NFL brethren, current and former players of the National Basketball Association (NBA) have occasionally embraced Waffle House both as a place to load up high-calorie fare without too much wallet-pinching expense and as a backdrop that reinforces their street cred through online postings and restaurant shoutouts. To wit:

- Current Los Angeles Laker phenom Dwight Howard gave his Instagram followers an up close glimpse of his dietary intake when he played for the Houston Rockets (2013–16) after posting before and after photos of his three-course Waffle House meal in 2015 that included a waffle, ribeye steak, scrambled eggs, grits, toast, and iced tea (Hill 2015).
- In January 2014, Golden State Warriors guard and future Hall of Famer Wardell Stephen "Steph" Curry II tweeted the following: "Just passed the nicest Waffle House I've ever seen in Atlanta. I mean the nicest" (Hill 2015).
- Basketball legend Shaquille "Shaq" O'Neal got pranked by his onetime girlfriend, reality television star Nicole "Hoopz" Alexander, while on a date at Waffle House. While the former Orlando Magic standout excused himself for a bathroom visit, Hoopz dumped salt into his plastic tumbler of orange juice. Upon returning and sipping from the tainted drink, Shaq and nearly everyone inside the eatery had a heartfelt laugh. Not one to get upset, Shaq left the restaurant server a thirty-dollar tip for a twenty-dollar meal (Hill 2015).

If sports serve as a viable distillation of contemporary American life just as Waffle House encapsulates so many of the South's enduring uniformities, idiosyncrasies, and mundanities, then it can be little wonder that the chain occasionally intersects with professional and amateur athletics in either profound or subtle ways. As the above examples demonstrate, Waffle House seemingly jibes well with the specialized (traveling) lifestyles of sports fans and players, offering a resonant context for asserting a regional and/or nonelitist identity. Like their entertainment industry counterparts, professional athletes have few qualms about posting their Waffle House experiences across various social media formats.

With a multidimensional profile that transcends so many sports and entertainment genres, Waffle House enjoys the sort of brand status that engages consumer sensibilities beyond the standard expectations of today's dining public. For a chain long averse to mainstream advertising or slick marketing campaigns, these restaurant depictions figure prominently in shaping or reinforcing popular perceptions of the twenty-four-hour eatery whether for good or ill. Such Waffle House portrayals wield considerable sway outside of the US corporate foodscape as many purveyors of pop culture content employ them as symbolic shorthand for various non-food-related subject matter including the American South, contemporary southerners, working-class identities, and/or Red State politics. Disaggregating the southern imaginary's influence from all of these Waffle House representations proves difficult because the two are so inextricably bounded up with one another, making an enduring restaurant chain all the more palatable to southerners and nonsoutherners alike.

Conclusion

Waffling on Waffle House? Post-Southern Possibilities

As the corporate reach of the South's quintessential roadside breakfast counter/greasy spoon encroaches into previously untapped territories, some far afield from its traditional regional stronghold in the American Southeast and Gulf Coast, new questions arise about Waffle House's putative identity as a southern icon. For a brand seemingly averse to touting its regional credentials in any overt or emphatic way, this gradual expanse outside of the Bible Belt may finally add some genuine credibility to Waffle House's underrecognized motto of "America's Best Place to Eat."

For those living on both sides of the Mason-Dixon Line, Waffle House provides an accessible entry point for understanding the mercurial American South. As a region of real and imagined landscapes, the South remains rife with complexities and contradictions, making it easy to caricature but not so easy to accurately categorize. Many have previously argued that Waffle House represents a veritable microcosm of today's Bible Belt, embodying all that is either admirable or problematic in the southern character. This work strives to move beyond such binary thinking, avoiding the strictures of the simple light/dark or Red State/Blue State dichotomies that so often characterize the chain's place within the region's increasingly corporatized foodscape and America's prevailing cultural ether.

In this book, I have critically examined the brand's unique sociocultural status, adding both depth and granularity to popular understandings of Waffle House. The analysis neither dismisses the eatery as a retail punchline nor overinflates Waffle House's symbolic significance as the restaurant equivalent of an indefatigable Southern Everyperson, one whose rough-around-the-edges image belies a simple heartfelt integrity that elitist tastemakers can never fully appreciate. Efforts at striking the right critical balance in this way speak to the genuine lack of consensus that Waffle House engenders in public thought. Without some general agreement as to what the 24-7 chain means to most Americans, Waffle House continues to invite split-screen characterizations that typically reinforce one of two popular sentiments. Definitively reconciling such opposing perspectives proves elusive even as findings revealed throughout this book represent positive steps in that direction.

When filtered through the refractive lens of the southern imaginary—where the region's sepia-tinted romanticisms and most obvious imperfections assume outsized or distorted dimensions—these dualistic conceptions work to obscure not only the mundanity of Waffle House operations but also the paradoxical tension that animates so much of what people find captivating about Waffle House, specifically, and the South, more broadly. The sometimes slight, sometimes significant misalignments between the long-cherished values and practices that serve to define both the restaurant and region to the rest of the world and the lived realities and daily hardships experienced by everyday folk variously situated within the socioeconomic strata of today's South creates a cognitive dissonance of sorts. Although such disjunctions seem all but evident to outside observers, they frequently go unnoticed by those cultural insiders inextricably immersed in the nitty-gritty and moment-by-moment minutiae of regional life.

In this way, the southern imaginary works for the interests of southerners and nonsoutherners alike in defining the people, places, events, traditions, and foodways that effectively define this particular region of the continental United States however positively or negatively. Neither group can rightly claim a propriety ownership over the southern imaginary as each seemingly engages it for their own ends. What remains particularly intriguing is how the southern imaginary provides a context for so many cultural insiders in the American Southeast and Gulf Coast states for articulating a hyperbolic if also controversial idea of what it means to be a "real," "true," or "patriotic" American, an identity or affiliation readily capitalized upon by groups and institutions such as the NRA, NASCAR, Southern Baptist Convention, and Republican Party.

Waffle House's enduring status as a cultural touchstone of an alternatively celebrated, alternatively denigrated southern identity appears to have emerged largely independent of company marketing efforts. From a strictly Business 101 perspective, not delving too deeply into the media-hyped incidents that routinely plague locations during weekend graveyard shifts makes absolute sense. Beyond occasional nods toward the after-hours party crowd that keeps the good times rolling at Waffle House well into the early morning, there is really little upside to drawing attention to the eatery's seamier side. Less understandable is Waffle House's apparent resistance toward directly capitalizing on its regional credentials. As a means to exploit America's longtime embrace of down-home southern cooking, never mind as a way of cementing its fast-casual grip throughout the US Southeast and Gulf Coast, the chain's ostensible indifference toward touting its regional heritage remains rather perplexing. While Waffle House arguably approaches the South's quintessential roadside diner/breakfast counter, it appears reluctant to openly acknowledge much less overtly publicize its southern affiliations, leaving rival restaurant chains Cracker Barrel or Bojangles ample space to assert such claims.

However muted or understated, Waffle House's attempts to brand itself as the highway travelers' and budget-conscious Americans' all-night eatery of choice include few, if any, overt mentions of the South. Over the years, the sit-down establishment has only obliquely referenced its regional bona fides through a limited public outreach that continues to avoid conventional advertising platforms like television and radio. Surprising for a chain with some 1,990 outlets operating in more than two dozen states, Waffle House favors a less-is-more approach when it comes to showcasing its brand profile within America's highly competitive (fast-)casual scene.

Whether by sponsoring a NASCAR race team or licensing product placement in select Hollywood features—typically ones with strong southern characters or settings—Waffle House only engages its regional pedigree rather sporadically or tangentially in restaurant promotions. Even with its more active social media presence from the mid-2000s onward, the twenty-four-hour eatery rarely acknowledges its putative southern affiliations. If anything, after replacing the "Good Food *Fast*" company slogan some decades back with the less geographically insular phrase "America's Best Place to Eat," Waffle House let it be known that its corporate orientation transcends the Bible Belt grounding of its formative years.

No matter how much the company avoids explicitly acknowledging its regional ties, most Americans view Waffle House as a southern brand. Countering these ingrained associations appears doomed to failure for multiple reasons none the least of which is how Joe Rogers Sr. and Tom Forkner's joint restaurant creation achieved that rare and, in Waffle House's case, largely unbidden status as a celebrated regional icon. Beyond the chain's unpretentious service format, countryfied cuisine, and roadside ubiquity, such deep-rooted characterizations persist in no small part due to the considerable sway the southern imaginary exerts over the US popular consciousness.

Southern Imaginary on the Skids?

The pan-southern South of the southern imaginary remains a place of sometimes mawkish sentimentality (e.g., "Look away, look away, look away Dixie land") that also encompasses a foreboding darkness where possibilities of violence, race-based or otherwise, can never be wholly ruled out. This amorphous assemblage of narrative, imagery, and sentiment continues to showcase overdetermined manifestations of regional identity that invariably gloss over the true messiness and complexity at the heart of past and present southern lifeways. Notions of subtlety, irony, contradiction, and ambiguity continually take a backseat to the more emotionally charged resonances articulated within this highly evocative amalgamation of conceptual and material expression. If anything, the southern imaginary provides a viable context for creating or envisioning particular versions of the South that best align with the aspirational experiences or darker impulses of countless individuals and communities both now and in the past.

As counternarratives and emergent voices coalesce to challenge many of the presumed certainties long holding currency about southern history, politics, race relations, class arrangements, gender dynamics, and faith, a reappraisal of what exactly it means to be southern increasingly comes to the fore. As relevant, given such shifting circumstances, is a reassessment of just how different this part of the country is from other US regions. When using Waffle House as a framing device, the probing of these questions assumes a certain level of relatability, if not actual immediacy, to many everyday Americans. The car-crash fascination so often associated with Waffle House media portrayals, coupled with the more recent tendency to view the eatery and its clientele as irrepressible underdogs, perpetuates a curious kind of yin and yang identity, one that few other chain restaurants readily experience. Waffle House's minimal efforts in concretely defining its brand in the public domain basically allows others to project their own ideas or labels onto the restaurant, sometimes to the detriment of Waffle House's popular standing.

Waffle House 2.0

Despite the hue and cry that sometimes inform public understandings of Waffle House, the chain continues racking up some impressive results, especially in terms of reaching important company milestones. Besides recently celebrating its sixty-fifth business anniversary, Waffle House appears on the cusp of opening its two thousandth restaurant sometime in the early 2020s. Barring a major COVID-19-related industry downturn in 2022 or afterward, the upward trajectory that began in Avondale Estates way back in 1955 appears ongoing and unyielding. Indeed, the familiar presence of Waffle House's yellow/black corporate logo in the street-level fabric of strip mall parking lots, near economy motels, or along roadside properties just off interstate exits shows little sign of fading away anytime soon.

As Waffle House's geographical reach encroaches into territories beyond its traditional stronghold across Red State America, questions arise as to whether or not this publicly designated southern icon will ever shed its imposed-from-the-outside regional affiliations much as other brands with distinctly southern roots previously have. Coca-Cola, Holiday Inn, Home Depot, Chick-fil-A, and Wal-Mart spring to mind as vivid examples of US companies launched decades ago that eventually transcended their regional origins, assuming newfound status worldwide. So widely encountered are these expansive brands nowadays, in fact, that most twenty-first-century consumers could be forgiven for not immediately recognizing their southern beginnings.

Writing about the national and now worldwide appeal of Krispy Kreme doughnuts in the 2008 volume *Dixie Emporium: Tourism, Foodways, and Consumer Culture in the American South*, noted sociologist John Shelton Reed ponders: "On the many southern things that have ceased to be southern, not because southerners gave them up but because we [southerners] exported them so successfully. Coca-Cola was an early example, going from a regional thirst-quencher to a symbol of American civilization, then—as opponents of 'coca-colonization' feared it would—teaching the world to sing in more than 100 languages. Holiday Inn and Wal-Mart have followed the same path. NASCAR, country music, and the Southern Baptist Convention may be doing the same" (2008:207).

At this point, it is probably premature to place Waffle House too far down the offramp of Reed's path away from a public persona largely subsumed in the trappings of a down-home southern identity. However, Waffle House appears well positioned to make this transition at some point, what with a retail presence in two dozen states and a business reputation that all but precedes itself nationwide. A nominal nationalization of Waffle House and by extension southern-inspired cuisine like that served at its eateries suggests new wrinkles in America's highly variegated and corporatized foodscape as well as a continued blurring of distinctions between various geographical regions.

Such prospects raise some intriguing possibilities for Waffle House. Consider the double irony of Waffle House—an iconic regional brand long resistant to such southern self-labeling—growing so successful and geographically diffuse that it loses its enduring place-based identity to no longer resonate as a southern brand to the wider world. Although the emergence of a post-southern Waffle House 2.0 would unlikely mean too much to company higher-ups given their already noted tepid enthusiasm for touting such regional affiliations, for others—particularly that swath of the dining public that continually embraces the chain as a southern institution—this transition would doubtless seem both inconceivable and unwelcome considering their deep-rooted fondness for the brand. The self-proclaimed "Master of the 88 Key Disaster," Rev. Billy C. Wirtz (see chapter 5) says as much in 2008, noting that Waffle House is "one of the few elements of Southern life that has stayed true and not been ripped off and exploited by outsiders and then handed back to us in some generic, watered-down form, as is the case with country music, NASCAR, rasslin', and TV preaching" (Dyer 2008:168).

For now, Waffle House remains firmly entrenched in US sensibilities as unequivocally southern, evoking everything from the sublime to the ridiculous in how it engages the American imagination. Its seeming inability to lock its doors or dim the lights makes the chain easy to take for granted, while its considerable corporate footprint across the Bible Belt and beyond provides continual solace to all of those night owls, party people, and cost-conscious travelers looking for coffee, hash, and reliable comfort food whenever or however the need arises. Although media accounts documenting on-site encounters cover a wide spectrum of human behavior, they frequently skew to the aberrant or outright criminal, making it difficult for more upbeat or charitable occurrences, as well as the long hours of mundanity that invariably characterize normative Waffle House operations, to gain much of a foothold within in the dominant 24-7-365 news cycle. All in all, Waffle House maintains a considerable symbolic richness that both reflects and reifies the unfinished tapestry of the American South, a region where the best and worst of the American character finds expression in sometimes the most ordinary of places.

Notes

Preface

1. Micah Cash's photo essay "Waffle House Vistas" was originally published in 2019 in the digital magazine the *Bitter Southerner*. Later that year, the *Bitter Southerner* released a hardcover edition of the work available for purchase on its online store. In August 2021, *The Bitter Southerner* made available a few of Cash's photos for purchase as signed art prints suitable for framing.

Introduction

1. Anecdotally, I can attest to Waffle House's near ubiquity along US interstate highways in the South having made the eight-plus-hour drive from Cedar Mountain, North Carolina, to Orlando, Florida, on the Saturday following Thanksgiving 2019. With the help of my wife and kids, we counted 32 Waffle House restaurants along both I-26 (South Carolina) and Interstate 95 (South Carolina, Georgia, and Florida). Most were less than a quarter mile from the highway exit. We even encountered the burnt-out shell of a Waffle House restaurant while getting gas in Georgia.

2. When the chain moved into Indiana sometime around 1990, another firm legally held the Waffle House name, leaving the Georgia-based brand to promote its eateries in the Hoosier State as Waffle & Steak for several years until finally securing the right to bring its local restaurants in line with company operations nationwide (Contrera 2013).

3. According to the data company *ScrapeHero* (2020), North Carolina has 185 Waffle House outlets, roughly 9 percent of all company eateries, boasting a per capita ratio of one Waffle House outlet for every 56,000 North Carolinians. Florida is only one restaurant behind North Carolina with 184 outlets, similarly comprising 9 percent of all Waffle House eateries and maintaining a per capita ratio of one Waffle House outlet for every 114,000 Floridians.

4. Outside of the United States, IHOP maintains a limited commercial presence in Canada, Mexico, and Central America as well as a handful of operations in South America, Asia, and the Middle East (Dine Brands 2018).

5. According to the Denny's website, the California-based company had approximately 115 overseas restaurants in 2016 including operations in Canada, New Zealand, Mexico, Costa Rica, the United Arab Emirates, the Philippines, Chile, Curaçao, and Honduras (Denny's 2016).

6. For Hurricane Michael, which slammed into the U.S. Gulf Coast in October 2018 with sustained winds of 155 mph before carving a path of destruction through Georgia and into the Carolinas, the company closed twenty-two restaurants in the Florida Panhandle and eight in southwest Georgia (McDonald 2018).

7. Incidentally, "Smothered, Covered and Chunked" is the name of the American hip-hop/horrorcore group Insane Clown Posse (ICP)'s thirteenth studio album. Released in

2012, the disc contains cover versions (hence the title) of hits made popular by other artists. The ICP record follows in the footsteps of two other albums released by major recording groups including a 2000 covers collection by the platinum-selling Hootie and the Blowfish, "Scattered, Smothered and Covered," and a 1995 record of original material by the noise rock trio Unsane, "Scattered, Smothered & Covered."

8. Brian Carpenter defines the first component of this subgenre in ways equally applicable to Waffle House clientele, stating in his introduction to *Grit Lit: A Rough South Reader* (2012) that a "grit" is "typically blue collar or working class, mostly small town, sometimes rural, occasionally but not always violent, usually but not always southern" (Carpenter, xvii).

9. Waffle House is known for its jukebox music. Every location sports a music player that features popular hits, college fight songs, and original tracks about the restaurant itself with titles including "Waffle House Thank You" and "Waffle House for You and Me." These latter songs are distributed on the company's very own record label (Locker 2017).

10. Of course, there are associations between waffles or more accurately "fried chicken and waffles" in the culinary traditions of American soul food even as assertions about their origins as distinctly southern fare have been scrutinized (Miller 2016). Some anecdotes suggest chicken and waffles may have taken root in southern foodways via the Chitlin Circuit—a network of Black-owned roadside nightclubs, theaters, and honkytonks spread across the South and Midwest before and during the civil rights era (1954–1968)—whereby entertainers traveling from New York and other points north "ordered chicken for breakfast after missing dinner on Saturday night because they were performing and ordered waffles as hot bread to eat with the fried chicken" (Opie 2010:122).

11. Although not a restaurant chain like Waffle House, Blue Bell Creameries, headquartered in Brenham, Texas, and manufacturer of the U.S.'s fourth-highest-selling ice cream brand, maintains a geographical sales reach that approximates that of Waffle House in most respects. Following a devastating 2015 Listeriosis outbreak that led to at least three deaths, an unprecedented product recall, and hundreds of employee layoffs, Blue Bell never lost public support in part because of its decades-long marketing efforts that touted an image of the company as the "Little Creamery" in the country replete with old-fashioned imagery and wholesome small-town aesthetics (Dinges and Herrera 2018).

12. Celebrated South Carolinian writer George Singleton (*The Half Mammals of Dixie*) echoes such thinking about the South in a 2002 interview, asking rhetorically, "Why do the conservative right wing people around here think the way they do; and why do the foreigners, the transplants, and liberals keep hanging around? Oh, it's a dichotomy, baby. It's a place where nothing but conflict can evolve." Native Floridian, Rock and Roll Hall of Famer, and music legend Tom Petty (1950–2017) reaffirmed such sentiments. When asked by *Rolling Stone* writer David Fricke how much of his fighting streak comes from growing up southern, Petty replied, "I don't necessarily agree with a lot of the Southern ethic. I'm grateful to the South. It's a beautiful place. There are wonderfully colorful people that are fascinating to me. There's also terrible ignorance and downright evil. That's part of the culture, all mixed together" (Fricke 2014).

13. Like Evoni Williams, thirty-year-old James Shaw Jr. received much deserved recognition for his actions at Waffle House that morning. His courage under fire prevented further bloodshed and loss of life among both restaurant staff and clientele. He even established a GoFundMe page to raise money for the deceased victims' families. Tennessee legislators passed a joint resolution soon after the shooting honoring Shaw's bravery.

14. Later identified as Doug Umland, the alleged aggressor was visiting the Pinson Waffle House with his wife, Ginger, for an after-hours meal. After the Mitchell's video went viral both Umlands were fired from their jobs at a local tractor company. Doug Umland

claims he was not threatening gun violence toward Mitchell but rather stating, "I'll sue you," for filming his wife (Thorton 2019).

15. This work should not be approached as a definitive or exhaustive Waffle House corporate history. Although formative chain events and personalities obviously greatly inform assertions made over subsequent pages, I leave it to other scholars to document Waffle House's remarkable rise and ongoing operations with more considered detail. Similarly, this book is not an ethnography in the classic sense, despite my training as a cultural anthropologist. Most of my previous research is rooted in data collected through interviews and participant observation, but this food studies analysis forgoes such traditional fieldwork techniques, relying on information culled from secondary sources.

Chapter 1

1. The recent success of Grubhub, DoorDash, Uber Eats, and other popular online food delivery platforms underscores this point. With streamlined ordering through user-friendly mobile apps and prompt doorstep service provided by self-employed takeout couriers, this kind of on-demand e-commerce simplifies the American dining public's access to menu offerings from nearby (non)chain restaurants to just a few easy cellphone swipes.

2. Of course, the scale and character of how we dine will likely change in unexpected ways as advances in automation, robotics, and other developments alter the future of work moving forward. In the past and continuing today, major technological innovations have punctuated the continual uncoupling of our eating behaviors from domestic home life. Advances in refrigeration/electrification expanded the ability of restaurant owner/operators to offer fresh and diverse menu items among other things. Similarly, the rise and eventual domination of the automobile in the twentieth century not only increased the range of travel for millions worldwide but also dramatically altered the dining landscape by introducing all sorts of consumer amenities that revolutionized modern food service including fast food, drive-through lanes, take-out service, and curbside pickup, especially in the United States and other parts of the global North.

3. For a list of common characteristics of restaurants, see Gillian Crowther's *Eating Culture: An Anthropological Guide to Food* (2013:185–90).

4. The Great Migration—sometimes called the Great Northward Migration or the Black Migration—refers to the movement of some six million rural African American southerners to the U.S. Northeast, Midwest, and West that occurred approximately between 1916 and 1970.

5. According to the *Washington Post* in 2018, "13.9 percent of workers are employed in blue collar professions, vs, 15 percent in government and 71.1 percent in the service sector" (Long and Van Dam 2018).

6. In interviews discussing his work on "ironic consumption," University of Arizona's Caleb Warren uses the example of pop sensation Bruno Mars dancing outside of and then eating at an Indiana Waffle House in 2017 (see chapter 5) as emblematic of ironic "high-status consumers adopting a low-status product as a way to distinguish themselves from middle-class consumers" (Schmitz 2018).

7. An entrepreneur from Providence, Rhode Island, Walter Scott, is generally credited with creating the first horse-pulled lunch wagon in 1872. A crude precursor to the twentieth-century roadside diner, his original mobile restaurant featured walk-up windows through which customers could place/receive meal orders. Some fifteen years later, Thomas Buckley began mass producing commercial lunch wagons in Worcester, Massachusetts. Following Scott's and Buckley's leads, Charles Palmer officially patented the first diner in 1893, dubbing his invention the Night-Watch Wagon (Gutman 2000).

8. The US population in 1951 was approximately 154.9 million (US Census Bureau 2021).

9. Of the twentieth century's ten leading US diner manufacturers—Bixler Manufacturing Company (Fremont and Norwalk, Ohio), DeRaffele Manufacturing Co. Inc. (New Rochelle, New York), Fodero Dining Car Company (Newark and Bloomfield, New Jersey), Jerry O'Mahony Diner Company (Elizabeth, New Jersey), Kullman Dining Car Company (Newark, New Jersey), Mountain Views Diners Company (Signac, New Jersey), Silk City Diners (Paterson, New Jersey), Tierney Dining Cars (New Rochelle, New York); Worcester Lunch Car Company (Worcester, Massachusetts), Sterling Streamline Diners (Merrimac, Massachusetts)—most were located in New Jersey (Hurley 2001:34–35).

10. As if to commemorate the diner's gradual decline and years-long marginalization during this timeframe, Rock and Roll Hall of Fame inductee and popular music's most successful duo of all-time, Daryl Hall and John Oates, released their sophomore album *Abandoned Luncheonette* (1973). Besides containing one of their signature tunes "She's Gone," the record effectively lived up to its quirky title with a cover photograph showcasing an actual railcar diner sitting derelict in a Pennsylvania field overgrown with vines and weeds, its metallic facade discolored by rust and neglect. Although limited in impact, this depiction reflected early 1970's sentiments about diners' collective status in American foodscapes where these once-commonplace eateries no longer enjoyed their ubiquitous status.

11. For simplicity's sake, I subsequently use the term *lunch counter(s)* in referring to *lunch/breakfast counter(s)*.

12. Only with the mid-1990s' emergence of online shopping did retail models so deeply rooted in fixed physical locations begin suffering their first major setbacks. In fact, by the early 2000s, e-commerce's paradigm-shifting impact left many traditional chains scrambling to capture whatever consumer dollars remained up for grabs as the convenience and endless array of shippable merchandise proffered by the likes of Amazon and eBay exerted an almost irresistible appeal. Notwithstanding how cybershopping's ripple effects permanently altered the fabric of US brick-and-mortar retailing right around the twenty-first century's onset, the decades leading up to these profound changes in global commerce—what can retrospectively be viewed as the ostensible heyday of shopping malls, big box retailers, and so-called category killers—was primarily characterized by an ongoing concentration of retail power to larger more highly capitalized corporate ventures.

13. Labor conditions within these stores and among their suppliers both at home and abroad, coupled with stagnating store employee wages and environmental impact of disposable packing/shipping materials, are some further problematic aspects associated with this new mode of retailing.

14. For example, the menus of (fast-)casual mainstay Hooters and emergent Chicken Salad Chick are similar in terms of food quality and price but strikingly different in terms of target audience, especially with regard to their gender-normative aesthetics and perceived culinary bents. Hooters primarily targets middle-class men and the Chicken Salad Chick mainly focuses on suburban women, so it is surely fair to suggest that each chain's core constituencies would feel decidedly out of place partaking of the other's on-site restaurant offerings. Such sentiments arise more by design than default as most industry players craft their retail concepts and brand images with considerable forethought and deliberation.

Chapter 2

1. Prior to becoming a world-class tourist showcase in Atlanta's Pemberton Place, Coca-Cola's namesake museum/attraction, the World of Coca-Cola, was housed in a three-story downtown indoor facility from 1990 to 2007. It was in this previous location where the soft-drink giant featured a Waffle House exhibit in 2005 to commemorate the breakfast chain's fiftieth anniversary. Many items currently on display at the Waffle House Museum in Avondale Estates come from this special presentation of restaurant memorabilia.

2. At one point, Waffle House sold Chick-fil-A sandwiches at their restaurants.

3. Rogers likens his "poor old cash customer" to the Dagwood Bumstead character from the *Blondie* comic strip: a patron who "might have missed the bus or carpool, didn't have any breakfast before they left home, and they're looking for a fight" (Rogers 2000:95). Rogers viewed Waffle House managers and waitstaff as akin to physicians, stating, "We can make people feel better, and most days they need that" (Rogers 2000:95).

Chapter 3

1. The title track of the Iggy and the Stooges' 2013 album *Ready to Die* is actually based on this case (see chapter 5). Moreover, it similarly echoes the planning stages of the criminal caper at the heart of the 2004 movie *The Ladykillers* (see chapter 5).

2. Even Waffle House's bargain retail counterpart Dollar General is now recognized as a hub of criminal activity, including armed robbery and felonious assault (Meyersohn 2020).

3. Under these circumstances the aforementioned "Waffle House Index" comes into play. Basically, this informal metric allows the federal government to ascertain (1) a natural catastrophe's severity, (2) the prospective recovery timeline for affected areas, and (3) approximately how much economic aid is necessitated based on the rare occurrence of a Waffle House shutdown. The number of locations temporarily closed during these periods of disruption alongside how long they take to resume normative operations all figure into this novel and by now well-publicized benchmark gauge. Waffle House is the retailer most conspicuously foregrounded in this namesake metric, but the operational status of other commercial chains including local Home Depot, Walmart, and Lowe's stores is also taken into consideration when evaluating disaster severity and community preparedness.

4. In a local job ad in September 2020 for a full-time Orlando-area Waffle House server job, applicants were deemed eligible for the following perks: (1) weekly pay; (2) available direct deposit; (3) paid time off; (4) available medical, dental, and vision insurance for employees and their kin; (5) seven-dollar to twenty-two dollars hourly wages; (6) no tip sharing; (7) flexible scheduling; and (8) ability to purchase company stock after one year's employment.

5. Again, only in 2006 did Waffle House begin accepting credit card payments. Before then, cash was the only tender accepted.

Chapter 4

1. Other notable and recent cases involving African Americans killed in law enforcement encounters include Atatiana Jefferson (1990–2019), Aura Rosser (1974–2014), Stephon Clark (1995–2018), Botham Jean (1991–2018), Philando Castile (1983–2016), Alton Sterling (1979–2016), Michelle Cusseaux (1975–2015), Freddie Gray (1989–2015), Janisha Fonville (1995–2015), Eric Garner (1990–2014), Akai Gurley (1986–2014), Gabriella Nevarez (1993–2014), Tamir Rice (2002–2014), Michael Brown (1996–2014), and Tanisha Anderson (1977–2014) (Chughtai 2020).

2. This memorial depicting a Confederate soldier standing sentry-like at the university's entrance had been a campus fixture since 1913. It had been repeatedly vandalized in recent years. In November 2019, the university ultimately agreed to donate the controversial statue to the Sons of Confederate Veterans.

3. An eighteenth-century Franciscan priest widely credited as spearheading the Spanish colonization and conquest of what is now the state of California.

4. Fort Bragg is named after General Braxton Bragg (1817–1876), Fort Hood is named after General John Bell Hood (1831–1879), and Fort Gordon is named after General John Brown Gordon (1832–1904).

5. Logos from Uncle Ben's and Aunt Jemima products feature affable likenesses of

African Americans seemingly in subservient roles. Both have long drawn criticism for perpetuating harmful racial stereotypes. While the 130-year-plus Aunt Jemima design was retired, the Uncle Ben's logo was slated to undergo significant revamping.

6. Country-pop acts the Dixie Chicks and Lady Antebellum both truncated their southern-inspired names to "The Chicks" and "Lady A," respectively. American hard-rock band Lynch Mob, which showcased the guitar talents of Dokken alumnus George Lynch, announced they would no longer record music or tour under this moniker.

7. For example, after the Floyd killing and resultant national protests, NASCAR announced it would strictly enforce a ban on the display of Confederate flags and related paraphernalia at its events or properties. NASCAR's 2015 request that fans voluntarily no longer bring such items to events resulted in a surge in their display on race day. The only major professional African American driver, William Darrell "Bubba" Wallace Jr. vocally supported BLM concerns in 2020, leading to this shift in NASCAR policy. On the heels of the NASCAR decision was news that the Washington Redskins would finally abandon their controversial name after years of ardently refusing to do so.

8. Notably, *Gone with the Wind* and *Blazing Saddles* are both honored by the National Film Preservation Board and enshrined in the National Film Registry, a rarefied group of films deemed worthy of preservation for posterity.

9. Regarding the lawsuits and legal proceedings featured in this section, nearly all garnered considerable media attention upon their announcement or filing. Yet information about how many are ultimately resolved or adjudicated proves more difficult to come by. The fact that so many claims have been raised suggests that they have some substance.

10. IHOP does tout itself as a brand that believes in social responsibility and diversity. The company website lists a number of philanthropic and outreach efforts along with a statement delineating how IHOP cultivates and supports an inclusive work environment for its thousands of rank-and-file employees (IHOP 2020).

11. In April 2018, cellphone video surfaced and quickly went viral showing the handcuffing and arrest of two Black men at a Philadelphia-area Starbucks for simply sitting at a store table and not ordering anything. Outrage over such heavy-handed company and law enforcement response spurred calls for boycott, which eventually led the chain to revamp its operational policies regarding customer occupancy (Orso 2019).

12. Rogers tells almost exactly the same story in an *Atlanta Journal Constitution* piece commemorating Waffle House's fiftieth anniversary (Osinski 2004). Rawson draws her analysis from this.

13. Indeed, securing the original *Atlanta Daily World* newspaper account would likely entail sifting through various databases to locate the microfiche article and then accessing it through something like a university's interlibrary loan services.

Chapter 5

1. Phillips had long wanted to include Waffle House in one of his movies but continually met with company resistance. According to Phillips, "Yeah, they're very strict about what they let you film there. I tried to film a scene in *Road Trip* [a 2000 Phillips comedy] there, where Horatio Sanz [*Saturday Night Live* alumnus] puts French Toast down his pants. But they turned us down" (Rich 2010). He adds, "Yeah, [Waffle House] has to know what you are shooting. That scene in *Road Trip* was an obvious no-go" (Rich 2010).

References

Abramovitch, Seth. "Man Found Living on Roof of a Waffle House." *Gawker*, May 10, 2011. https://gawker.com.

AP News. "IHOP Restaurant Reaches out of Court Settlement in Discrimination Suit." December 24, 1992. https://apnews.com.

Atlanta Business Chronicle. "Waffle House Hit with Discrimination Suits." January 18, 2005. https://www.bizjournals.com.

Atlanta Daily World. "12 Are Served at Restaurant." January 16, 1964.

Auchmutey, Jim. "The Little Restaurant That Started the Big Chain Has Become a Museum Near Atlanta." *Atlanta Journal-Constitution*, September 2, 2008. https://www.ajc.com.

Baicker, Katherine, Oeindrila Dube, Sendhil Mullainathan, Devin Pope, and Guz Wezerek. "Is It Safer to Visit a Coffee Shop or a Gym?" *New York Times*, May 6, 2020. https://www.nytimes.com.

Baker, Deborah. "Introduction: The Southern Imaginary." In Baker and McKee, *American Cinema and the Southern Imaginary*, 1–24.

Baker, Deborah, and Kathryn McKee, eds. *American Cinema and the Southern Imaginary*. Athens: University of Georgia Press, 2011.

Baker, Margaret. "Graphic Video Reveals Details about Killing of Waffle House Waitress." *SunHerald*, December 16, 2015. https://www.sunherald.com.

Balko, Radley. *Rise of the Warrior Cop: The Militarization of America's Police Forces*. New York: PublicAffairs, 2014.

Bell, Kandice. "Waffle House CEO on Success: Just Eggs and Bacon." *Newnan Times-Herald*, July 24, 2016. https://times-herald.com.

Beriss, David, and David Sutton. "Restaurants, Ideal Postmodern Institutions." In *The Restaurant Book: Ethnographies of Where We Eat*, edited by David Beriss and David Sutton, 1–13. New York: Berg Publishers, 2007.

Bernarde, Scott. "Waffle House Pitchfork Robber Charged with Murder in Tennessee." *Patch*, May 12, 2019. https://patch.com.

Berrios, Laura. "Lucy Shelton, 85: 47-Year Waffle House Employee." *Atlanta Journal-Constitution*, August 11, 2012. https://www.ajc.com.

Bhasin, Kim. "Apparently Chuck E. Cheese Has a Problem with Adults Getting into Violent Brawls." *Business Insider*, March 9, 2012. https://www.businessinsider.com.

Blinder, Alan. "Portrait of the South, Served Up One Waffle House at a Time." *New York Times*, April 25, 2018. https://www.nytimes.com.

Bottoms, Anthony E., and Paul Wiles. "Environmental Criminology." In *The Oxford Handbook of Criminology*, 3rd ed., edited by Mike Maguire, Rod Morgan, and Robert Reiner, 620–56. Oxford: Oxford University Press, 2004.

Brasch, Ben. "Waffle House Is Selling Beer for the First Time." *Atlanta Journal-Constitution*, April 19, 2018. https://www.ajc.com.

Brown, Larry. *A Miracle of Catfish*. New York: A Shannon Ravenel Book, 2007.

——. *The Rabbit Factory*. New York: Atria Books, 2003.

Brown, Robbie. "A Large Side of Drama at Waffle House Diners." *New York Times*, November 26, 2011. https://www.nytimes.com.

Burns, Rebecca. "This Week in Atlanta History: The King Funeral, 1968." *Atlanta*, April 9, 2012. https://www.atlantamagazine.com.

Campbell-Schmitt, Adam. "Waffle House Has Its Own Record Label Just to Release Songs about Waffle House." *Food and Wine*, January 8, 2020. https://www.foodandwine.com.

Carpenter, Brian. "Introduction: Blood and Bone." In *Grit Lit: A Rough South Reader*, edited by Brian Carpenter and Tom Franklin, xiii–xxxii. Columbia: University of South Carolina Press, 2012.

Carson, Clayborne. *In Struggle: SNCC and the Black Awakening of the 1960s*. Cambridge, MA: Harvard University Press, 1995.

Cash, Micah. "Waffle House Vistas." *Bitter Southerner*, March 12, 2019. https://bittersoutherner.com.

Catte, Elizabeth. *What You Are Getting Wrong about Appalachia*. Cleveland: Belt Publishing, 2018.

Cavendish, Steve, Neil MacFarquhar, Jamie McGee, and Adam Goldman. "Behind the Nashville Bombing, a Conspiracy Theorist Stewing about the Government." *New York Times*, February 24, 2021. https://www.nytimes.com.

Charlotte Observer. "Waffle House Suit Alleges Racism." May 24, 2001.

Chughtai, Alia. "Know Their Names. Black People Killed by the Police in US." *Al Jazeera*, 2020. https://interactive.aljazeera.com.

Clark, Kevin. "The Carolina Panthers' Secret Weapon: Waffle House. Players See Proximity to the Popular 24-Hour Restaurant Chain of the South as a Homefield Advantage." *Wall Street Journal*, January 20, 2016. https://www.wsj.com.

Cobb, James C. *Away Down South: A History of Southern Identity*. New York: Oxford University Press, 2005.

Cohen, Lawrence E., and Marcus Felson. "Social Change and Crime Rate Trends: A Routine Activity Approach." *American Sociological Review* 44 (1979): 588–608.

Comparably. "Waffle House Executive Team Score." 2020. https://www.comparably.com.

Contrera, Jessica. "The End of Waffle House. Regulars Say Goodbye to Bloomington's Second Oldest Restaurant." *Indiana Daily Student*, October 21, 2013. https://www.idsnews.com.

Cook, Rhonda. "2 Georgia Men Found Guilty of Plotting Terrorism at Waffle House." *Atlanta Journal-Constitution*, January 17, 2014. https://www.ajc.com.

Cooley, Angela Jill. *To Live and Die in Dixie: The Evolution of Urban Food Culture in the Jim Crow South*. Athens: University of Georgia Press, 2015.

Cooper, Christopher A., and H. Gibbs Knotts. *The Resilience of Southern Identity.: Why the South Matters in the Minds of Its People*. Chapel Hill: University of North Carolina Press, 2017.

Craig, Robert M. "Atlanta's Modern Diner Revival: History, Nostalgia, Youth and Car Culture." *Studies in Popular Culture* 19, no. 2 (1996): 67–90.

Crane, Emily. "Waffle House Restaurants in Georgia Begin Dine-In Again As Other Eateries across the State Also Reopen after Coronavirus Restrictions Are Lifted." *Daily Mail*, April 27, 2020. https://www.dailymail.co.

Crowley, Chris. "Fast-Food Companies Still Don't Care." *Grub Street*, June 3, 2020. https://www.grubstreet.com.

Crowther, Gillian. *Eating Culture: An Anthropological Guide to Food*. Toronto: University of Toronto Press, 2013.

Daniel, Pete. *Lost Revolutions: The South in the 1950s.* Chapel Hill: University of North Carolina Press, 2000.

Denny's. "Denny's Continues Its Global Expansion of America's Diner with the Opening of Its First Restaurant in the Philippines." October 10, 2016. http://investor .dennys.com.

———. "Diversity." 2020. https://www.dennys.com.

Dine Brands. "Dine Brands International Continues Global Expansion, Entering South America with Deal to Bring IHOP' Restaurants to Peru." July 9, 2018. https:// investors.dineequity.com.

Dinges, Gary, and Sebastian Harris. "3 Years after Listeria Scandal, Blue Bell Back in Growth Mode." *Austin-American Statesman,* September 16, 2018. https://www .statesman.com.

Dodero, Camille. "The Story of the 450-Pound Rapper Who Loved Waffle House Too Much." *Gawker,* June 14, 2013. https://gawker.com.

Dostal, Erin. "Waffle House: CEO Litigation a Personal Matter. Family-Dining Chain CEO Accused of Sexual Harassment, Denies Allegations." *Nation's Restaurant News,* November 14, 2012. https://www.nrn.com.

Dowdy, G. Wayne. *Lost Restaurants of Memphis. American Palate.* Mount Pleasant, SC: History Press, 2019.

DuPlessis, Jim. "Discrimination Claims Hurt Business Even If False." *State* (Columbia, SC), October 21, 2006.

Dyer, Carol. "Scattered, Smothered, Covered, and Chunked: Fifty Years of the Waffle House." In *Cornbread Nation 4: The Best of Southern Food Writing,* edited by Dale Volberg Reed and John Shelton Reed, 166–71. Athens: University of Georgia Press, 2008.

Edge, John T. *The Potlikker Papers: A Food History of the Modern South.* New York: Penguin, 2017.

Edge, John T., Elizabeth Sanders Delwiche Engelhardt, and Ted Ownby, eds. *The Larder: Food Studies Methods from the American South.* Vol. 7. Athens: University of Georgia Press, 2013.

Editorial Board. "The Companies Putting Profits ahead of People. As the Coronavirus Spreads, the Public Interest Requires Employers to Abandon Their Longstanding Resistance to Paid Sick Leave." *New York Times,* March 14, 2020. https://www .nytimes.com.

Egerton, John. *Cornbread Nation 1: The Best of Southern Food Writing.* Chapel Hill: University of North Carolina Press, 2002.

Elder-Vass, David. *The Casual Power of Social Structures: Emergence, Structure and Agency.* New York: Cambridge University Press, 2010.

———. "Social Structure and Social Relations." *Journal for the Theory of Social Behaviour* 37 no. 4 (2007): 463–77.

Ergun, Özlem, Jessica L. Heier Stamm, Pinar Keskinocak, and Julie L. Swann. "Waffle House Restaurants Hurricane Response: A Case Study." *International Journal of Production Economics* 126, no. 1 (2010): 111–20.

Fausset, Richard, and Rick Rojas. "Across the South, 'Walking a Tightrope' While Awaiting the Worst. Public Health Officials Fear Underlying Problems, from Poor Health to Poverty, Could Exacerbate the Effects of the Coronavirus in the South." *New York Times,* April 9, 2020. https://www.nytimes.com.

Ferguson, Lana. "Here's What Police Say about Hardeeville Waffle House Knife Fight That Made International News." *Island Packet,* February 4, 2019. https://www.islandpacket .com.

Ferris, Marcie Cohen. *The Edible South: Food and History in an American Region.* Chapel Hill: University of North Carolina Press, 2014.

Filloon, Whitney. "Everything You Need to Know about Waffle House. A Brief History of the Beloved Southern Icon." *Atlanta Eater*, May 2, 2017. https://www.eater.com.

Forbes, Paula. "Man Crashes Truck into Waffle House Trying to Kill His Wife." *Eater*, August 16, 2011. https://www.eater.com.

Frazier, Eric. "Group Sues Waffle House for Civil Rights Violations." *Washington Post*, May 24, 2001. https://www.washingtonpost.com.

Freeman, Nik. "A Map of All the Waffle House Locations in America. The Visualization Stems from My Irrational, Lifelong Infatuation with Waffle House, the Always-Open Dive Joint That Manages to Provide a Low-Cost, Consistently-Satisfying Breakfast Meal at Its 1,600+ Locations." *Huffington Post*, December 6, 2017. https://www.huffingtonpost.com.

French, Rose. "Cracker Barrel Rebuilding Its Image." *Associated Press*, June 19, 2005. https://www.tuscaloosanews.com.

Fricke, David. "Tom Petty's Rock & Roll Refuge." *Rolling Stone*, August 14, 2014. https://www.thepettyarchives.com.

FundingUniverse. "Waffle House Inc. History." 2020. http://www.fundinguniverse.com.

Gaffigan, Jim. "Waffle House." *King Baby*. New York: Comedy Central Records, 2013.

Garreau, Joel. *The Nine Nations of North America*. Boston: Houghton Mills, 1981.

George, Cindy. "Biker Group, Eatery Named in Discrimination Suit." *Houston Chronicle*, December 29, 2015. https://www.houstonchronicle.com.

Georgia Historical Society. "The Waffle House." Historical Marker. 2012.

Gettys, Travis. "Meth Clowns, Nude Brawls and Shootouts: How Waffle House Became the 'Florida Man' of Restaurants." *Raw Story*, June 7, 2016. https://www.rawstory.com.

———. "'They Crushed My Spirit': Texas Teens Leave Racist 'KKK' Message for Server at IHOP." *Raw Story*, January 1, 2018. https://www.rawstory.com.

Giles, Harry. *Tonguit*. Edinburgh: Stewed Rhubarb Press, 2015.

Goad, Jim. "6 Things That Could Happen to You at Waffle House." *Thought Catalog*, April 19, 2014. https://thoughtcatalog.com.

Grant, Gavin. "George Singleton Interview." Indiebound.org, 2002. https://www.indiebound.org.

Greene, Andy. "Iggy and the Stooges Are Ready to Die. First Record with Reunited Guitarist James Williamson Hits Shelves on April 30th." *Rolling Stone*, April 15, 2013. https://www.rollingstone.com.

Guta, Marin. "12 Things You Didn't Know about Waffle House." *Atlanta Journal-Constitution*, January 29, 2018. https://www.ajc.com.

Gutman, Richard J. S. *American Diner Then and Now, Expanded Edition*. Baltimore: Johns Hopkins University Press, 2000.

Haag, Matthew. "Black Woman's Violent Arrest at Alabama Waffle House Was Justified, Police Say." *New York Times*, April 24, 2018. https://www.nytimes.com.

Haley, Andrew P. *Turning the Tables: Restaurants and the Rise of the American Middle Class, 1880–1920*. Chapel Hill: University of North Carolina Press, 2011.

Hays, Sharon. "Structure and Agency and the Sticky Problem of Culture." *Sociological Theory* 12, no. 1 (1994): 57–72.

Heath, Trina, Charnae Knight, Pat Warner, and Linsey Bill. *The Waffle House Experiences: A Celebration 50 Years*. Decatur, GA: Looking Glass Books, 2005.

Held, Amy. "As S.C. Waffle House Worker Sleeps, Customer Mans the Grill." NPR, December 5, 2017. https://www.npr.org.

Hicks, Bill. *Love All the People: The Essential Bill Hicks*. Berkeley, CA: Soft Skull, 2004.

Hijek, Barbara. "Report: Angry Hubby Crashes through Waffle House." *South Florida Sun-Sentinel*, August 17, 2011. https://www.sun-sentinel.com.

Hill, Sienna. "A Brief History of the Most Iconic Rap and Athlete Moments at Waffle House." *First We Feast*, October 10, 2015. https://firstwefeast.com.

Himes, Geoffrey. "James McMurtry Melds Literature and Lyrics." *Los Angeles Times*, July 21, 2008. https://www.latimes.com.

Hoff, Madison. "This Map Shows How Many Confederate Monuments and Symbols Still Stand in the US." *Business Insider*, June 13, 2020. https://www.businessinsider.com.

Holley, Peter. "Massive Fight at Florida Chuck E. Cheese Caught on Video." *Washington Post*, October 6, 2016. https://www.washingtonpost.com.

Hood, Patterson. "The South's Heritage Is So Much More Than a Flag." *New York Times Magazine*, July 9, 2015. https://www.nytimes.com.

Horne, Jay M. *As the Waffle Burns: 10th Anniversary Edition*. Bradenton, FL: Bookflurry, 2018.

Horton, Alex, and Rachel Siegel. "A Woman Was Tackled by Officers at an Alabama Waffle House. Police Are Defending Actions." *Washington Post*, April 24, 2018. https://www.washingtonpost.com.

Hurley, Andrew. *Diners, Bowling Alleys and Trailer Parks. Chasing the American Dream in Postwar American Consumer Culture*. New York: Basic Books, 2001.

IHOP. "See What Social Responsibility Means to Us." 2020. https://www.ihop.com.

Isenberg, Nancy. *White Trash: The 400-Year Old Untold History of Class in America*. New York: Penguin Books, 2016.

Jitchotvisut, Janaki. "Surprise! Map Shows Greater Incidence of Obesity in States with More Waffle House Locations. We Know Correlations Isn't Causation, but Taking Your Hash Browns 'All the Way' Does Have Its Consequences." *First We Feast*, July 18, 2014. https://firstwefeast.com.

Jones, Robert P. *White Too Long. The Legacy of White Supremacy in American Christianity*. New York: Simon and Schuster, 2020.

Junod, Tom. "An Ode to Waffle House: Never Mind the Waffle Themselves. The American South's Homogenous, Twenty-Four Hour Homage to Breakfast Has a Place for All of Us." *Esquire*, March 25, 2009. https://www.esquire.com.

Kaiser Family Foundation. Kaiser Family Foundation Analysis of the Centers for Disease Control and Prevention (CDC)'s Behavioral Risk Factor Surveillance System (BRFSS) 2013–2018 Survey Results. 2018. https://www.kff.org.

KARE Staff. "Waitress Receives Kind Gesture from Mom of Waffle House Survivor." *KARE 11*, July 20, 2018. https://www.kare11.com.

Klein, Allison. "The Lone Employee at an Alabama Waffle House Was Swamped. So Customers Jumped behind the Counter to Help." *Washington Post*, November 11, 2019. https://www.washingtonpost.com.

Knipple, Paul, and Angela Knipple. *The World Is a Skillet. A Food Lover's Tour of the New American South*. Chapel Hill: University of North Carolina Press, 2014.

Knowlton, Andrew. "What It's Like to Work at the Waffle House for 24 Hours Straight." *Bon Appétit*, February 17, 2015. https://www.bonappetit.com.

Kogler, Christian. "This Map Correlates Cardiac-Related Deaths with Waffle House Locations." *Wide Open Eats*, November 21, 2017. https://www.wideopeneats.com.

Kwate, Naa Oyo A. *Burgers in Blackface: Anti-Black Restaurants Then and Now*. Minneapolis: University of Minnesota Press, 2019.

Labaton, Stephen. "Denny's Restaurants to Pay $54 Million in Race Bias Suits." *New York Times*, May 25, 1994. https://www.nytimes.com.

Lamour, Joseph. "From High-End to Waffle House, Why Do Some Restaurants Just Feel Racist?" *Mic*, September 22, 2020. https://www.mic.com.

Langdon, Philip. *Orange Roofs, Golden Arches: The Architecture of American Chain Restaurants*. New York: Alfred A. Knopf, 1986.

Lassiter, Matthew D., and Joseph Crespino, eds. *The Myth of Southern Exceptionalism*. Oxford: Oxford University Press, 2009.

Lauderdale, Vance. "Toddle House." *Memphis*, March 9, 2011. https://memphismagazine.com.

Lemann, Nicholas. *The Promised Land: The Great Migration and How It Changed America*. New York: Knopf, 1991.

Leonardi, Roey L. "Contemporary Romance: Scattered, Smothered, and Covered." *Harvard Crimson*, February 13, 2020. https://www.thecrimson.com.

Leslie, Jennifer. "No Cushy Office or Holidays for Waffle House Execs." *Dunwoody 11Alive*, June 25, 2012. http://dunwoody.11alive.com.

Levine, Jon. "Atlanta Rioters Spared Beloved Waffle House during George Floyd Protest." *New York Post*, May 30, 2020. https://nypost.com.

Locker, Melissa. "14 Things You Didn't Know about Waffle House." *Southern Living*, May 29, 2017. https://www.southernliving.com.

———. "The 10 Best Songs You'll Hear at Waffle House." *Southern Living*, June 1, 2017. https://www.southernliving.com.

London, Julie. "A Letter to the Editor." *Inc: A Waffle House Diversity Magazine*, October 2006.

Long, Heather, and Andrew Van Dam. "Under Trump, the Jobs Boom Has Finally Reached Blue-Collar Workers. Will It Last?" *Washington Post*, September 9, 2018. https://www.washingtonpost.com.

Lotz, C. J. "Scattered and Smothered: How Do You Like Your Hashbrowns?" *Garden and Gun*, February 9, 2015. https://gardenandgun.com.

MacGillis, Alec. "How Dollar Stores Became Magnets for Crime and Killing. Discount Chains Are Thriving—While Fostering Violence and Neglect in Poor Communities." *ProPublica*, June 29, 2020. https://www.propublica.org.

Maddock, Jay. "5 Charts Show Why the South Is the Least Healthy Region in the US." *Conversation*, February 5, 2018. http://theconversation.com.

Manfred, Tony. "Bubba Watson Left a $148 Tip at Waffle House after Winning the Masters." *Business Insider*, April 15, 2014. https://www.businessinsider.com.

Matejowsky, Ty. *Fast Food Globalization in the Provincial Philippines*. Lanham, MD: Lexington Books, 2018.

McBrayer, Ronnie. *The Gospel According to Waffle House: Reimagining the Community of Faith*. Los Angeles: Match Point, 2013.

McDonald, Leah. "It Must Be Bad! Waffle House, the Restaurant Chain Which Opens 24hrs a Day 365 Days a Year, Is Forced to Close THIRTY Stores in Florida and Georgia as Hurricane Michael Wreaks Havoc." *Daily Mail*, October 10. 2018. https://www.dailymail.com.

McKibben, Beth. "Atlanta Activists, Bernice King Call for Boycott of Waffle House. Bernice King, Daughter of Martin Luther King Jr., Takes to Twitter Urging Boycott Following Incident at North Carolina Waffle House." *Atlanta Eater*, May 11, 2018. https://atlanta.eater.com.

Melbin, Murray. *Night as Frontier: Colonizing the World after Dark*. New York: Free Press, 1987.

Mencimer, Stephanie. "Alleged Waffle House Terror Plotters Inspired by Former Militia Author." *Mother Jones*, November 2, 2011. https://www.motherjones.com.

Meyersohn, Nathaniel. "Dollar General Is Cheap, Popular and Spreading across America. It's Also a Robbery Magnet, Police Say." CNN, June 26, 2020. https://www.cnn.com.

Miller, H. D. "Chicken and Waffles: The Most Complete Expression of Southern Culinary Skill." *Eccentric Culinary History*, September 4, 2016. https://eccentricculinary.com.

Miller, Mary. *The Last Days of California: A Novel*. New York: Liveright, 2014.

Mitchell, Corey. "Data: The Schools Named after Confederate Figures." *Education Week*, August 19, 2020. https://www.edweek.org.

Mohdin, Aamna. "To Understand America's Race-Issue, Look at Its Fast-Food Chains." *Quartz*, May 11, 2018. https://qz.com.

Molina, Brett. "Good Samaritan Paying for Others' Meals at Waffle House Shot to Death, Police Say." *USA Today*, April 9, 2019. https://www.usatoday.com.

Moraitis, Mike. "See It: Titans' Julio Jones Wears Waffle House Cleats to Practice." *Titanswire*, July 28, 2021. https://titanswire.usatoday.com.

Morrison, Maureen. "How Annie Helped Popeyes Find Its Brand Identity—Louisiana." *Ad Age*, June 24, 2014. https://adage.com.

Moser, Bob. "What Waffle House Means to Southerners: The Tennessee Waffle House Shooting Will Resonate in Ways That Past Events Have Not." *Rolling Stone*, April 25, 2018. https://www.rollingstone.com.

Mote, Dave, and Christina M. Stansell. "Waffle House, Inc." International Directory of Company Histories. May 19, 2020. https://www.encyclopedia.com.

MTV News Staff. "ICP Puts Waffle House Brawl behind Them, Moves on to Music." *MTV News*, June 11, 1998. http://www.mtv.com.

Murphy, Bill, Jr. "People Are Boycotting Waffle House after Its 4th Alleged Racial Incident in 12 Days. Here's Who's Leading It." *Inc*, May 11, 2018. https://www.inc.com.

Nagle, James L. "Makers of Diners Seek Fresh Fields. Aim to Enter Areas Thus Far Left Untapped Because of High Freight Rates Now Has 2-in-1 Combination." *New York Times*, September 23, 1951. https://www.nytimes.com.

National Restaurant News. "NRA: Restaurant Sales to Hit $799B in 2017." February 28, 2017. https://www.nrn.com.

Nelson, Andrew. "The Holiday Inn Sign. Exploding with Color, Optimism, and Razzle-Dazzle, the Now-Extinct Holiday Inn 'Great Sign' Was a True Design Landmark of the American Century." *Salon*, April 30, 2002. https://www.salon.com.

Newkirk, Vann R., II. "The Coronavirus's Unique Threat to the South. More Young People in the South Seem to Be Dying from COVID-19. Why?" *Atlantic*, April 2, 2020. https://www.theatlantic.com.

Newman Andrew Adam. "Yes, the Diner's Open. How about a Seat at the Counter?" *New York Times*, February 1, 2011. https://www.nytimes.com.

Norman, Bob. "Who Is Florida Man?" *Columbia Journalism Review*, May 30, 2019. https://www.cjr.org.

Olmeda, Rachel. "Waffle House Murderer Again Sentenced to Death." *South Florida Sun-Sentinel*, December 18, 2018. https://www.sun-sentinel.com.

Opie, Frederick Douglass. *Hogs and Hominy. Soul Food from Africa to America*. New York: Columbia University Press, 2010.

Orso, Anna. "One Year Later: A Timeline of Controversy and Progress since the Starbucks Arrest Seen 'Round the World." *Philadelphia Inquirer*, April 12, 2019. https://www.inquirer.com.

Osinski, Bill. "The Cornerstone of Waffle House. At 50, Chain Still Reflects Co-Founder's People Skills." *Atlanta Journal-Constitution*, December 24, 2004. https://www.ajc.com.

Oxford, Cliff. "Waffle House Shows Atlanta How to Handle a Snowstorm." *New York Times*, February 17, 2014. https://boss.blogs.nytimes.com.

Page, Sydney. "He Opted to Skip Graduation and Work a Shift at Waffle House. His Boss

Was Not Having It. 'I Was Going to Get Him There No Matter What.'" *Washington Post*, June 14, 2021. https://www.washingtonpost.com.

Pallasch, Abdon M. "Cracker Barrel Settles Illinois Workers' Harassment Claims." *Chicago Sun-Times*, March 12, 2006. http://www.highbeam.com.

Pardue, Derek. "Familiarity, Ambience and Intentionality: An Investigation into Casual Dining Restaurants in Central Illinois." In *The Restaurant Book: Ethnographies of Where We Eat*, edited by David Beriss and David Sutton, 65–78. New York: Berg Publishers, 2007.

Penman, Susie. "Cracker Barrel's Culture: Exporting the South on America's Interstate Exits." Master's thesis, University of Mississippi, 2012.

Peterson, Kim. "Waffle House Almost Denies Waitress Big Tip." CBS News, June 11, 2014. https://www.cbsnews.com.

Phifer, Donica. "Florida Woman Arrested after Dancing Naked in Waffle House Parking Lot, Licking Employee's Face." *Newsweek*, January 23, 2019. https://www.newsweek.com.

Plunkett-Powell, Katherine. *Remembering Woolworth's: A Nostalgic History of the World's Most Famous Five-and-Dime*. New York. St. Martin's Press, 1999.

Prentzel, Olivia. "Bogus Employee Took Orders, Then Cash from Local Waffle House: NOLA." *Times-Picayune*, March 7, 2019. https://www.nola.com.

Prince, Chelsea. "Waffle House Employees Fired after Pouring Food on Passed-Out Customer, Sharing Video Online." *Atlanta Journal-Constitution*, January 11, 2019. https://www.ajc.com.

Prior, Anna. "Calling All Cars: Trouble at Chuck E. Cheese's, Again." *Wall Street Journal*, December 9, 2008. https://wsj.com.

Prior, Ryan. "When a Waffle House Was Short on Staff, Customers Jumped behind the Counter to Help Out." *CNN*, November 8, 2019. https://www.cnn.com.

Randle, Aaron. "Teen 'Distraught and Upset' after KC-Area IHOP Server Prints N-Word on Her Receipt." *Kansas City Star*, May 2, 2018. https://www.kansascity.com.

Raub, Kevin. "The Mayer of Atlanta." *American Way*, June 1, 2006. https://www.kevinraub.net.

Rawson, Katie. "'America's Place for Inclusion': Stories of Food, Labor, and Equality at the Waffle House." In *Larder: Food Studies from the American South*, edited by John T. Edge, 216–39. Athens: University of Georgia Press, 2013.

Reed, John Shelton. "*Introduction: Southern Eats*." In *Dixie Emporium: Tourism, Foodways, and Consumer Culture in the American South*, edited by Anthony J. Stanonis, 205–7. Athens: University of Georgia Press, 2008.

———. *Mixing It Up: A South-Watcher's Miscellany*. Baton Rouge: Louisiana State University Press, 2018.

Rich, Katey. "Interview: Due Date Director Todd Phillips on Waffle House and Pushing Boundaries." *Cinema Blend*, 2010. https://www.cinemablend.com.

Richards, Kimberly. "A Black Woman Was Violently Arrested inside an Alabama Waffle House after a Disagreement over Utensils." *Blavity*, April 23, 2018. https://blavity.com.

RoadsideAmerica.com. "Decatur, Georgia: Waffle House Museum." July 6, 2002. https://www.roadsideamerica.com.

Rogers, Joe W., Sr. *Who's Looking Out for the Poor Old Cash Customer?* Decatur, GA: Looking Glass Books, 2000.

Romano, Andrew. "Pancakes and Pickaninnies: The Saga of 'Sambo's,' the 'Racist' Restaurant Chain America Once Loved." *Daily Beast*, July 12, 2017. https://www.thedailybeast.com.

Ruggles, Ron. "Waffle House Rolls Out Faster POS. Chain Speeds Transaction Times to Three Second Average." *Nation's Restaurant News*, March 27, 2015. https://www.nrn.com.

Russell, Kent. *In the Land of Good Living: A Journey to the Heart of Florida*. New York: Knopf, 2000.

Russo, Jared. "Facebook Users Flock to Follow Waffle House as It Announces Rare Closings." B2, March 25, 2020. https://www.businessofbusiness.com.

Sarder, Sarah. "Pair Robbed 4 Waffle Houses in 80-Minute Spree, Fort Worth Police Say." *Dallas Morning-News*, March 18, 2019. https://www.dallasnews.com.

Scheiber, Noam. "Joseph W. Rogers, a Founder of Waffle House, Dies at 97." *New York Times*, March 7, 2017. https://www.nytimes.com.

Schenke, Jarred. "For Waffle House, Most Things Will Never Change, Including Its Headquarters." *Bisnow*, February 22, 2019. https://www.bisnow.com.

Schmit, Julie, and Larry Copeland. "Cracker Barrel Customer Says Bias Was 'Flagrant.'" *USA Today*, May 7, 2004. https://usatoday30.usatoday.com.

Schmitz, Amy. "Irony Is the New Black." *UA College of Eller Management*, September 5, 2018. https://uanews.arizona.edu.

Schulman, Bruce J. *From Cotton Belt to Sunbelt: Federal Policy, Economic Development, and the Transformation of the South, 1938–1980*. Durham, NC: Duke University Press, 1994.

ScrapeHero. "Number of Waffle House Locations in the United States." 2020. https://www.scrapehero.com.

Searcey, Dionne, and Matt Richtel. "Obesity Was Rising as Ghana Embraced Fast Food: Then Came KFC." *New York Times*, October 2, 2017. https://www.nytimes.com.

Seattle Times Staff. "A Look at Claims of Racial Bias in U.S. Restaurants." *Seattle Times*, April 15, 2018. https://www.seattletimes.com.

Sewell, William H., Jr. "A Theory of Structure: Duality, Agency, and Transformation." *American Journal of Sociology* 98, n0.1 (1992):1–29.

Sharon, Susan. "Auburn IHOP Manager Reacts to Facebook Post: 'We're Not Racist.'" *Bangor Daily News*, March 13, 2018. https://bangordailynews.com.

Sharp, John. "Waffle House Violence Raises Security Concerns." AL.com, April 24, 2018. https://www.al.com.

Sharpe, Joshua. "Waffle House Co-Founder Dies at 98, a Month after Business Partner." *Atlanta Journal-Constitution*, April 27, 2017. https://www.ajc.com.

Sharpless, Rebecca. *Cooking in Other Women's Kitchens: Domestic Workers in the South, 1865–1960*. Chapel Hill: University of North Carolina Press, 2010.

Sherman, Chris. "Neighborly Toddle House Coming to Town." *Orlando Sentinel*, January 11, 1987. https://www.orlandosentinel.com.

Sheumaker, Helen. *Artifacts for Modern America. Daily Life through Artifacts*. Santa Barbara: Greenwood, 2017.

Sides, Hampton. *Americana: Dispatches from the New Frontier*. New York: Anchor, 2004.

Sleep Judge. "Crimes That Happen While You Sleep." 2019; revised July 28, 2020. https://www.thesleepjudge.com.

Smith, Daniel P. "How Popeyes Clawed Its Way to Chicken Elite: Popeyes Louisiana Kitchen Reclaimed Its Heritage and Its Momentum—Just in Time to Take On KFC." *QSR Magazine*, 2016. https://www.qsrmagazine.com.

Snider, Mike. "Waffle House to Go. Restaurant Chain Uses Food Truck to Cater Events." *USA Today*, August 20, 2018. https://www.usatoday.com.

Soong, Kelyn. "At the Waffle House, She Cut Up a Customer's Food for Him. It Changed Her Life." *Washington Post*, March 16, 2018. https://www.washingtonpost.com.

Sorvino, Chloe. "Crippled by Coronavirus, Waffle House Faces a Harsh Reality. 'We've Never Seen Anything Like This.'" *Forbes*, March 29, 2020. https://www.forbes.com.

Spang, Rebecca L. *The Invention of the Restaurant: Paris and Modern Gastronomic Culture.* Cambridge. MA: Harvard University Press, 2000.

Specker, Lawrence. "Covered: Waffle House Customers Step In to Fill Gap at Birmingham Restaurant." *AL.com*, November 8, 2019. https://www.al.com.

Stanonis, Anthony J. "Introduction: Selling Dixie." In *Dixie Emporium: Tourism, Foodways, and Consumer Culture in the American South*, edited by Anthony J. Stanonis, 1–16. Athens: University of Georgia Press, 2008.

———. "Just Like Mammy Used to Make: Foodways in the Jim Crow South." In *Dixie Emporium: Tourism, Foodways, and Consumer Culture in the American South*, edited by Anthony J. Stanonis, 208–33. Athens: University of Georgia Press, 2008.

Steger, Manfred B., and Paul James. "Levels of Subjective Globalization; Ideologies, Imaginaries, Ontologies." *Perspectives on Global Development and Technology* 12, no. 23 (2013): 1–2.

Stern, Michael, and Jane Stern. *Roadfood. The Coast to Coast Guide to over 400 of America's Great Inexpensive Regional Restaurants All within 10 Miles of a Major Highway.* New York: Random House, 1978.

Suggs, Ernie. "Waffle House Smothers Customers with Surcharge at Underground Location." *Atlanta Journal-Constitution*, February 16, 2013. https://www.ajc.com.

Swenson, Kyle. "Waffle House: America's All-Night Stage." *Washington Post*, April 24, 2018. https://www.washingtonpost.com.

Szczesiul, Anthony. *The Southern Hospitality Myth: Ethics, Politics, Race and American Memory.* Athens: University of Georgia Press, 2017.

Tamen, Joan Fleischer. "Cracker Barrel Accused of Bias to Black Customers." *South Florida Sun-Sentinel*, December 14, 2001. https://www.sun-sentinel.com.

Taylor, Kate. "For Chick-fil-A, Impact Trumps 'Any Political or Cultural War' When It Comes to Controversial Donations." *Business Insider*, May 15, 2019. https://www.businessinsider.com.

Thompson, Hunter S. *Songs of the Doomed: More Notes on the Death of the American Dream. Vol. 3 of The Gonzo Papers.* New York: Summit, 1990.

Thorton, William. "Alabama Woman Says Waffle House Offered Her $15 Coupon after Locking Her Out." *AL.com*, May 3, 2018. https://www.al.com.

———. "'It's Been Pure Hell': Woman Suing Thomson Tractor after Firing for Viral Video." *AL.com*, October 23, 2019. https://www.al.com.

Toast. "What Is Fast Casual Dining?" 2021. https://pos.toasttab.com.

Tolentino, Jia. "Letter of Recommendation: The Cracker Barrel." *New York Times Magazine.* January 28, 2016. https://www.nytimes.com.

Tran, Ho Hai, and Chloe Cahill. *Pizza Hunt.* Sydney: Cursa Major, 2016.

Turner, Cal. *My Father's Business: The Small Town Values That Built Dollar General into a Billion-Dollar Company.* New York: Center Street, 2018.

Underhill, Maxwell. "Maxim's Super Bowl Party Catered by Waffle House Sounds Absolutely Awesome." *12UP*, January 28, 2019. https://www.12up.com.

US Census Bureau. "US Population by Year." September 20, 2021. https://www.multpl.com.

Vance, J. D. *Hillbilly Elegy: A Memoir of a Family and Culture in Crisis.* New York: Harper Collins, 2016.

Vernon, Zackary. "Romanticizing the Rough South: Contemporary Cultural Nakedness and the Rise of Grit Lit." *Southern Cultures* 22, no. 3 (Fall 2016): 77–94.

Vestal, Christine. "The South May See the Largest Share of Coronavirus Misery." *Pew*, April 13, 2020. https://www.pewtrusts.org.

Victor, Daniel. "15 Hours and 9 Waffles Later, a Fantasy Football Punishment Is Complete." *New York Times*, June 18, 2021. https://www.nytimes.com.

Wang, K. S. "Celebrity Drive. Bob Watson, CEO of 5 & Diner. Car Enthusiast Loves His Vintage American Iron." *Motortrend*, October 19, 2012. https://www.motortrend.com.

Warren, Caleb, and Gina S. Mohr. "Ironic Consumption." *Journal of Consumer Research* 46, no. 2 (August 2019): 246–66.

Welch, Mary. "Is Waffle House Cooking Up Changes? Restaurant Halts Franchise Growth." *Atlanta Business Chronicle*. September 19, 1988.

Wells, Bob. "Georgia Waffle House Customers Volunteer to Help Due to January 2014 Snow Storm." *YouTube*, January 29, 2014. https://www.youtube.com.

Westin, David. "Inductee Made Most of Trip." *Augusta Chronicle*, January 7, 2007. https://www.augustachronicle.com.

Wilson, Charles Reagan. "Religion and the US South." *Southern Spaces*, March 16, 2004. https://southernspaces.org.

Wilson, Dave. "Is This Heaven? No, It's a Waffle House." *ESPN*, October 19, 2017. http://www.espn.com.

Wyatt, Kristen. "Waffle House Still Dishin' Diner Food at 50. Chain Still Retains Down-Home, Blue Collar Aura." *NBC News*, August 15, 2005. http://www.nbcnews.com.

Yamato, Jen. "John Legend Dishes on Epic Double Date with Kayne West and Kim Kardashian at Waffle House." *Daily Beast*, April 14, 2017. https://www.thedailybeast.com.

Zak, Sean. "Brooke Pancake, Waffle House Re-Up Deal for Another Season." *Golf*, December 18, 2015. https://golf.com.

Ziegbe, Mawuse. "Kid Rock's Waffle House Brawl Results in $40,000 Payout." *MTV News*, September 17, 2010. http://www.mtv.com.

Index